FADED
DREAMS

FADED DREAMS

More Ghost Towns of Kansas

DANIEL C. FITZGERALD

University Press of Kansas

© 1994 by the University Press of Kansas
All rights reserved

Published by the University Press of Kansas (Lawrence, Kansas
66049), which was organized by the Kansas Board of Regents and is
operated and funded by Emporia State University, Fort Hays State
University, Kansas State University, Pittsburg State University,
the University of Kansas, and Wichita State University

Library of Congress Cataloging-in-Publication Data

Fitzgerald, Daniel.
Faded dreams : more ghost towns of Kansas / Daniel C. Fitzgerald.
p. cm.
Includes bibliographical references and index.
ISBN 0-7006-0667-X (alk. paper) — ISBN 0-7006-0668-8
(alk. paper : pbk.)
1. Ghost towns—Kansas—Guidebooks. 2. Kansas—Guidebooks.
3. Kansas—History, Local. I. Title.
F679.3.F57 1994
917.8104'33—dc20   93-42117

British Library Cataloguing in Publication Data is available.

Printed in the United States of America
10 9 8 7 6 5 4 3 2 1

CONTENTS

CHAPTER NINE: SOUTHWEST KANSAS

INTRODUCTION

My interest in Kansas ghost towns began when I was barely twelve years old, growing up in Topeka. My grandparents owned a farm just west of town that I explored from one end to the other. The farm came complete with its very own ghost town—the remnants of a small community known as "Plowboy," which developed in the 1880s. Plowboy consisted of three or four buildings including a post office, general store, blacksmith shop, and livery barn. Three buildings were eventually torn down, but the livery barn somehow survived and still marks the townsite. I took every opportunity I could find to walk the cold, empty field where that town once stood, picking up cans full of square nails, broken china, assorted pieces of metal, and other junk left to disintegrate by earlier generations. If this ghost town had not piqued my interest, then others, such as Uniontown (in Shawnee County) and Palermo certainly would have.

In time I was guilty of bribing my parents to take me and my ever-growing list of ghost town possibilities on trips around Kansas; it would be another three years before I could legally drive. I soon wore out two vehicles in my hot pursuit of the next ghost town that lay in ruins just around the bend.

This is actually the fifth book I've written on Kansas ghost towns. The first three, entitled *Ghost Towns of Kansas, Volumes I-III*, were published privately from 1976 to 1982. The fourth volume, *Ghost Towns of Kansas: A Traveler's Guide*, published in 1988 by the University Press of Kansas, revised the first three volumes and provided some new material. I might have stopped there, but over the years I discovered more old towns that deserved proper attention. Hoping that others would continue to find the subject interesting, I decided to write a final fifth volume on Kansas ghost towns. This subject has been close to me now for nearly twenty years. Never in my wildest dreams did I imagine that it would result in five books, and it is with a little sadness that I have decided to end it with this volume. However, the time seems right now to move on to other things, and I deeply thank the hundreds of ghost towns fans out there who have made this topic both a rewarding and a popular one for me.

The sometimes impossible task of locating and researching Kansas ghost towns has been made easier by a list I discovered when I first began working at the Kansas State Historical Society. This "dead town list" consists of nearly forty cloth-bound notebooks containing the names of over six thousand communities that either never saw the light of day or, if they did exist, are no longer around. Had all these towns been built and survived, they, combined with the incorporated towns of Kansas today, would have resulted in a density of one town for every twelve square miles. One could not have walked, ridden, or driven more than seven miles in any direction without encountering another community. These dead towns are excellent examples of major entrepreneurial activity in Kansas from 1854 to 1890. Potential promoters and investors perceived town building as a money-making venture destined to make them rich overnight. A small percentage of these investors succeeded. Most of them, however, lost their fortunes and eventually moved somewhere else to play the "town game" again.

DEFINITIONS
A primary question that readers constantly ask is, "What is a ghost town?" Many of us have the same visual impression of one. We generally see a "prop" created in a Zane Grey western or a Clint Eastwood movie. There stands the completely deserted town with a long block of false-fronted buildings, tumbleweeds blowing from one side to the other, and perhaps a saloon with the proverbial swinging doors and the big fogged-up mirror behind the bar. Unfortunately, these places exist only in fantasy, and ghost town hunters are very fortunate if their towns even remotely resemble this description.

My definition of a ghost town comes from years of examining what other ghost town writers, including the father of the genre, Lambert Florin, said about the subject. In general terms, my definition of a ghost town is a town that is a shadowy remnant of what it once was: if a particular community has lost two-thirds of its business district, and/or two-thirds of its population, I would consider it as a possible contender. Other factors must be considered as well, such as the town's growth over a twenty-year period and the town's possibilities for making a comeback. Some communities listed in this book still have life, or community spirit, although nothing to compare with the prosperity they enjoyed in their heyday. Even though they are too small for more than a post office and a few stores, some still have hopes for a brighter future. Whether this optimism is warranted is yet to be seen.

After the traveler's guide was released in 1988, I was surprised to find how controversial the label "ghost town" was for some of these towns on the verge of abandonment. One example was St. Paul. A few St. Paul residents were less than pleased to see their proud community included in my last book. Some feelings turned to anger, and these citizens did not hesitate to let me know that their town was not a ghost town and that it did not deserve the "stigma" attached to the title. During this controversial time, I was a national celebrity of sorts. The wire services had picked up on the story and ran it in newspapers and on the radio from coast to coast. I learned the valuable lesson that I should be more specific in my categorization of small towns. St. Paul is still around today, although its status, according to my definition, has not improved.

GHOST TOWNS: WHAT HAPPENED?

The reasons for the abandonment of communities are sometimes quite diverse. If all the warning signs could be identified during their formative stages, then there certainly would be some economic advisers on the unemployment lines. It's important to remember that the era that witnessed the decline of many of our small country towns is not over. Small towns are still being abandoned today. If there are any doubts about this, you need only compare a highway map from the 1950s with a current highway map. Dozens of communities shown on the map of forty years ago no longer exist.

Specific conditions or warning signals preceded the abandonment of many of these communities. I have developed eight categories that describe in general terms what happened to force the desertion of most of the towns in this book.

TRANSPORTATION

Kansas has always played a major role in moving people and supplies from one region to another. A large percentage of what are now ghost towns were established to capitalize on the potential trade involved in catering to the needs of this transitory element. In fact, the first communities in Kansas were known as "trail towns," established to service the needs of emigrants and freighters traveling on any one of a number of overland trails, such as the Oregon-California Trail, the Santa Fe Trail, and the Mormon Trail. When the trails were bustling with activity, these communities, with their blocks of trading stores, thrived. As the trails began to decline, these towns also declined if they had no other economic base. The residents usually packed up their wares and moved on to greener pastures. Towns such as 110 Mile Creek, Allison's Ranch, and Old Clear Water are good examples of these early trail towns.

The next transportation development that played an active role in creating townsites was the steamboat. Until the arrival of the first rail connection to the region in 1859, the steamboat was the primary mode of transportation for emigrants seeking homes in the West. Once Kansas Territory was open for settlement, river towns such as Palermo, Kickapoo City, and Quindaro were established along the Missouri River from Kansas City to White Cloud. Their raison d'etre was the business brought by the steamboats. Competition was intense, and many of these river towns quickly attracted several thousand residents.

The steamboat, however, proved to be an inefficient mode of transportation on the Missouri River. It could follow only primary water routes; its trading season was usually limited to eight months a year because of winter ice; and it was accident prone, succumbing to snags, high winds, sandbars, man-made obstacles, and boiler explosions. The steamboat also had difficulty maintaining a fixed schedule, often arriving several hours (or several days) late. Towns that based their existence on this transportation giant were successful only while the steamboat enjoyed a monopoly on the trade. After railroad companies began to construct their spiderweb of lines across the state, the steamboat trade dropped dramatically. Many river towns, unable to secure a more efficient means of transportation, declined or disappeared entirely. Of the thirty-six river towns established along the Kansas border in the 1850s, only six remained by 1900.

The advent of rail transportation brought civilization to Kansas. Inland towns that established themselves on rail lines had a direct, vital link with cattle and grain markets for the local farmers and with passenger and freight transportation for their residents and suppliers. In the nineteenth century, attracting a railroad was so important that several towns, missing a rail connection by only a few miles, actually were moved on log rollers to the new railroad site.

The great era of railroad "colonization" lasted in Kansas from the post-Civil War period through World War I. Towns established on railroad lines prospered. Unfortunately, the depression years of the 1930s reversed this prosperity, as many railroad companies consolidated their lines. Many communities, left without rail connections, plunged into economic nightmare. Their stories of decline and abandonment were replicated all across the state, if not across the Central Plains. Towns such as Blaine in Pottawatomie County and Miller in Lyon County quickly became memories.

Since the 1920s, the building of roads and highways has also played an important role in the rise and fall of communities. Like the trails and the railroads in their time, roads serve the vital function of moving people and supplies from one point to another. Accordingly, towns located along major highways have been able to prosper by establishing gas stations, restaurants, motels, repair shops, and other businesses oriented toward travel.

Soon, with the ease and speed allowed by paved roads, people began traveling farther to do their shopping. Larger communities offering a wide variety of goods benefitted from an efficient network of roads. Towns unable to satisfy the tastes or pocketbooks of their clientele slowly declined. In the last thirty years, the problem has become more serious as middle-sized towns attract larger trading networks at the expense of small-town neighbors.

POLITICS
Although economic conditions have been the primary force behind the success or failure of given townsites, politics has played a role in at least two different ways. First, many of the state's earliest communities were founded by settlers with strong proslavery or abolitionist beliefs. During the first two years of Kansas Territory, the proslavery view dominated, and several successful towns aligned themselves with these beliefs. However, as increasing numbers of abolitionists from the northeastern United States began to settle in the territory, the political atmosphere changed. Towns established as abolitionist centers were the prosperous ones; proslavery communities were attacked, boycotted, and threatened with abandonment if they refused to change their stand. Those that resisted abolitionist pressure disappeared, such as Paris in Linn County.

Second, politics governed the selection of the county seat. The town that won the county seat contest usually became the dominant town in the county, and those that lost the election either remained small or dwindled to nothing. It comes as no surprise, then, that a great deal of emotion and rivalry preceded many county seat contests. Usually at least two towns in each county had an equal chance of becoming the county seat. A few examples of the importance of winning the election can be found in this book—Defiance and Kalida in Woodson County; Abram, Lincoln County; Kickapoo City, Leavenworth County; and Eustis in Sherman County.

INDUSTRY AND EMPLOYMENT
An important indicator of a town's success is its ability to employ its citizenry and to attract outside business. A community with a wide economic base is generally more successful than one that depends upon a single primary industry. For when the industry closes its doors, the town usually cannot provide sufficient employment, and residents then must move where economic conditions are better.

As Kansas developed an industrial base in the heartland in the late nineteenth century, many towns were established with an uncertain dependence on one or two employers. Quite a few, including Treece, Le Hunt, and Yocemento, which I discuss in this book, lost a primary business and folded as a result. Major industries, many of them resource oriented, such as coal, lead, and zinc, cement manufacturing, brickmaking, and oil production, created scores of boomtowns across Kansas. As these industries overproduced and their markets collapsed, some places stopped growing. In the mid–twentieth century more and more small towns were unable to provide jobs for their residents. Consequently, a massive migration of people from the small town to the larger cities began in the 1930s. The trend in Kansas from rural to urban has transformed some of our small towns into ghost towns. As technologies continue to improve and work forces are depleted, the trend will become even more severe.

LEADERSHIP

Blame for town abandonment also belongs to civic leadership. Most communities that survived for any length of time had the strong support of at least one individual, if not a handful of leaders, who cared about and promoted the town's existence. If no new leadership appeared in the next generation, usually twenty or thirty years after the town was established, the town suffered economically. This factor can determine the success or failure of a certain town, for the lack of leadership leads to factionalism, and important civic decisions go unmade. Many towns described in this book suffered a lack of leadership after the town founders were gone.

INFRASTRUCTURE DEVELOPMENT

The basic needs of a community must be met in order for that town to continue to prosper. The first three decades of the twentieth century placed a greater demand on towns to develop and modernize. These civic improvements included a sufficient and modern waterworks, street paving, telephone service, residential electricity and electric street lighting, sewage service, natural gas lines, access to a local hospital or town physician, public parks, athletic fields, and community halls. Towns unable to provide their citizens with the basic needs were at a disadvantage, especially when other nearby communities could. Most towns in this volume failed to provide at least half of the services mentioned here.

SCHOOLS

A relatively recent problem confronting small towns is schools. Since 1947, school consolidations across the state have eliminated many small rural districts, lumping them with larger ones. Towns that lost their local school due to consolidation also lost a sense of community spirit, identity, and pride. No longer would townspeople cheer for their local football or basketball teams or watch a school performance. Their children moved suddenly to a school in a neighboring town, perhaps one that was a previous football rival. The loss of a school not only brings its share of economic problems but also deflates civic pride. And to citizens who fear their town is becoming a ghost town, an abandoned schoolhouse provides just another nail for the coffin.

NATIONAL ECONOMIC PANICS AND DEPRESSIONS
The general economic picture can lay the groundwork for financial disaster in small towns. Our vision of these places as isolated pastoral islands is false. Financial panics have had adverse affects on small Kansas towns since the mid–nineteenth century, when the Panic of 1857 wiped out real estate investment and inflation in the territory. Depressions in the 1870s and 1890s crippled the local farm economy, but none rivaled the Great Depression of the 1930s, the watermark decade for the small town. Hundreds of state banks closed their doors, and residents left by the thousands for better opportunities in large urban areas. More recently the farm crisis of the late 1970s and early 1980s disrupted small town growth. Farm prices dropped and farmers went bankrupt. The effect on surrounding small towns was devastating, and indeed many of them, some of which I describe here, declined dramatically in the last fifteen years.

EMINENT DOMAIN AND FLOOD CONTROL
Since the 1951 flood, which inundated communities in the Kansas River valley and its tributaries, the U.S. Army Corps of Engineers has actively sought to establish flood control dams on rivers in Kansas. With recourse to eminent domain policies, the corps has taken land and moved or destroyed entire towns that lay in the path of their dams and reservoirs, resulting in the loss of over thirty small towns since the 1950s. Richland in Shawnee County is just one example.

FINAL OBSERVATIONS
The loss of a community, for whatever reason, is sad. Though the world may call it progress, this loss, psychologically, symbolizes defeat. The twentieth century has witnessed so many changes that it is difficult to keep up with all the technological advances. We now think nothing of traveling fifty or a hundred miles to shop, whereas in 1900 such a trip would have required extra preparation and an overnight stay. In those early years when

people stayed close to home, a small town every few miles was a necessity. Our trading networks, even our social networks, were so restricted that a grocery store or a blacksmith shop had to be located within a few miles of home. This is no longer true. Better transportation, better roads, better connections with others who can provide needed services, have made many small communities obsolete. The small town is no longer important, and the residents have moved on to larger cities and better opportunities.

Much attention has focused in the last ten years on saving the small town, perhaps even spending millions of federal dollars to do so. However cold and callous I may sound, such an expenditure would be a waste of money and an antihistorical gesture. Towns that can keep up with our changing world deserve to retain an identity and usefulness—they are true survivors. Towns that can't will just naturally disappear. Would society benefit a hundred years from now if Matfield Green were still around? I don't believe that life would be any different whether it were a dot on the map or a vignette in someone's ghost town book. We can, however, learn about the past by studying the reasons behind the loss of the small town: that is the goal of this book. You will find no shocking new theories here, nothing for college professors to argue about, but perhaps the avid ghost-town hunter or armchair historian will find a town or two that strikes a chord and brings back memories.

A trip to a Kansas ghost town differs a bit from going to one in other western states. Kansans have always found a use for lumber and brick from deserted buildings. As a result, little remains of many of the communities featured here, for the sites of most of these old towns have been plowed for crops or used as pasture by farmers. More often than not, all that remains is a foundation or cemetery headstones; imagination is the key.

I hope readers will enjoy the following anecdotes about some of the more colorful Kansas ghost towns. As you tour the sites of these towns, I also hope you will appreciate the subtle beauty Kansas reveals to those who take the time to look for it—from the chat piles of southeast Kansas against a late summer sunset to the lush green of the Flint Hills against the backdrop of a huge thunderhead. A final remark: please remember that the sites of many of these towns are now on private property and that permission should be obtained before visiting them.

Horace Greeley once stated, "It takes three log houses to make a city in Kansas, but they begin calling it a city as soon as they have staked out the lots."[1] In the following histories of ghost towns, it is apparent that "three log houses" were significant enough to change the course of our state's history.

FADED
DREAMS

The Regions of Kansas

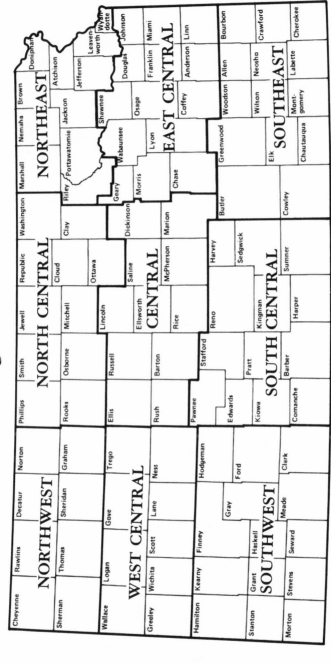

Laura Kriegstrom Poracsky

Scale in Miles

0   50   100

1

NORTHEAST KANSAS

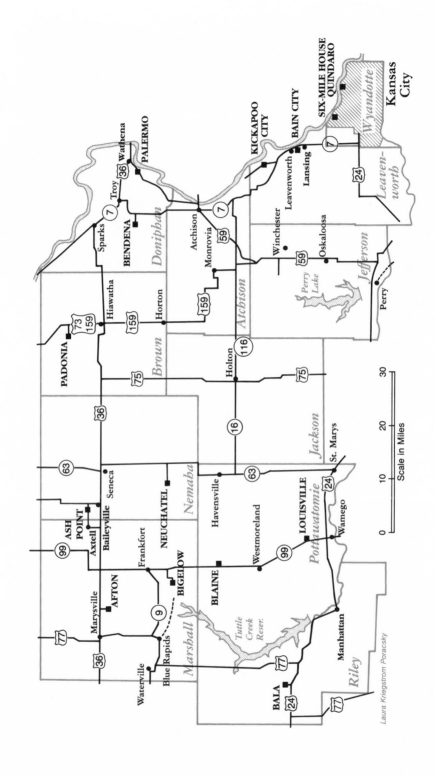

Kansas
City

SIX-MILE HOUSE
QUINDARO

Wyandotte

*Leaven-
worth*

KICKAPOO
CITY

BAIN CITY

Leavenworth

Lansing

24

7

PALERMO

Wathena

36

Troy

7

Sparks

BENDENA

Doniphan

Atchison

Monrovia

59

7

Winchester

Oskaloosa

Jefferson

*Perry
Lake*

Perry

59

Hiawatha

159

Horton

159

Atchison

Brown

Holton

116

73
159

PADONIA

159

75

75

36

63

Seneca

Baileyville

Nemaha

16

Havensville

63

St. Marys

24

Westmoreland

LOUISVILLE

Wamego

Pottawatomie

Jackson

30

20

10

0

Scale in Miles

ASH
POINT

Axtell

Frankfort

NEUCHATEL

99

AFTON

Marysville

BIGELOW

BLAINE

99

9

Marshall

*Tuttle
Creek
Reser.*

Manhattan

77

Riley

77

Waterville

Blue Rapids

36

77

BALA

24

77

Laura Kriegstrom Poracsky

PALERMO
Doniphan County

Surveyors originally platted Palermo in 1855, and in 1856 William Palmer formed the Palermo Town Company.[1] According to the *Atchison Globe,* the settlers chose the name Palermo "after a city in Italy, which is noted for the production of macaroni and anarchists." Neither the macaroni nor the anarchists, however, ever found their way to Kansas Territory.

The founders of Palermo promoted the town as a major steamboat port on the Missouri River. For a brief time in the mid-1850s, the community showed promise of achieving this goal. Businesses were established without delay. Rush Martin, the town lawyer, opened the first general store; Dr. B. G. Beaumont was the town's first physician; the partners of Mahan & Kimber built an "elegant" steam grist mill; and Granville Livermore erected a sawmill. A newspaper, the *Palermo Leader,* was started by the firm of Emery and Perham and remained in business for many years. Other early buildings constructed were a schoolhouse, a church, and a brickyard.[2] The settlers built a wharf on the Missouri River that stretched along the banks for more than a hundred feet. When the steamboats anchored at the landing, freighters' wagons were always there waiting to take the ships' merchandise to some western point in the territory.

A trio of so-called real estate men established a banking and investment business in Palermo. One was a noted gambler who had been barred from playing cards on the steamboats because of his cheating habits, and the other two were his card-playing accomplices. This group of "investors" tried to pass bogus banknotes bearing the name of a Leavenworth bank. Thankfully, little of this "wildcat currency" was actually circulated. The citizens refused to deal with these men and soon forced them out of business.

The town continued to grow during the late 1850s. Another physician, Dr. Joseph Hastings, located in Palermo, and Hardy & Swenson operated a general store there for several years. The legal profession in town passed from Rush Martin to Charles Madoulet, who advertised that he would attend to all "road cases in justice court."

After the steamboat business collapsed before the Civil War, a railroad was built through Palermo. It became known by such cute names as the "Bob-Tail" and the "Cork Screw" because the tracks meandered along the winding Missouri River. The railroad had no depot, just a platform where the passengers who wanted to board had to wave a flag to stop the train.[3]

Unfortunately, the railroad remained in operation only a few years, and its short stay hastened the town's downfall.

One of the founders' plans for the town included the building of a university, and by a special act of the Kansas legislature on February 18, 1858, a charter was granted for the establishment of Wayland University at Palermo. At that time the town was prospering, and its citizens were working hard to lay the groundwork for such an institution, believing that it would increase the town's population and stimulate the economy. The money necessary for building the university, however, was never appropriated, and the project never materialized.

In the 1860s Lucretia Herrington Bowers, a local settler, reminisced about Palermo.

The best houses were framed in St. Louis and brought by boat to Palermo; many I remember were beautiful and some were equal in beauty to some of the best homes in Troy at this time. The wharf was a busy place; at times several boats were tied up for unloading merchandise for the several merchants at Palermo and the taking on of wheat, corn, hogs, and cattle to be delivered at St. Joseph, Omaha, and other Missouri River points. The thickly timbered hills yielded cordwood that boats used for fuel at that time. Several fine hotels did a flourishing business, and pleasure boats from St. Louis would frequently come for a ball at those places.[4]

The Civil War brought to Palermo the threat of rebels and bushwhackers from across the Missouri. With most of the men gone to war, the town's population consisted mainly of women, children, and old men, perfect targets for the Missouri rebels. Mrs. Bowers recounts the Civil War years in Palermo as follows:

"Bushwhackers" . . . cared not whether their depredations were made on the northern or southern branch. Old men would take turns every night in patrolling the river front for a mile along Palermo; the women in their homes keeping watch as best they could; my mother who kept a maid during father's absence, took the first watch from dark to midnight, then the maid took over the watch; a gun on one side of the latched window, and an ax on the other side; we four children were put in the one bed in the front room, mother or the maid on a pallet on the floor, nearby to be aroused if molested; one midnight as my mother aroused the maid for duty, a galloping of horses was heard, then a fearful scream from a lady, then silence; the mornings investigation showed a trail of blood from the road to the edge of the river; nightly, these marauders tried to cross from the Missouri side to reach Palermo.[5]

After the Civil War and on into the 1880s and 1890s, Palermo went slowly downhill, and many businesses closed down. The post office, established on December 19, 1855, closed on December 15, 1904. By 1910, even though the population was still rather high—listed at 279—most of the businesses were gone. Today Palermo is a peaceful rural hamlet eight miles southeast of Troy and two miles from Wathena. The steamboats and railroads are gone, but ruins of a few townsite buildings can still be seen through the prairie grass.

BENDENA
Doniphan County

Old Doniphan County towns usually fell into two specific types—the earliest was the Missouri River community that prospered during the golden age of steamboat navigation; however, when the steamboat trade on the river diminished during the post–Civil War years, most of these towns disappeared. The second type was the inland community established on railroad lines that catered to the local farmers and merchants. Bendena was one of many railroad towns that prospered when the locomotives made frequent stops but declined during the depression years of the 1930s when rail service was interrupted and eventually terminated.

The town was established in 1886 when the Rock Island Railroad laid track through the county. The railroad depot was named Albers in honor of John Albers, owner of the land and the original founder of the town. When the station was completed, Albers decided it would be profitable to lay off a portion of his farm into town lots. Albers's success in selling lots inspired several local farmers and merchants to seize the opportunity to build stores close to Albers or to purchase lots with the intention of building in town.

In the fall of 1886, the first business was constructed in Albers: a general store operated by William Macklin. Macklin's store existed for a few years before it burned to the ground when someone carelessly overturned an oil lamp. Other businesses soon followed. Victor Ladwig and John Severin built another store, and Jake Bastin opened a blacksmith shop. In 1890, Councilman & Company built a new elevator. The government had already established a post office in 1888 and appointed Victor Ladwig as the first postmaster. After the Macklin store and J. W. Howard's elevator were completed, residents were at a loss to come up with a more appropriate name for the town. They left the matter to the station agent, Evie Morgan, who promptly named the town Bendena as a tribute to his girlfriend. The young lady evidently did not appreciate the honor, for she soon bestowed her affections on another man.

The population grew slowly but steadily. By 1910, however, there were still only about a hundred people in town. According to a 1916 history of Doniphan County, Bendena's population was small, but "they are prosperous and get along on brotherly love. The farmers adjacent are making all manner of fortunes and for a town its size Bendena gets its share of trade. . . . The town is very well situated from a commercial standpoint."

Bendena's boom period occurred from the 1890s to about World War I. During this time, the citizens established several more businesses and added some public improvements. St. John's Lutheran Church was built in the early 1900s. A hotel opened in 1896 with F. W. Reipen as "host." A lumbermill was built in the 1890s (though it was destroyed by fire on December 27, 1900). Around this time, S. A. Severin built another general store. Other businesses included a hardware store, a drugstore, two restaurants, the Bendena State Bank, a livery stable, a grocery store, three blacksmith shops, a photography lab, a barber, and a telephone office. In 1889 the partnership of Gray & Morgan established the first telephone service. They used two cigar boxes and some binder wire, which they strung between the depot and the post office. In the same year the railroad made improvements in Bendena when they dug a large well twenty-four feet across and eighty feet deep and erected a 55,000 gallon water tank.

Among the town's most colorful residents in the 1890s was "Uncle Johnny" Valmore Hudson, who was a first cousin to President Ulysses Grant and a veteran of the Mexican War who had assisted in the capture of General Santa Ana. Another resident, Gabriel Gerardy, invented the first disc pencil sharpener.[1]

Bendena remained an active community until the depression years of the 1930s forced the closing of the bank and several other businesses. Today several original stores, a few homes, and various other structures are all that remain of Bendena.

KICKAPOO CITY
Leavenworth County

When John P. Smith came to the Midwest in the spring of 1832, the only "civilized residents" in the area were "the soldiers sent to keep the Indian tribes in order; the missionaries sent to convert them; the traders who made friends with them; and those 'natives' who had attained some measure of civilization from their association with the 'whites.' "[1] Smith, a pioneer blacksmith from Tennessee, brought his family as far west as Clinton County, Missouri, in hopes of finding a new life in the West. On October 24, 1832, a treaty with the Kickapoo Indians stated that the government would support a blacksmith for the Kickapoo nation at a salary of $1,000 a year. Smith was fortunate enough to secure this position, and he immediately moved his family across the Missouri River to the Protestant mission previously established by the Reverend J. C. Berryman.[2]

In March 1834 Berryman started a day school, and Mary Smith, daughter of John, was one of his students. Mary described the mission.

> The old mission building was a large, plain log house with two large rooms, one of which was a dining room. In the other was a fireplace. There were also two small rooms in the back part of the house and a kitchen. This house sat on a hill. The school room was off from the main building. Down the hill toward the spring and above it was our house. We all carried water from that spring and I think my father walled it with rock. Fifty yards below the spring was father's shop. [Lawrence] Pensoneau, the French trader, I remember well. His place was below father's shop and on the river.[3]

In the 1830s a church society began to flourish. An 1834 church census showed 2 white members and 230 Kickapoo and Pottawatomie Indians. By 1838 the figures had changed to 3 whites and 161 Indians. Berryman's mission continued to thrive until July 1839, when the son of Chief Kennekuk killed the local blacksmith. After this unfortunate incident, the Kickapoo Indians became reluctant to let their children attend the mission school. Henceforward it was operated chiefly as a boarding school with as few as sixteen children living there at one time.[4]

Evidently the murder of the mission blacksmith by Chief Kennekuk's son was the turning point in Indian-white relations in the area. Mary Smith related the tragedy:

> After we left Kickapoo, the son of the "Wild Chief" killed the blacksmith who succeeded my father. I don't remember the Indian's name but that of the blacksmith was Potter. The Indian was passing the field where the Potter boys were cutting grass and when he was opposite them they said something that he thought was making fun of him for he was hideous looking, had a terribly scarred face and was very sensitive about it. The children often made

fun of him. When he started for the boys they ran to the house and he followed them. The father of the boys met him at the door and asked him what the trouble was, when the Indian deliberately stabbed him to death in his own door.

The Indian boy was John Kennekuk, who later succeeded his father and became chief of the Kickapoos. According to legend, he was killed by his jealous wife in 1867 and buried in a small cemetery south of Horton.[5]

In 1836 the Annual Register of Indian Affairs noted that the government had constructed a saw and grist mill at the Kickapoo Mission; meanwhile, the settlers built a new church costing $700.[6] On June 1, the Catholics established the Kickapoo Mission at a site a mile west of Lawrence Pensineau's fur trading post located near both Kickapoo settlements (Chief Pa-sha-cha-hah's village and Chief Kennekuk's town). The first Catholic mission building was ready for use in October and served as mission headquarters that winter. But although twenty Indian students attended Father Christian Hoecken's school, the mission church had only two Kickapoo members. The biggest obstacle to converting the Indians was the opposition of Chief Kennekuk. He not only had his own religion and a government-built church in which to preach, but he also thought the school was unnecessary, since they already had the government school run by Rev. Berryman, the Methodist missionary.

When the religious order replaced Father Hoecken and Father Felix Verreydt with two other priests in July 1837, Chief Pa-sha-cha-hah and his tribe moved some twenty miles away, leaving the Catholics with few supporters. The school dwindled to eight students, and the government withdrew its $500 per annum support in 1840, the same year the Kickapoo Catholic Mission closed.[7]

Two early visitors to Kickapoo were Charles Murray, the noted English traveler, who visited the site in the 1830s, and Francis Parkman, the American author, who mentioned Kickapoo in his book *California and the Oregon Trail* in 1846. The Reverend William Patton conducted a tour of Methodist Indian missions in Kansas in 1843 and noted in his journal that "in sight of the mission house" there was a "Roman Catholic establishment . . . which has not been in operation for some two or three years," and that there was also a house belonging to Kennekuk, "a heathen prophet," whose followers had shrunk to a bare quarter of the 250 he once led.[8]

The Catholic mission building stood abandoned for many years. The *Horton Headlight,* April 20, 1922, noted that it was the oldest building in Kansas still standing at that time, but its demise came a few months later when the new owner tore the building down and replaced it with a farm-house.[9] Known as the "cradle of the Catholic church in Kansas," the mission was constructed of immense native walnut logs, notched at the ends and fastened with wooden pegs. In 1854 the building operated as a hotel and later housed the *Kansas Pioneer,* one of the first newspapers in Kansas.

Major Robert Wilson established a trading post at Kickapoo and occupied it until 1852 when he sold it to Major M. P. Rively. It was at Rively's store that the first squatters' meeting in Kansas Territory was held. By 1854 plans were under way for Kickapoo City, one of the oldest towns in the state. As early as September 20, 1853, politicians held a convention there in order to nominate a delegate to Congress. Among the more important early settlers of the city were John Freeland, chairman of the county board for many years and a state senator; Isaac Cody, father of "Buffalo Bill" Cody and a store and hotel owner; Merrill Smith, government freighter, hotel keeper, and farmer; and David Harley, builder of Eight-Mile House, a tavern and inn near Kickapoo.

Some citizens from Weston and Platte County, Missouri, laid out Kickapoo City in July 1854. Much of the township was open to preemption, unlike nearby Leavenworth, which had grown around the confines of the military reserve. Accordingly, the founders hoped that Leavenworth would find it hard to compete with Kickapoo. Unfortunately, trouble began to develop between the settlers and some "claim jumpers," people who actually had no legal right to the land. In one instance, Captain J. W. Martin staked off his claim and returned to his former home in Liberty, Missouri, to get his family. His claim was "jumped" while he was away, and he had to employ H. Miles Moore, a personal friend, to go to court and argue his case before the U.S. marshal. The man who had been the "jumper" fled, leaving his wife behind to defy the law. After the coaxing, threats, and force of the marshal, she departed, but when he was out of sight, she returned and threatened to burn down the cabin. Captain Martin had to hire two men to guard his property until he could return permanently.

In the fall of 1854, a party of men from Leavenworth traveled to Kickapoo City to attend a sale of town lots. One man recalled his impression of the town:

> Some energetic business men have taken hold of this place, who will contribute greatly towards building the town. A brisk and spirited sale of lots took place on the premises. The lots generally brought from 30 to 70, 80 and 100 dollars each and one or two, we think, were as high as 110 dollars each. We understand there were some 40 or 50 lots sold.

In November 1854 the *Kansas Pioneer* made its appearance. A. B. Hazzard, the editor, was stoutly proslavery, and for three years he published bitter editorials in his anti-Leavenworth newspaper. The earliest known document connected with the territorial history of Kansas was printed by Mr. Hazzard in the *Kansas Pioneer*.

Businesses in Kickapoo City boomed overnight. A steam ferry busily carried passengers across the Missouri River; sawmills, grocery and dry goods stores, hotels, saloons, and lawyers' and doctors' offices were constructed in town. A newspaper census in 1854 counted 1,500 people in the city. By 1855 three more saloons, a livery stable, and a blacksmith shop completed the town's business directory.[10]

In April 1855 the settlers held their first election to decide the county seat of Leavenworth County, and Delaware City triumphed over both Kickapoo City and Leavenworth. The court declared these returns fraudulent, however, and a second election was held on March 18, 1857, which Leavenworth won. The citizens of Kickapoo City hardly noticed, for businesses continued to grow and the town prospered.[11]

The proslavery element around Kickapoo was strong. The Reverend Cyrus R. Rice gave this description of the vicinity in 1856 when border troubles were accelerating:

Kickapoo, a new town a few miles above Fort Leavenworth, was chosen as the meeting place for the first annual conference in Kansas Territory, (missionaries) and the bishop G. F. Pierce, fixed the time Sept. 12, 1856. Mrs. Rice and I left . . . for Kickapoo, Sept. 6, . . . The Missourians were invading Kansas in those days, and one did not feel very safe traveling over the prairies. . . . We reached the Mission in safety. Our business went pretty smoothly until Friday evening, when we were startled by news that (Col. Alexander) Doniphan and his men had crossed the river making for Lawrence and that Lane and his men were coming out to meet Doniphan, and might clash at Kickapoo or near there. The town was thrown into a furor of excitement in a little while, and some of the men went out on the different roads to stand guard and give the alarm if need be. No one was sleepy that night, for a little after midnight a fellow fired both barrels of his shotgun and came running and shouting "Lane is coming! Lane is coming!" . . . The men gathered in squads to defend the city while the women and children cried and gathered under the bluff near the river. But the alarm proved to be false. The fellow who gave it was declared drunk and was soon put under guard, and for the rest of the night all was quiet.

Proslavery voters at the polls in Kickapoo, 1855, as they appeared in Albert D. Richardson's book Beyond the Mississippi.

The term "Kickapoo Rangers" applied to the northern division of the militia in the Kansas Territory, and nearly 300 of these men defended the Missouri proslavery settlers in Kansas. David R. Atchison, a Missouri senator, was one of their leaders and advisors. Many of these Kickapoo Rangers were involved in the sacking of Lawrence on May 21, 1856. Senator Atchison gave the following speech concerning the raid:

> Boys, this day I am a Kickapoo Ranger. This day we have entered Lawrence with Southern rights inscribed on our banner, and not one Abolitionist dared to fire a gun. And now, boys, we will go in again . . . and test the

strength of that Free-State hotel and teach the Emigrant Aid Company that Kansas shall be ours. . . . If one man or woman dare stand before you, blow them to hell with a chunk of cold lead.

An unfortunate incident occurred in Leavenworth County on January 18, 1856. A few of the Rangers were involved in the murder of Captain Reese P. Brown at Easton following a quarrel over an election. These proslavery forces were attempting to take the ballot boxes by force from the home of T. A. Minard. The free-state men thwarted their attack, but not before one of the Rangers killed Captain Brown.[12]

Kickapoo City's residents were active players in the slavery issue in Kansas and were the proud owners of a six-pound brass cannon nicknamed "Old Kickapoo." American forces first captured this cannon during the Mexican War in the Battle of Sacramento on February 28, 1847. "Old Kickapoo" eventually turned up in Weston, Missouri, from whence it was stolen by a band of Kickapoo Rangers who retained possession of the cannon for two years and used it to sway elections and threaten free-staters. On January 5, 1858, a party of sixty angry free-state men from Leavenworth went to Kickapoo City and removed "Old Kickapoo" while the residents were sleeping. The next day the group returned to Leavenworth "with drums beating and flags flying—some of the victorious army on foot, some on horseback, parading the streets, dragging glorious 'Old Kickapoo' after them." Kickapoo City had lost its brass "protector."

The indignant citizens of Kickapoo City held a meeting and passed a resolution proclaiming the free-state men a bloodthirsty mob who had broken into dwellings and stores, trying to draw innocent citizens into a fight for the purpose of "bringing on a general battle, destroying the town and murdering the inhabitants." The essence of the proceedings was that "Old Kickapoo" must be recaptured "peaceably if we can, forcibly if we must." Nothing was ever accomplished either way, and "Old Kickapoo" is now a museum piece at the Kansas State Historical Society.[13]

During the Civil War, the population of Kickapoo City began to wane. A land treaty signed in 1862 moved the Kickapoo tribes sixty miles west to the Pottawatomie reservation near Holton. After the Civil War, the town was a large farming community. In 1868, when the Leavenworth Coal Company purchased twenty acres in order to operate a coal mine, Kickapoo City experienced a small business boom. In 1871 the Rock Island Railroad came through Kickapoo City, and the company constructed several roundhouses and a terminal. But in spite of the railroad, Kickapoo residents were forced to accept the inevitable. Kickapoo City had become little more than a small

The U.S. Land Office at Kickapoo in disrepair in the late nineteenth century.

agricultural town and coal center. The men who had promoted Kickapoo City had originally planned to make the town the capital of Kansas. Indeed, Cyrus K. Holliday, on his way to Kansas in 1860, was told to settle at "the greatest city on the continent—and that city, sir, is Kickapoo."[14] That statement certainly held little truth by the 1880s.

Andreas, in his *History of Kansas,* offers the following description of Kickapoo City around 1880:

> The once busy village is almost deserted, containing two little churches, a schoolhouse, two or three stores and a physician. . . . There are two Catholic churches in the township—one in the village—under charge of Father Bernard Fink. They have a combined membership of about 75. There is also quite a flourishing Methodist Episcopal Church.[15]

On January 23, 1902, Kickapoo City became just plain Kickapoo. By this time the main source of income in the area was coal, and the city of Leavenworth had five coal mines in operation twenty-four hours a day. Gradually the residents, along with the stores and shops, moved to Leavenworth. In 1910 Kickapoo's population was 200, a far cry from its busier days. On August 31, 1920, the post office closed its doors.

Today Kickapoo stands at its original location three miles north of old Highway 7. A few new homes been built, and the street locations have been changed, but the town remains basically the same. You can still find arrowheads in the vicinity, also parts of old wagon wheels, military buttons, scrapers, bone knives, and a few coins. Old foundations and abandoned buildings mark the place where people came with high hopes of a new life but ultimately found only the sound of creaky wagons, the ring of the blacksmith's hammer, and the gunshots at the local saloons.[16]

BAIN CITY
Leavenworth County

With the stroke of a pen in 1964, Bain City disappeared. The thousand-acre community between Leavenworth and Lansing had become a victim of annexation—to Leavenworth. At this time about 300 residents living along ten unpaved streets composed the town. The business district consisted of two grocery stores and a school with eighty pupils. Life in Bain City was far from boring, however, and its disappearance signaled the end of a long, exciting era in the Leavenworth community.

J. W. Bain first platted Bain City as a 400-acre community on May 30, 1867. Within ten years, it was located next to the Civil War veterans' center and soldiers' home, later known as Wadsworth, which gave Bain City its identity. The town soon became a haven for veterans. Among its many nicknames was "Klondike," recalling the gold rush and the fact that veterans then were paid in gold. Bain City was also known as "Uniontown," which reflected its popularity among northern Civil War veterans.[1]

The early establishments in town catered to soldiers of the nearby home; therefore, quite a few taverns and houses of ill repute thrived. In time, Spanish-American War and World War I veterans found the night life offered by Bain City merchants just as attractive as their Civil War counterparts had years earlier.[2]

Edward Chapman, Leavenworth County Attorney, once remarked that "Bain City is a perennial trouble spot. Assaults and disturbances average more than one a month." Albert Bodde, a general merchandise operator in 1919, offered his own opinion on the origin of this trouble. "There are good people living in Bain City. . . . Its reputation has been made by outsiders who came here looking for trouble." Bodde claimed that since the platting of Bain City four hundred people had died within its boundaries. Although some of these people were stabbed, shot, or beaten, most of them died of natural causes. Certainly Bodde himself was familiar with some of the more violent incidents. Near his store a huge elm tree once stood. In 1927, a World War I veteran named Harris was killed, and his murderer dumped his body under the tree. Subsequently, Bain City endured a period of martial law that included twenty-four-hour patrols by the sheriff's department.

Bain City's many saloons and centers of nightlife were not elegant, but they were exciting. A veteran police officer told the story of two visitors from St. Louis who found Leavenworth's spots uninteresting and decided to go to Bain City. They were seated at a wooden table in an unnamed establishment when another customer accused the bartender of failing to mix alcohol with the near beer in the pan of liquid that he served for a quarter. After arguing for a few minutes, the customer threw the contents of the pan in the bartender's face. The bartender, in turn, grabbed his baseball bat. As fists, chairs, and bottles flew in the melee that followed, the visitors huddled behind the table they were using as a barrier. When the action subsided, they fled, crying "Get us out of here quick!"[3]

After Leavenworth's first annexation move in the city's history, Bain City ceased to exist, giving the lie to Bodde's prediction that "Bain City will always be Bain City." Recent business expansions have overlapped the area to the point that it is difficult to find the former community at all.

QUINDARO
Wyandotte County

"Why one town should live and another die; why should one flourish continually and another's glory fade in a day are problems which often vex the wisest," wrote Andreas in his *History of Kansas*. The reason for Quindaro's decline is relatively clear: Quindaro was a prosperous boom town whose location near a big city ensured its demise.[1]

Charles Robinson, the first governor of Kansas, was one of the original promoters of Quindaro. He helped found the town in the early 1850s, when the proslavery forces outnumbered the free-state settlers. In 1856 the proslavery factions made several attempts to control Kansas politics, and the settlers believed these attempts were almost certain to succeed. For some time Missourians had been stopping much of the free-state emigration by forcibly turning back the westbound settlers and by searching for and confiscating firearms and other supplies coming into Kansas. Because the free-state partisans sorely needed a friendly home, free-state leaders in Lawrence explored the banks of the Missouri River for a suitable townsite. At a point six miles above the mouth of the Kansas River, on Wyandotte Indian land, the men found a natural rock ledge where the river ran about twelve feet deep, just the necessary depth for an ideal steamboat landing. They also found plenty of wood and rock that could be used for building purposes.

The men formed a town company in January 1857, and Charles Robinson and Abelard Guthrie took charge of most of the town's legal affairs. Since Guthrie's wife was a Wyandotte Indian, the land was easily acquired from the tribe. Mrs. Guthrie's Indian name was Quindaro, meaning a "bundle of sticks," and the town company decided to name the town in her honor.

On May 13, 1857, J. M. Walden started a weekly newspaper, the *Chindowan*—meaning "Leader," and Mrs. Clarina I. H. Nichols, a noted Kansas suffragette, became assistant editor.[2] The settlers built three or four more buildings that spring, including the Quindaro House, the second largest hotel in the territory.[3]

The first issue of the *Chindowan* reported that trees had been removed from several acres on the townsite and thirty-four houses and sixteen businesses were under construction. A second hotel soon opened, along with two commission houses, a few land agencies, a carpenter shop, a surveyor, a stone yard, a sawmill, a cabinetmaker, and several blacksmiths. By the fall of 1857, professional men were plentiful and included land agents R. P. Gray, Charles Chadwick, H. J. Bliss, M. B. Newman, R. M. Ainsworth, and Charles Robinson of the Boston Land Trust, as well as Dr. George Budington, physician, Charles Ellis, civil engineer and surveyor, and A. C. Strock & Co., drugs and medicines. Quindaro's sawmill was the largest in Kansas at the time of its construction; and Captain Otis Webb operated one of the biggest ferry boats on the Missouri River between Quindaro and Parkville.

Prospects looked good for the proposed Quindaro, Parkville & Burlington Railroad, which was supposed to connect with the Hannibal & St. Joseph Railroad in northeastern Kansas. Henry Wilson, an early Kansas judge, arrived at Quindaro on May 24, 1857, and made a short but inspirational speech to the citizens. These events inspired townspeople to buy into the town company for $100 a share. With their motto "In union there is strength," the citizens of Quindaro were pulling together to make their city the "Queen of Kansas."[4] Unfortunately, the queen's reign was destined to be short.

The new town initially found it difficult to gain recognition as a good steamboat landing. The steamboats were mostly Missouri-owned and -operated, and their officers refused to stop at Quindaro because of its free-state politics. The officers actively pressured the passengers to pass up Quindaro for Leavenworth or Kansas City, both proslavery towns, and charged fares accordingly. Passage from Leavenworth to Quindaro was $3, but from Leavenworth to Kansas City, a much longer trip, the cost was $2.50. A threat by the free-state people to start their own steamboat line

Ruins of a Quindaro hotel around the turn of the century. The largest building in town, this made for the most noteworthy ruin. The once-thriving steamboat town was later designated a park, and children raced among its ruins.

broke up this swindle, and soon the passengers regarded Quindaro as having the best landing on the river. Traffic was heavy; for example, there were thirty-six steamboat landings at the levee during one week. In 1857, the *Chindowan* reported that fifty-five steamboats were operating on the Missouri at that time, and the celebrated "Polar Star" was one of Quindaro's regulars.

The steamboats brought to the free-state advocates of Quindaro much-needed supplies that were later transported overland by stage across the Delaware Indian reservation to Lawrence, a distance of thirty-one miles. For the first fifteen miles, the stage coaches went through heavy timber to a halfway house where the Indians served them lunch—not exactly the best meal as they used stale, mushy corn in most of their food. The settlers built another road south to Osawatomie, where the Quindaro Town Company maintained a free ferry, and later a stage line ran from Wyandotte to Lawrence by way of Quindaro.

In August 1857, the *Chindowan* reported that Quindaro had a population of 600 living in more than 100 buildings and that much of the grading of Kanzas Avenue had been completed. George Park, of Parkville, Missouri, had enough faith in this enterprising town that he built a large three-story stone hotel. Albert D. Richardson, a New York newspaper correspondent, spent some time in Quindaro and lectured to the Literary Society on "Out West." Also in late summer of 1857, O. H. Macauley and James Redpath attempted to bring a cannon into Kansas to Quindaro, but when they learned there was a proslavery party waiting for them to reach the territory, they buried the cannon near the Kansas-Nebraska line. When Macauley felt it was safe to move it, Quindaro had its cannon. In the 1860s a "committee" from Wyandotte quietly "borrowed" it.

In October 1857 the settlers celebrated the Quindaro-to-Parkville ferry by firing the cannon, signaling the beginning of Quindaro's own transportation system. In 1858 the legislature granted a charter for Otis Webb, Charles Robinson, and Charles Chapin to establish another ferry across the Missouri River. Charges were as follows: One-horse carriage, 75 cents; each passenger, 10 cents; two-horse team loaded, $1.25; each additional horse, mule, ass, oxen, cow, calf, 15 cents; each score of sheep or swine, $1.00; lumber, $1.50 per 1,000 feet.

In 1858 Quindaro became involved in steamboat travel on the Kansas River, but the entire enterprise was a failure. The *Minnie Belle,* one of the best steamboats in the area, took more than four days to reach Lawrence. Another steamer, the *Lightfoot,* was more successful, but it could only make seasonal trips because water on the river was consistently low.

Meanwhile, however, shares of stock were selling well in Quindaro. Business lots on the levee sold for $500–750, and on Kanzas Avenue from $500–1,250. Charles Robinson's manipulative stock deals and the settlers railroad "fever" were two major factors in Quindaro's economic success. Many Quindaro men joined with George Park of Parkville in organizing the Quindaro, Parkville & Grand River Railroad. The line was surveyed and projected across the Missouri River at Parkville, then on to southern Kansas. In May 1858 the Quindaro steamer *Otis Webb* carried a load of citizens to Wyandotte for an important railroad meeting. Unfortunately, they hit the Wyandotte ferry as they came into the landing, putting it out of business for several days.

Life was pleasant in Quindaro during its boom days. According to the *Chindowan*, J. V. Fitch served ice cream and soda at his store, the Literary

Society was well attended, and the library committee offered more than 200 volumes of good reading material. During the summer and winter of 1857, the townspeople organized a "Shanghai" court and arrested some poor soul nearly every night for an alleged misdemeanor. When the court convened each day, a regular trial was held, and the jury invariably found the prisoner guilty. The fine was usually a box of cigars or a bushel of apples.

Reality intruded on the idyll, of course, as the free-state movement gained ground. The Topeka convention organized a free-state militia, and sixty-eight citizens of Quindaro enrolled. The citizens also formed a Temperance League, and in January 1858 they resolved to close the liquor shops. Within five days, the town voted seventy-seven to twenty-five to make liquor illegal. This proclamation influenced many pioneer women to persuade their husbands to settle there. Not long after this self-proclaimed prohibition was in effect, the members of the Temperance League discovered whiskey hidden in a shack west of the Quindaro House. After holding a council meeting, the men quickly hauled the offensive barrel from beneath the owner's bed, broke it, and poured the whiskey out into the street.

Legend has it that runaway slaves on their way north used the Underground Railroad at Quindaro. Only one slave is said to have been caught there while escaping to freedom. They reportedly stayed in an isolated cabin near the town before heading north. One slave girl remained hidden with some local citizens at Quindaro for several days while slave hunters from Missouri searched the area for her.

By mid-1858 Quindaro's prospects for economic growth slowly faded. Times were changing rapidly. That year the newspaper experienced financial difficulty, and the editor suspended publication. Hard times continued through 1859. Wyandotte County was formed, and Wyandotte City, only a few miles from Quindaro, became the county seat. Yet business in town was still brisk. The *Wyandotte Gazette* confessed that more business was conducted in Quindaro in one day than in Wyandotte in a week.

By the end of 1859, there were no new settlers in Quindaro, and business had come to a standstill. After George Park built his hotel three stories high, he roofed it over and never finished the inside. The lot on which O. H. Macauley carefully built his warehouse had once been leased to the *Chindowan*. Macauley eventually sold both the building and the lot to Alfred Gray for $5.00 and a pair of Chester White pigs. The town company's income dwindled, and it was unable to meet routine expenses. Abelard Guthrie had invested heavily in land and lost his money because of the

Residence of Charles Calhoun Dar of Quindaro, 1906.

town company's debts. He became very embittered by his misfortune and blamed Charles Robinson, one of the founders who came out of the economic crisis in good shape financially.

Quindaro's economic collapse took several years to culminate. Various schemes still looked promising to the townspeople, and Guthrie spent some time in Washington trying to secure for the town the terminus of the projected railroad. Thaddeus Hyatt and Robinson were appointed agents of the city to promote appropriations of land for the extension of the Parkville & Grand River Railroad to Quindaro. In 1860, George Veale, Fielding Johnson, Julius Fisk, and Abelard Guthrie were granted a charter by the legislature to maintain a ferry at Quindaro for a period of ten years. This was the last ferry at Quindaro, for in 1861 at the start of the Civil War the Missourians sank the ferry boat to prevent their slaves from escaping.

From January 20 to March 12, 1862, the Ninth Kansas Volunteer Infantry quartered their men in the empty business buildings of Quindaro and reorganized themselves into the Second Kansas Cavalry. Officer control was slack, and the men gutted the town. They tore up everything movable for firewood and abandoned the buildings to weather, fire, and theft.

C. M. Chase wrote a series of letters to the Sycamore (Ill.) *True Republican and Sentinel*, in which he noted in 1863: "We visited Quindaro and found only one family there—a poor man and a crazy wife had strayed into the hall of the hotel and occupied a bunch of rags." In 1873, he revisited the place and reported to the *Vermont Union* of Lindon, Vermont: "Quindaro was, but now she is not. One store with a granite front and iron posts stood as good as new and various other buildings were in good preservation, but empty. . . . Small cottonwoods had sprung up in the street and the owls were making a selection of choice localities for places of abode. The solitary family of 1863 even has abandoned the place."[5]

The legislature of 1862 repealed the act that incorporated Quindaro, and the town company was officially out of business. Today what little is left of the town is within the city limits of Kansas City in Quindaro Park.

SIX-MILE HOUSE & STAGE STATION
Wyandotte County

Just west of Quindaro stood "Six Mile House," a notorious saloon and an important stopping point on the stage route from Independence to Leavenworth. The house was six miles from the Wyandotte ferry, hence its name. The polished black-walnut tavern is still standing on land acquired by J. A. Bartles from the original Wyandotte Indian owner. Bartles and his son Theodore operated the stage stop for many years. The two-story tavern once boasted nine rooms with a wine cellar and secret closets, but over the years its appearance has changed. The owners cut the tavern in two in 1894; one section became a barn, the other a shed.

During the Civil War, the timber around Six-Mile House was an ideal hiding place for bushwhackers, guerrillas, and army deserters, who made a habit of terrorizing the local settlers. On August 3, 1861, the *Wyandotte Gazette* noted that thirteen people had been murdered in the county during the past two years and none of their murderers had been caught. The paper gave many accounts of robbery, horse stealing, and the kidnapping of free blacks by "visitors" from across the Missouri River. Six-Mile House was well known as a rendezvous for these gangs. On July 17, 1862, the citizens of Quindaro and Wyandotte held a meeting at the county courthouse and formed a "Committee for Safety" whose objective was to tear down Six-Mile House. When the committee arrived at the tavern, they were surprised to find a company of soldiers camped outside. Bartles had learned of the committee's plans and had gone to Fort Leavenworth to appeal for protection. General James G. Blunt's orders were "no destruction of personal property," which saved Six-Mile House.

On December 18, 1862, a man named Smith was shot at the saloon by a posse looking for horses stolen near Westport. In July 1863, Missourians made plans to burn Six-Mile House and the town of Wyandotte, but the local sheriff arrested them before they could cross the river.

Theodore Bartles, a notorious character and son of owner J. A., was famous for being fast with a gun. In fact he had once defeated "Wild Bill" Hickok in a shooting contest. One evening at his tavern Bartles overheard some men talking about Quantrill's plan to attack Lawrence. Using his skills in the cause of abolition whenever possible, he sent a Shawnee Indian named Pelathe to warn the settlers of the coming raid. Unfortunately, Pelathe arrived in Lawrence too late. Quantrill's men were already firing the first shots.

After the Civil War other businesses sprang up near the tavern, including a blacksmith shop, a store, a hotel, a tobacco factory, a church, a schoolhouse, and the post office that later moved to Braman Hill, one mile south. Still, crime was rampant in the area around Six-Mile House. Someone shot Dr. J. B. Welborn and his wife through their front window as they were sitting quietly at home. Miraculously, both recovered. A traveler and his son were hanged from a tree near Six-Mile House after being robbed by bushwhackers. Neighbors claimed that the ghosts of these victims haunted the area for many years.

About a mile beyond Six-Mile House on the road from Quindaro to Leavenworth stood a trading post called Young America. The trader there carried a variety of merchandise, but "grog" was his biggest seller. Abelard Guthrie recalled stopping at Young America and finding the Indians in various degrees of intoxication. He noted that they were lying about on the ground as though they had been in a battle.

All these particular sites were part of the Quindaro vicinity, an area steeped in Kansas history.[1]

PADONIA
Brown County

James H. Lane, a free-state leader in Kansas Territory, laid out three towns during the 1850s: Padonia, Plymouth, and Lexington, the latter two located in the northwestern part of Brown County. Unfortunately, Lane's attempts to establish permanent free-state settlements in Kansas were unsuccessful, and only Padonia existed for any length of time.

In Plymouth, Lane's men mounted a small cannon on some earthworks for defense against the Missouri border ruffians; in Lexington, they erected a small log fort for further protection. Upon leaving the county, Lane was supposed to have buried the cannon, but after making several unsuccessful attempts to locate it, the Missourians learned that the cannon had been taken to White Cloud and secretly loaded onto a steamboat.[1]

Padonia was the site of a skirmish known as the Battle of Padonia, a bloodless encounter between Kansas settlers and the Missourians. Both before and after the Civil War, Kansas "Jayhawkers" often crossed into Missouri to steal horses. In fact one Jayhawker nicknamed "Cleveland" and his partner made horse rustling a lucrative business. In return, gangs of Missourians rode over into Brown County and stole horses, cattle, and personal property, then returned by way of the Missouri River between Rulo, Nebraska, and White Cloud.

Orville Root, storekeeper and postmaster and one of Lane's officers, formed a vigilante committee. He had stacks of prairie hay placed on high ground near the town. These stacks were to be set on fire if anyone saw the Missourians approaching the settlement. On October 4, 1861, a gang of over 100 border ruffians split their forces at Falls City, Nebraska; one force headed for Padonia and the other for Salem, Nebraska. A free-state man who saw them ride out went to the nearest house south of Falls City and sounded the alarm. That night other free-state men warned the settlers along Walnut Creek that the Missouri border ruffians were coming. The "Minute Men," ready at a moment's notice, rode as far as Hiawatha and alerted the militia, who then went to Padonia and set the stacks of hay on fire.

By early morning about 100 settlers, armed with every conceivable type of weapon, met in Root's storeroom at Padonia and waited anxiously for dawn to break. Meanwhile over seventy-five Missourians arrived just outside of town at the homestead of James Leavitt, a known free-state man, and forced him to kill a hog and prepare a meal for them. The free-state men in Padonia, who had been informed of the ruffians' whereabouts, rode out to the Leavitt homestead and positioned themselves on the north side of the house. A Missouri sentinel discovered them and immediately warned the rest of his men, who left their meal, ran out to their horses, and hid behind them for protection. The ruffians hesitated to start shooting, for Root's men had them surrounded. Hoping to avert bloodshed, Root sent in two men under a flag of truce. These men told the Missourians that they must lay down their arms or face the consequences. The Missourians agreed and marched in front of Root's men to lay down their weapons in true military style. Root's men took possession of the arms, then forced the ruffians to take the oath of allegiance to the United States, a bitter pill for them to swallow. Eight of the Missourians were discovered to be Confederate soldiers and were held as prisoners of war for the U.S. authorities. Root ordered the rest of the men to leave Brown County on foot. What could have been a major encounter ended in a peaceful victory for Padonia's citizens.[2]

Padonia remained a typical small country town for many years and had a post office off and on from October 1857 to May 1933. Today the site of Padonia lies amid a cluster of residences and a few farm fields in Brown County.

ASH POINT
Nemaha County

For the two glorious years of 1859 and 1860, Ash Point, ten miles northwest of Seneca at the junction of two overland stage routes, enjoyed a short-lived boom. James Parsons and Josiah Blancett founded Ash Point, but the town's principal backer was John O'Laughlin, builder of the first general store and hotel. These few dwellings and the overland stage buildings comprised the entire town at that time.

The U.S. government established a post office in Ash Point in 1859 and hired Horace Bemus as the first postmaster. After the settlers built the stage station that year, the site became known as Ten Mile Point, denoting its distance from Seneca. If not for its strategic location on these overland stage routes, the town probably would have been abandoned within a short time, but in fact Ash Point flourished as a stage stop until 1870. The town hit a peak population of thirty inhabitants in 1860. That same year the pony express started at St. Joseph, and Ash Point became one of its relay stations.

In the mid-1860s, settlers established another town called Okeeta in an attempt to divert the overland traffic away from Ash Point. In an argument sparked by the rivalry existing between the two towns, Josiah Blancett shot and killed an unidentified resident of Okeeta.[1] Okeeta citizens did not soon forget this tragedy.

Albert D. Richardson, early American author and explorer, traveled through Ash Point on his way to Pike's Peak. In a letter dated May 22, 1860, Richardson made this humorous reference to the town:

We camped the second night near Seneca—a rapidly growing village in Nemaha County. . . .

At that point settlements began to grow scarce and the principal sites of residents along the road consisted of the cabins and tents of enterprising gentlemen of a commercial turn who inform the public through very primitive signs that they are in the grocery business and sell beer and gingerbread. . . . At Ash Point a grocer seeks to captivate the hearts and purses of emigrants by informing them that he dispenses "Butte Reggs, Flower and Mele." Another sign that read "Flower & Mell, Chese, Egse; Lagar Bear; Liker, 5 cents a glass." At present he does not seem to be over-run with customers.

In 1870, when both the St. Joseph trail and the Fort Leavenworth military road became inactive, the settlers abandoned the town. Today both Okeeta and Ash Point have disappeared into the prairie, their once busy streets now filled with stalks of corn.[2]

NEUCHATEL
Nemaha County

In May 1857 two brothers, Charles and Ami Bonjour, arrived on the site of what became the town of Neuchatel. They were the first French-speaking persons to settle in the region, and through their influence their brother, Frederic Bonjour, his wife, Julia, and L. August Zurcher also took up claims. In the summer of 1857, the government hired Zurcher and the Bonjour brothers to cut hay, which was one of the few ways for the settlers to make money before their land could be broken for farming. The homesteading continued with the arrival of the Simon and Mouton families, as well as additional Bonjours.

Alfred Bonjour and his wife built the large stone house that now stands on the property belonging to his grandson, Donald Bonjour. In the early 1860s, Alfred was commissioned a notary public, elected justice of the peace, and served as postmaster. Alfred and his wife were parents of thirteen children, including one set of triplets. Sadly, only four children survived infancy.

Settlers thronged to Neuchatel in the 1860s, bringing the surnames of Freziere, Gaume, Sauvageot, Dulace, Labbe, Dockler, Junod, Mentha, Pinet, and Rossier. Peter Dockler, a French physician, came to Neuchatel in 1862. When Onaga became a larger town in the region, he moved there and lived to be over a hundred years old. Most of the settlers in the area were from France, Switzerland, and Belgium, making Neuchatel quite an international community.

A general merchandise store opened in an old log house in 1867. Fred Bonjour and Henry Labbe owned the second frame store erected just south of the Neuchatel Hall in 1869. On one occasion Labbe sued a customer, J. H. Everts, for refusing to pay his bill. Shortly thereafter, Everts walked into the store carrying a gun and tried to force Labbe to withdraw the suit. Instead, Labbe added the charge of assault to his case. This lawsuit turned out to be one of the biggest and most expensive in Nemaha County, and the court summoned many residents of the area to serve as witnesses. In the end, Evert was forced to pay $15 in court costs plus the $12.50 unpaid bill he owed Labbe.

On a Saturday evening around the turn of the century, Henry Labbe's son Sam was tending the store when a robbery occurred. At the time, Labbe was expecting a few of his friends in for cards, so he moved the cheese and crackers to the back room, tied a gunny-sack over the sugar barrel and, after throwing the store cat into the ash can, sat down to await his guests. By 8:00 p.m., ten of his friends, neighbors, and customers had arrived and were engaged in lively conversation when an unknown man flourishing a large revolver stepped through the front door and yelled "Hands up, Gentlemen!" The man had a red handkerchief tied over the lower part of his face, completely hiding his mouth and chin, and it was not until he had ordered every man to stand in line and threatened to shoot one of them that the group really grasped the reality of the situation. He ordered the men to advance, one at a time, and contribute their money and valuables to a bag he held in his hand. After he had emptied the cash register, the robber ordered them to follow him out on the porch. When the last man had passed over the threshold, the robber made a rush for a horse tied nearby. As he mounted the animal he remarked, "So long boys, I'll see you later," and disappeared. Later that evening the robber calmly ate his dinner at the home of an unsuspecting Mr. Noble who lived close by. The holdup later became known as one of the "coolest" robberies in that part of the country.[1]

In May 1907 the Neuchatel store caught fire. Everything burned except a few of the owner's personal effects. A large crowd gathered and saved the remaining buildings on main street, but the loss of the store hurt the town.[2]

The townspeople dedicated the new Neuchatel church on December 13, 1905, and they held regular services there until 1932. Until the 1940s, the Reverend Milliard Marshall of the Osage Congregational church in Onaga offered communion services occasionally, and the Reverend Robert Williams conducted services once a month. After the ministers' departure from Onaga, the residents abandoned the church until its restoration in 1950.[3] In 1964 the church closed again, but today it has been restored to excellent condition with the help of neighborhood friends. In 1970 the church celebrated its 100th anniversary. The cemetery adjoining the church is well-

kept; the schoolhouse and meeting hall have been restored. They stand together, side by side, marking the old townsite. It's worth a visit just to see
how community spirit saved a landmark. Without local interest, more of
Neuchatel might have disappeared, as have many other nearby towns.

BLAINE
Pottawatomie County

Imagine, if you can, a completely deserted main street with tumbleweeds,
worn-out rock business buildings crumbling in the sun, and grass covering
the cracks in the sidewalks. This is Blaine today. Nearly gone, but still one
of the most picturesque ghost towns in Kansas. The panorama of decay and
neglect would be complete were it not for the St. Columbkille Catholic
church, which still stands on the north side of town, the last vestige of life
in the community.

Like many small towns founded in the late 1880s, Blaine's existence re-
volved around the life of the church. Indeed, the two were dependent
upon one another. In 1875 a priest from St. Marys conducted services for
sixty families in the area, thus starting the Blaine parish. He often arrived
on horseback and performed baptisms, marriages, funerals, and other religious rites. In 1877 Father Ambrose Butler was assigned to the church at St.
Marys. As he traveled around the area, he could see it was just the right
place for certain hardworking immigrants from the slums of St. Louis. Father Butler established the St. Louis Colony Association and bought some
land near Blaine. He then persuaded about sixty families from St. Louis to
make the trip west. Butler founded one of only twelve Catholic parishes in
the United States formed by direct colonization. Blaine retained its pre-
dominantly Catholic population throughout its existence. In the 1870s a
Methodist bishop tried to attract a religious following. He constructed a
church and parsonage, but his services were somewhat irregular and his
congregation often failed to materialize.

The town was first called Butler City, but because a town by that name
already existed, the settlers changed it to Blaine, after James G. Blaine, a
popular Republican presidential nominee at that time.[1] During the mid-
1880s, the town developed rapidly. On January 7, 1886, the *Westmoreland Re-
corder & Period* described Blaine as

> a prosperous little town on the line of the Kansas Central railroad about 95
> miles west of Leavenworth and has a population of about 200. It was laid
> out October 14, 1884. The best men are wide awake and left no stone un-

A Union Pacific locomotive stopped for fuel at the Blaine water tank, 1908.

turned that may lend to the prosperity of their stirring berg. The Catholics have a church building, built in 1881 at a cost of $2,500 - Father Hudson, pastor. The Methodists have a neat building, recently completed and have a large membership. The schools are prosperous and have a large enrollment.

At its peak, Blaine had two hotels, two livery stables, a newspaper, two barbers, a bank, a hardware store, a drugstore, a real estate office, a physician, a blacksmith shop, a general store, and a meat market. The population peaked in 1910 at 250. After the Santa Fe Railroad purchased the Kansas Central's interests in town, rail stops became more numerous. For a brief time, more cattle were shipped from Blaine than from anywhere else on the line.

After World War I, Blaine began to go downhill. The Santa Fe discontinued its regular rail service, and businesses closed their doors during the depression years of the 1930s. The ability of the local residents to travel farther for goods and services also hurt Blaine's economy. The grade school closed in 1956 and the private Catholic school in 1958. The priest at the beautiful St. Columbkille Catholic church had to limit the number of masses held each week and after August 1966 he cut back drastically.[2]

Today Main Street is completely deserted and most of the business buildings are in ruins. The church still stands, however—a lasting monument to the community's spirit. Stop and visit; the chapel's beautiful stained glass windows and ornate woodwork remind visitors of churches in much larger cities.

LOUISVILLE
Pottawatomie County

The countryside surrounding the Louisville townsite was once part of the Pottawatomie Indian hunting grounds, and Louis Vieux, chief of the tribe, shares the honor for the origin of the town's name with Louis Wilson, son of the town's founder. Vieux, of Indian and French descent, served as both business agent and interpreter for the Pottawatomies and made many trips to Washington on their behalf. He was quite a wealthy landowner at the time of his death in 1872. In his will he bequeathed to his wife and children the entire townsite of Louisville, though legally he didn't own it.[1] Today his grave and those of his immediate family can be found in a small country cemetery a few miles east of town.

Louisville, first known as Rock Post, was located near the Oregon Trail, which passed a few miles northeast of the town. At the Vermillion crossing of the trail rest the graves of some of those '49ers who died of cholera five years before Louisville came into existence. Their graves are still marked with the rocks that someone placed there over a century ago.

Robert Wilson, the town's first postmaster and a government blacksmith

A 1907 bird's-eye view of Louisville looking north from a hill just south of town.

Curious spectators survey the smoldering wreckage of a fire that destroyed the Vermillion store in Louisville in 1908.

to the Pottawatomies, was the first settler at the Louisville townsite. Wilson's log cabin became a stopping place for travelers and the first "hotel" in Pottawatomie County. When Horace Greeley made his trip across the Plains in 1859, he spent several days at the hotel waiting for the high waters of Rock Creek to recede. During the spring, the settlers used an area south of town as a campground, and occasionally large numbers of pioneers in covered wagons camped for several days, resting and waiting for the high water to subside.[2]

The town was platted in 1857 after the arrival of a large group of settlers, many of whom were associated with the Pottawatomie Indian Reservation or the commerce on the Oregon Trail. After the Indians received their annuities from the government, they transacted much of their business in Louisville.

When the legislature organized Pottawatomie County in 1861, St. George became the county seat, but since Louisville was growing so fast, the townspeople decided to contest this action, and on November 5, they held an election. Louisville received the necessary majority of votes and became the county seat. However, although the town's population continued to grow, the commissioners moved the county seat in 1882 to Westmoreland, a much larger town in the area.[3]

During the early 1860s, Louisville furnished the site for a popular health resort on the south side of Rock Creek; its waters were well-known for their medicinal qualities. The town was also an unsuccessful candidate for the temporary location of the state capital at the Wyandotte convention in July 1859.[4]

In the 1860s the Civil War caused some periodic uneasiness to Louisville residents. One incident is recounted in 1863 by Mrs. Harriet Smith Spaulding in her "Bridal Trip in the Early Days" article in the *Club Member* paper:

When Quantrill was making his raid in Lawrence, the news came to Louisville that they were coming that way, so the men thought best to guard the town. The women doing their part, stayed up and made hot coffee for the men. Then the militia was organized. One day they had gone to Manhattan for general drill and there were only two or three men left in the town. Just about noon two men on horseback came riding rapidly through the town, followed closely by the U.S. Marshal and two other men. They stopped at the well to water their horses so we asked them what the trouble was. They would give us no satisfaction but shortly afterward came back with the two horses that had passed through town just before them. The men had stolen horses near Lawrence, so the marshal shot the men and captured the horses. Some of the articles that were found in the men's pockets were given to me to keep until they were called for by their friends. . . .

It was now nearing the Fourth of July, and as we had no flag the women met together and made one. At this time there was in our midst two Sesesh soldiers who had taken the oath of allegiance to the United States. They had gotten into trouble with some colored men farther west, and were arrested and brought to Louisville. We had no jail so they were kept with a ball and chain. With their assistance the flag was raised and we enjoyed our first Fourth of July celebration.[5]

During the 1860s and 1870s, Louisville was a central trading point in the county. Early businesses included George Travis, hardware; Eli Bartholemeu, tin shop; Billy Telcamp, harness shop; John Balderson and Justin

Main street of Louisville looking north, 1910.

In 1914 this ice gorge created a fantastic image next to the flour mill at Louisville. Today the mill lies in ruins.

Chilcott, blacksmiths; Charles and Val Bittman, general store; J. W. Shaw, general store; and Dr. Heddiner, physician. The town also sported two hotels, a flour mill, a drugstore, a courthouse, a pool hall, a barber shop, and a cheese factory. Louisville had a newspaper called the *Louisville Lyre,* edited by Billy Hauldren, who also printed the *St. George News.*

The first school was a two-story brick building built by J. U. Allen, who made the bricks from clay found at the south edge of town. He also operated an ice house by using ice from Rock Creek, storing it during the winter, then selling it to residents in the summer. The brick school was later replaced by the present rock building. A large home known as the Hultz House was built near a dam on Rock Creek. In later years, vacationers from Kansas City used the house as a summer resort cabin.

On November 8, 1875, the town experienced an earthquake, and the *Kansas Reporter* made the following comments: "The shock of an earthquake was perceptibly felt here on the morning of Nov. 8, between four and five o'clock. In some places stoves and crockery and window panes were rattled about. A door in C. W. Bittman's residence was jarred open."[6] This earthquake left a lasting impression on Louisville residents, who became suddenly aware that they might be living on a fault line.

The Union Pacific Railroad did not build directly to Louisville. The workmen laid the tracks along the high banks of the Kaw River because of the wide flood plain and because there were just too many swamps, hills, and buffalo wallows around Louisville. In the 1880s when the town of Wamego became firmly established, Louisville's population dropped considerably. In 1875 the population was 776, and in 1880 it was 1,101—probably its peak. Just two years later the county seat moved to Westmoreland, and many of Louisville's residents moved along with it.[7]

From the 1880s to the present, the population of Louisville has gradually declined. Fire has destroyed portions of the business district, although a few handsome stone structures still stand. Today a visitor can see a collection of homes, churches, an old school, a two-story stone house, and two old business buildings, reminders of Louisville's better days.

In 1960 Mayor Owen Stratton and the Louisville Rod and Gun Club, the town's leading booster organization, attempted to secure funds for an authentic restoration of the town in a manner similar to Williamsburg, Virginia. At the time only two businesses were still in operation, a feed store run by Albert and Gordon Menheusen and a general store owned by Guy Noll. Louisville citizens were hoping to receive both federal and state funds in the amount of $100,000 for the project. Thirty years have passed and no

An 1890s view of the Louisville schoolhouse and students. Note the students hanging out of the second-story windows.

Fishing at the Louisville dam, ca. 1915.

restoration has occurred. If it had, Louisville could have risen again as in its boom days, a memorial to the pioneers who founded our state.[8]

AFTON
Marshall County

In 1893 when wagons and buggies were the vehicles of choice for farmers on Walnut Creek, the need for a store to serve these settlers resulted in the organization of the Afton Store Company. The newly formed company purchased a tract of land from Thomas Cox and built a two-story structure that became the nucleus of the future townsite. On June 19, 1893, the government established a post office in the store, and Cox was the first postmaster.

During the 1890s, the small town of Afton prospered. At its peak, it offered its people a store, a post office, a dance hall, a saloon, a creamery, a church, a physician's office, and a blacksmith shop.[1] The dance hall was particularly popular with the townspeople, who loved to polka, waltz, square dance, and schottische. When masquerade balls were held there several times a year, the best-costumed couple received prizes. The music was furnished by local fiddlers such as the Wippels, Yungbergs, and Pecekas from Hanover. Occasionally, fights broke out with rowdies from another town or as a result of disagreements over women, but for the most part the local lawmen maintained order.

After much local opposition, a saloon keeper built a building west of the store to house his saloon. At that time, Kansas was a "dry" state, but many saloons still operated under what was known as the "fine system." A fifty-dollar fine was levied each month by a local judge. As long as the owners paid the fines, their taverns could remain open. Before long the saloon in Afton became the town's main source of entertainment and a haven for drunks. One cold winter morning when the saloon keeper arrived late, he was surprised to find all the whiskey bottles broken and bits of glass strewn all over the floor. No one found any clues as to the identity or gender of the "culprit." Another incident occurred when some local drunks forcibly took the saloon keeper, John Steglin, to the Afton bridge and threatened to hang him if he didn't comply with their unreasonable demands for free whiskey. The rope was in place when Adam Sachs, a local farmer, rode by, stopping just long enough to talk the rowdies out of lynching Steglin. After the saloon closed, new owners used the building as a tenant house, and later moved it to the James Cox farm where it became a granary.

In 1895 John Guenther moved his family to Afton and set up a blacksmith shop, but after his wife died in 1905, he sold his business and real estate to the Lutheran church. His residence became the parsonage and his blacksmith shop a barn.[2]

In 1904 the Charles Nider family purchased the store building from Lu Beiter and added several rooms on the west side for living quarters. In 1907 John Minge purchased the business from the Niders and kept it open for several years. R. E. Brase became the last owner in 1910, but after five years he closed the store and moved to Bremen. The old Afton store remained empty for many years before Henry Stohs purchased it and used it as a parochial school. In 1920 Stohs sold the school to Joseph Bruna, who a year later razed the building for its lumber.

A local character known as "Indian John" moved to Afton and built a shack on a high bank overlooking Walnut Creek. He was an Indian medicine man who brewed herbs, roots, bark, and cockleburs in a large container on the back of his stove. His patients came from miles around in search of cures. Luther Hanson remembered Indian John and had this to say about him:

> This gentleman spent one week or eight or nine days [a year] at my parents and grandparents, . . . I was around him 18 years during my boyhood.
>
> I have heard a lot of people call him a fake, especially some MD's. He was genuine in every respect. I saw him cure a bad case of cataract on my aunt's eyes. Also saw a case of creeping paralysis cured in less than a year and a half. Also a number of other ailments too numerous to mention. He could tell by looking at you what was wrong, and was a mind reader.
>
> His mother was a full-blooded Indian, his father was a white man, and he was raised in Sitting Bull's tribe. He was . . . also a participant in the Custer battle. He died in the fall of 1924. I attended his funeral with my parents. I was 18 years old then.
>
> His mind was clear until he died. His tales of the Custer battle were most interesting. He personally knew the six chiefs who were in that battle, and of course, he was not in sympathy with General Custer.

In 1906 Richard Ruetti organized the Afton Band, which played at local weddings and parties. Clarence Behm once noted that "we were not great musicians but we sure had a lot of good times." Band members in 1908 included Alfred and Paul Ludicke, Noah and William Wandel, W. E. Wippel, Henry Marquardt, and John Minge. In 1912 the band broke up as the members had all married and lost interest.

Many Danish settlers chose the Afton area to farm. Twenty years before the organization of the town, they built a Danish Lutheran church two miles northeast of the town and laid out a cemetery nearby. For several years, the German Lutherans used the Danish church for their services. Today only this building, the neighboring parsonage, and the cemetery mark the approximate site of Afton.[3]

BIGELOW
Marshall County

Two mounds of rocky earth in Marshall County known as the Twin Mounds are located south of the Bigelow townsite and southwest of the California-Independence branch of the Oregon Trail. These mounds first attracted travelers in the 1840s when men stopped to carve their names and dates on the limestone outcropping.

Legend has it that a great battle was fought on top of the mounds, and Grant Ewing of the *Marshall County News* wrote of the incident in his weekly column, "Notes By the Wayside":

On the morning of June 9, 1842,[1] a three day battle began between 300 white men and 1,500 Indians. The white men had muzzle loading rifles and only a few Indians had rifles and the rest had spear bars to battle with. The white men went up on the Twin Mounds 1 1/2 miles south of Bigelow where they could see a long distance and could shoot the Indians while they were climbing the hill. Here were 14 men killed besides a lot wounded. After the battle the white men buried their dead partners, seven on the center of each mound. . . .

A bird's-eye view of Bigelow, ca. 1900. Note the school building at right under construction.

The Bigelow Christian church ca. 1900. Most of Bigelow's structures disappeared with the construction of Tuttle Creek Reservoir during the 1950s and 1960s.

A lot of limestone from the hills were piled up over the graves making a base 10 feet in diameter. They continued to build these stones 6 or 8 feet high with a slope from the ground to the top so the top was 5 feet wide. The Indians buried their dead in a ravine and the white men buried a few Indians northwest of the mound.

As this legend has been repeated through the years, the actual number of white men and Indians supposedly engaged in the battle varies with each account. In fact, quite a few Indian arrowheads and artifacts have been found at the site.

Bigelow's beginnings can be traced to the early 1880s. Located twenty miles southeast of Marysville on the Missouri Pacific Railroad,[2] the town, named for General Alfred Bigelow, was a shipping point for the limestone quarries that operated in the vicinity. Jacob Inman opened the first limestone quarry on his land just south of the townsite. He built a few stone houses to provide homes for the workers and turned forty acres of his farm into town lots that became known as the Inman Addition. The limestone quarried there was the finest in the world for the construction of railroad

The old public school building in Bigelow, 1910.

bridges, and the Missouri Pacific purchased the entire output of the quarries. Over 600 cars of limestone were shipped from Bigelow in one year. At that time 300 men were working in the quarries. The workmen cut the stone in large slabs, three feet wide by eighteen inches thick by six feet long, and hauled these slabs down the hills on low-bedded, small-wheeled wagons pulled by six or eight horses. The railroad, however, had finished building bridges by 1910 and had no further need for the limestone, which caused the quarries to close. They reopened for a short time in the mid-1940s but later closed again permanently.

In its prime the town had a bank, a newspaper, a lumberyard, a doctor's office, a jewelry store, a drugstore, and several general merchandise stores. A post office opened on November 2, 1881, and closed on July 31, 1960. By 1910 Bigelow had a population of 200.

Between 1909 and 1941 the only unusual events in the town's history were two attempted robberies of the State Bank of Bigelow. In neither instance were the thieves apprehended.

The town continued to be a fairly busy community and probably would have endured had it not been for the Tuttle Creek Dam project. When construction began on the reservoir, people were forced to leave their homes. The move was especially hard on the older citizens. "It is killing them inside," Mrs. Lena Potter, the postmistress, said. For many long-time residents, their homes in Bigelow were the only ones they had ever known. "There is something sad and undefinable about the demise of a once thriving community. It can be seen on the faces of the few persons who still remain," Mrs. Potter noted. By 1960 deserted buildings and empty houses lined the streets. Some were demolished and others moved to different communities, but a few survived. The railroad closed the depot and moved the roadbed north of the river.

By 1960 the town consisted of twenty people and two businesses—the grain elevator owned by Ralph Miller, and Jesse and Irene Saville's cafe. Miller continued to operate the elevator to accommodate the nearby farmers until the rising water and the lack of customers caused him to close permanently.[3]

Mrs. Potter pointed out that everyone was glad the Antioch cemetery, located one mile west of town, was spared so that even those who had left town would know where to find their dead relatives. "Folks have scattered here and there. Some went to California, some to nearby towns, and others to places unknown without leaving a forwarding address," she said. Today, other than the cemetery, a deserted field near the reservoir is all that remains of the site of Bigelow.[4]

BALA
Riley County

In 1870 the Welsh Land and Emigration Society of Utica, New York, was formed for the purpose of establishing Welsh emigrants in suitable locations across the West. The colony of settlers near the Bala site was the third one founded in Riley County.

In 1862 a few individual settlers had moved into western Riley County. On Timber Creek south of the Bala site, A. D. Phelps took an eighty acre claim and established a post office appropriately named Timber Creek. Twelve miles north, Roland Spurrier settled on Fancy Creek, and eight miles east, Aaron Silvers took up residence near Riley Center. These settlers were the closest neighbors to Phelps and Timber Creek until the Bala colonists arrived. James H. Jenkins, the leader of the colonists, was an active member of the Welsh Emigration Society and was able to buy a large section of land on time payments from the Kansas Pacific Railroad. After he subdivided this land, he sold it to the settlers at cost.

On June 18, 1870, William H. Jones brought colonists from Maryland, New Jersey, and Pennsylvania, who were financially strapped but eager to build homes on the Kansas prairie. They arrived in Manhattan by train and stayed at the Cottage Hotel. At that time of the year, the air was hot and humid, and the rooms were stifling. Some travelers tried to sleep on the floor or the porch of the hotel, but most of them were so desperate for a little cool air that they went to the depot and stretched out on the bare ground.

The society had arranged for John and William Hughes to meet the Jones party and take them to their destination some twenty miles farther west. When they left Manhattan on the morning of June 19, the sun was broiling hot and the vegetation parched and brown. One of the settlers lit his pipe and thoughtlessly tossed the match on the dry grass, causing it to burst into flames. The fire spread quickly, burning several thousand acres of prairie grass before it could be contained. That afternoon, the settlers cautiously moved on to their colony, not arriving until late in the evening.

The scarcity of water in the area eventually defeated the colonists. The creek near the settlement went dry and the closest source of water was over two miles away. While excavating a well they had decided to dig in a ravine close to the town, the men had a strange experience:

> The men took turns digging which progressed with increasing difficulty . . . to around eighty feet when rock was struck. Having worked in the slate mines in Wales and Pennsylvania, the men resorted to powder which was obtained from Manhattan. A young man of seventeen years—Ellis Davies—was let down with ropes to light the fuse and barely escaped when the blast was heard. After the smoke cleared, a curious phenomenon occurred. There were rumbling noises, strange, uncanny sounds that chilled the spines of the well diggers. They waited a half hour, then an hour and still the next day the noise was louder than before. They waited a week and were curious but never solved the mystery by digging deeper.

What the diggers probably encountered was shale gas, which occurs at depths nearer the surface than oil pools. After this unfortunate incident, the settlers decided against any further excavations and moved the town two miles west near a large spring that had been the main source of their water supply. Several ministers in the colony suggested the new location be named Bala after a theological center in Wales.

The new village was laid out in 1871 on land owned by Richard Jenkins and James Sharples, founders of the Bala Town Company. The town had two avenues running north and south—Park and Powys. Other street names were Kansas, Caroline, Louisa, John, Davies, Laura, Emma, Broad-

Bala school scene during the cold winter of 1904.

way, and Genesee. The settlers moved a hotel and several other structures from their original site, known as Powys, to Bala. By the end of 1871, the town had four general stores, a drugstore, a blacksmith shop, a carpenter shop, a shoemaker shop, a feed mill, a cheese factory, and three churches.

The colonists centered the town on a square and placed businesses on all four sides. Rowland Davies opened a general store and advertised himself as a "dealer in everything." James Sharples, who started another general store across from the Davies store, also operated a successful feed mill and cheese factory. Mrs. Mary Jenkins operated another store and millinery shop. The government established a post office on February 24, 1871, and Davies became the postmaster.

By the end of the decade, Bala was busy and thriving, though life for the early inhabitants was by no means easy. Fifty families lived within five miles of the town. The Kansas Pacific Railroad brought the colonists plenty of seed for planting their gardens and their first crops of corn and wheat; nevertheless, their crops failed as a result of extremely dry weather. Furthermore, food for people and animals alike was difficult to find. For many settlers pioneer life was just too hard during those dry years and they returned to their former homes in the East.

The colony faced another problem: payments had to be made to the Kansas Pacific for the land that had been purchased. When the railroad demanded the money and the colonists were unable to pay, the land reverted to the railroad. The settlers, however, turned to the Homestead Act of 1862, which promised them free land if they made the required improvements. Still more difficulties arose in the form of prairie fires, hail storms, and grasshopper plagues. Even when crops were good, the grain markets were twenty miles away, and teams and wagons were the farmers' only means of transporting grain and livestock to these rail centers. The trips were long, slow, and tedious.

The building of the Kansas Central Railroad across Riley County through Leonardville in 1881 brought the closest market within six or eight miles and was hailed with relief by the settlers. But the railroad also meant greater business opportunities in Leonardville, and merchants from Riley Center, Winkler, and Bala began moving their stores there. Bala was not as badly affected as the other towns, but the cheese factory did go out of business that year. Davies opened another general store at Leonardville but continued to operate his Bala store for several more years. J. H. Jenkins remained in Bala to help the townspeople in his role of notary public and legal advisor. He also used his drugstore as a doctor's office and prescribed country remedies for illnesses until a physician could set up practice in the community. Jenkins later opened a store in both Clay Center and Leonardville.

The first of several tornadoes struck Bala on the night of June 7, 1882, destroying two churches, the schoolhouse, and many homes. Another shock to the town came five years later. The local politicians had consistently promised a railroad through Bala, but in 1887, when the Rock Island laid their tracks across the county, they built the depot a mile southwest of the village and named the station Bala City. The settlers saw the possibilities of a trade boom if the town could be moved closer to the tracks, so they relocated the stores, offices, one church, and seven dwellings nearer the depot. Among those making the move were the Watkins grocery store, the Robert Lewis Hotel, a coalyard, the blacksmith shop, the Presbyterian church, and two drugstores operated by Jenkins and Doctors Hulet and McNally. A newspaper called the *Bala Advance* was established in the new town on May 24, 1890, but was discontinued a year later.

Bala produced several talented individuals, including one Humphrey Jones, a graduate of Kansas State University in 1888. While a student, he composed the K-State alma mater. The wording has since been changed slightly, but the tune remains the same. Other compositions attributed to him are the Topeka High School song and the Kansas song, ''Kansas,

The Bala railroad depot, 1904. A second floor was added as business steadily increased.

Sunny Kansas.'' The Jones family's melodeon is now on display in the Riley County Historical Museum.[1]

In 1903 another tornado ravaged Bala. The storm demolished the Chris Daub home, killing two daughters and injuring Mrs. Daub and the Daubs' son Frank. The wind plucked all four of the Daubs out of the cellar and tossed them through the air. The tornado also destroyed the Calvinist Church, the John Younkin barn, the Henry Hollen homestead, and the George Thomas home, injuring both Mr. and Mrs. Thomas. The town never completely recovered, and by 1910 the population had dropped to 100.[2]

During the First World War Bala experienced more change. In response to the increasing popularity of the automobile, the state built a hard-surfaced road through the county, bypassing the town. The bank established immediately after the war became fiscally unsound by the 1930s. During the depression the Rock Island Railroad discontinued the Bala depot because there was too little business to warrant the expense of a station agent. The post office closed on March 25, 1966, and a rural carrier from Riley delivered the mail. The grocery, drugstore, and almost all other businesses closed their doors, and by 1964 even the Bala school had to close due to decreasing enrollment.

Fort Riley has now expanded to the southern edge of what was the Bala city limits. Today only a church and a few farm homes are left of this rural community that has seen its share of disasters, a victim of changing times in Kansas.[3]

2

EAST CENTRAL
KANSAS

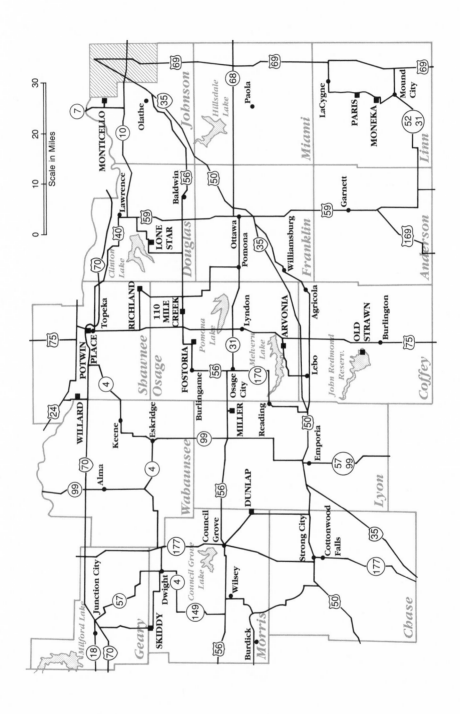

MONTICELLO
Johnson County

During the territorial period, the northern portion of Johnson County was inhabited by Shawnee Indians. A few white traders came to the area prior to white settlement and married Indian women. Three of these men adopted by the Shawnee tribe were Isaac Parish, Samuel Garrett, and John Owens.

The county was not opened to settlement by whites until 1857, when the town of Monticello, named after Thomas Jefferson's home, was laid out by the town company. Among those who moved to Monticello were J. M. Reed, proprietor of a large hotel, and Rich & Rively, operators of a dry goods store. The settlers constructed the first school in the area about a mile west of town, and the federal government established a post office in January 1858.[1]

"Wild Bill" Hickok was just twenty-two years old when he was elected constable of Monticello, and the townspeople often saw him patrolling the streets. It was his first job as a lawman and apparently not too difficult, for there were complaints that he spent most of his time either playing cards or target shooting at bottles. He was constable at Monticello for two years and boarded with John Owens, a farmer in the area.

In 1858 Monticello had a population of 250 people, and the city limits extended just west of the present cemetery. The townspeople named the main street Cherry Street after the many cherry trees that grew in and around the town. According to most newspaper accounts, there were at least eight business buildings in town: the hotel, the general store, the blacksmith shop, the harness shop and livery stable, two saloons, and a building that served as the land office and city hall. In the spring of 1858 a tornado ripped through Monticello, doing a great deal of damage, and some of the town was never rebuilt.

In the 1860s the fate of the town rested on the outcome of the county seat issue. Monticello, unfortunately, was not located in the middle of Johnson County, which was important for county planning. Olathe, the rival town, was more centrally located, and therefore the voters chose Olathe.

Tragedy avoided Monticello until the fall of 1864, when the settlers hanged Peter Bassinger for horse stealing. They most likely did not bury him in the Monticello cemetery, although it's hard to be sure since many of the old tombstones are weathered and generally indecipherable today.

The settlement remained fairly peaceful until 1874 when, along with most of Kansas, it suffered from the "great grasshopper plague." The following summer, many grasshoppers remained, but they were not quite as devastating to the crops. A column entitled "Grasshopper Notes" in the *Topeka Daily Commonwealth* for May 23, 1875, noted that "the farmers on Bull Creek, in Johnson County, captured three-hundred bushels of grasshoppers with a 'grasshopper machine,' whatever that is. On last Tuesday a son of Mr. William Reynolds of Johnson County, caught 18 bushels of grasshoppers. On the same day, the citizens of Paola drove into and captured 50 bushels of hoppers in the public square of that city."

By 1880 the town was much smaller and contained only two general stores, a blacksmith shop, a schoolhouse, fifteen residences, and about sixty inhabitants.[2] The decline continued after the post office closed on May 15, 1905. Today, almost all traces of the town have disappeared. Suburban houses now cover the land, and most of the old buildings are gone. Only Cherry Street remains, locked in a housing development that occupies some of the original land of the city of Monticello.[3]

PARIS
Linn County

Paris, the first county seat of Linn County, was named for Paris, Kentucky, the former home of James Barlow, one of the town's most prominent citizens. Paris was laid out on a claim owned by James Fox, a lawyer by profession and a "typical exponent of the fire-eating Southerner." He had a vocabulary of "invective abuse, and an abundant supply of cuss words, which he used without stint in addressing a jury or haranguing a crowd." A board of county commissioners appointed Fox the first treasurer of Linn County on January 8, 1856. These men also located the county seat on his claim and paid him $100 for his cabin, which was to be used as a courthouse. Fox's stay in Linn County, however, was not long, for at the request of some free-state men in 1858, he opted to move to a healthier and safer climate.[1]

James Barlow was also a lawyer of considerable ability, a Kentuckian by birth, a suave gentleman, and the owner of several slaves, some of whom remained with him until the last days of the Civil War. Unlike Fox, he was mildly conservative in his speech and actions and was generally respected and esteemed by those who knew him. He remained on his farm adjoining the town for several years after the war and then moved back to his native Kentucky.

The first free-state convention in Linn County was held in a sawmill just outside Paris in 1857. The first county election was held in Fox's log courthouse, where the voters stepped up to a small window and called aloud the names of those for whom they wanted to vote to the judge and clerks inside the building.[2]

At the start Paris was a proslavery town located on the roughest, dreariest rock pile in the county. Rogers, Badolet & Company and Zadock Lewis opened two stores; Gwynn & Bronson owned the first sawmill; and Jesse Brown became the postmaster. The town's population had grown to about four hundred people by 1859, the year they moved the county seat from Paris six miles north to Mound City.

Between 1857 and 1859 the Paris community gradually changed its political organization from proslavery to free-state because the proslavery party was losing ground, and the "Jayhawkers," violent upholders of free-state justice, were becoming more common in southeastern Kansas. In 1859 President James Buchanan sent U.S. Marshal James Russell, a proslavery sympathizer, to Paris to try to suppress the power of the Jayhawkers. It was a futile effort. James Montgomery, a free-state man, threatened Russell's life and sent him packing to Lecompton, the territorial capital, "a wiser if not a better man."[3]

When an election was held on November 8, 1859, to relocate the county seat, Paris received 471 votes and Mound City 508. The county officials at Paris steadfastly refused to move the records to the new county seat, whereupon some citizens of Mound City, armed with pistols, shotguns, Sharpe's rifles, and a cannon known as "Brass Betsy," appeared early one morning on the Paris public square and demanded all the county books and records. At first the officials refused to comply, denying all knowledge of the location of the county records. After some forceful persuasion, however, they brought the records out from under the treasurer's bed, from a potato hole, and from under the floorboards of several store buildings and delivered them into the hands of the intruders.[4] Later, Paris citizens discovered that the formidable-looking cannon, "Brass Betsy," had not a grain of powder in her firing chamber.[5]

Though Paris was a lively trading point for several years before the coming of the railroad, no one had enough confidence in the town's future to invest in any improvements. When all efforts to establish the county seat there failed, the citizens abandoned Paris. Nothing now remains of the townsite.

MONEKA
Linn County

Moneka, or "morning star," named for an Indian woman, was founded in February 1857 by John B. Wood, Erastus Heath, Andrew Stark, Julius

Keeler, and Augustus and John Wattles. Most of these town incorporators were abolitionists, as were the settlers who lived on the site. Stark was the first clerk of the supreme court, serving from 1861 to 1867, and John Wattles was an ardent advocate of Spiritualism,[1] an enthusiastic educator, and an optimist "of the most pronounced type." Through his influence, the town company erected an academy, and for several years Moneka was the educational center of Linn County. The company also built a large hotel that, at various times, sheltered several territorial governors and most of the free-state leaders of the territory.

Augustus Wattles came to Kansas in 1855 from Ohio and first located near Washington Creek in Douglas County, where he was associated with G. W. Brown, editor of the Lawrence *Herald of Freedom*[2] newspaper. Wattle's influence in town speculation led to several newspaper advertisements beginning on April 11, 1857, announcing Moneka's merits and showing its location on Little Sugar Creek near the center of Linn County.[3]

O. E. and O. S. Morse operated the first store in Moneka; F. C. Bacon opened a tin shop; and William Hobson built the first sawmill in Linn County. The first term of school at the Moneka Academy started in April 1858, and Miss Sarah Wattles, daughter of Augustus, was the teacher. By that time, Moneka had a population of over 200.[4]

The Reverend Samuel Young Lum visited Moneka in 1857 and described the town in a letter dated October 5:

> From Ohio City, it is about 30 miles S.E. to Moneka—on Sugar Creek—about 12 miles from the Mo. line—but little has been done on the town. . . . I was told that at any time a congregation could be secured, of at least 100, some of the leading men are desirous to be supplied from your Soc. though in the vicinity there quite a number of "spiritualists" who of course would not look with favor upon such a movement. . . . Moneka derives some prospective importance—from the fact that as the Pacific R. R. looks for a passage away from the Mo. River & less expensive—southern Kansas presents itself fertile & fast filling with a dense population. . . . This matter has been already under discussion by the director of the R. R.[5]

One of the most important political issues in 1858 was the proposed railroad from Jefferson City, Missouri, to Emporia by way of Moneka. John Wattles, the promoter of this project, hoped to make the town one of the great emporiums of the West, and he organized a company, obtained a charter, and solicited endorsements from the directors in both Missouri and Kansas. He went to Congress that winter to obtain a grant for the right-of-way and to acquire an appropriation of public lands. Wattles had the preliminary surveys made and had arranged for the breaking of ground at the state line. Congress granted the right-of-way, but Wattle's untimely death and the beginning of the Civil War changed all the well-laid plans and halted any further progress.

Failure to secure a railroad meant that Moneka's days were numbered, and free-state/proslavery troubles in the area only added to the turmoil in the town. Soon after the Marais des Cygnes massacre at nearby Pleasanton in May 1858, Augustus Wattles brought John Brown to Moneka. Brown and his free-state forces made Moneka their frequent headquarters until Brown left the state, successfully taking a dozen slaves from Vernon County, Missouri, with him. Wattles corresponded with Brown for some months, and in his own home he concocted the plan to free Brown from the jail at Harper's Ferry. In order to perfect the scheme, Wattles went east to see Brown and only Brown's refusal to sanction the whole idea, together with the deep snow in the Appalachians, prevented Wattles from carrying out his strategy. After Brown's death, Wattles was summoned to Washington to tell an investigating committee about Brown and his "traitorous" activities.[6]

During the 1850s, there was an unwritten law that no saloons could exist in either Moneka or Mound City, but in 1863 an enterprising individual arrived in Mound City and opened a barroom. Before long this saloon business became an intolerable nuisance to the citizens of both towns. Drunken soldiers from nearby Fort Scott became a common sight. Since nearly all of the male population was away fighting the war, the women took it upon themselves to cope with the situation. One morning a wagonload of ladies from Moneka drove into town, carrying with them hatchets and axes. A squad of their Mound City friends joined them, and the group marched to the open door of the saloon and walked in. Although one man made a move to intervene, he was promptly stopped by a revolver in the hands of a bystander, who told him that he would shoot anyone who interfered with the women. After driving out the barkeepers and the loungers, the women deliberately broke every bottle, glass, and decanter in sight and knocked in the heads of every barrel and keg. The saloon was out of business in Mound City. The long-range result of the women's movement was prohibition in both towns without recourse to laws or courts.[7]

By the 1860s most of Moneka's inhabitants had left for other localities. The academy building was first moved to Linnville and then to Pleasanton in 1871. Soon only the hotel building was left on the site of the little village, and today almost no traces of the town remain.

LONE STAR
Douglas County

Situated along Washington Creek in Douglas County, Lone Star has not declined significantly in population in the last fifty years, but the town did lose its entire business district during this period.

James Tally, one of the town's earliest residents, chose an eighty-acre tract near present Lone Star Lake in 1854. When the local Indians burned his cabin and drove him out, he retreated to Missouri, where he stayed a few years before returning. By then the Indians posed little threat to the settlers, and Tally and his brother preempted a quarter section of land along the creek.

An 1855 census of the Lone Star area lists a few of the settlers, most of them proslavery, including Enoch and Margaret Reed, James Evans, George and Nancy Brians, James and John Campbell, D. C. Halbert, Darwin and Sarah Bowen, Fields and Elizabeth Bledsoe, George Rhodes, and three Todhunter brothers.[1] Raids by free-state sympathizers on these proslavery settlers became so frequent that by June 1856 eleven families had returned to Missouri. A cabin owned by the Burton family was burned on June 8 following the family's departure, and by the end of that summer, the free-staters' threats of violence reached an all-time high. Acting territorial Governor Daniel Woodson reported that "the settlement on Washington Creek was . . . threatened with extermination, and the settlers, driven by instincts of self-preservation into the log house of James P. Saunders, Esq., one of the oldest and best citizens in Douglas County, began to fortify it." A subsequent raid resulted in the remaining settlers fleeing for their lives. "Fort Saunders," as the cabin was called, was used as a stronghold by one young man, a woman, and her two children, but they were unable to defend themselves and ran into the woods. The free-staters robbed the cabin and burned it.

By 1860 proslavery and free-state factions at Lone Star were even more divided. Joseph Gardner operated an underground railroad and transported slaves to freedom. He hired one of these slaves, Napoleon Simpson, to construct a stone wall, which caused widespread dissension in the area. On June 9, at 1:30 in the morning, some gunshots were exchanged between the proslavery men and Gardner and Simpson, who had barricaded themselves inside Gardner's log cabin. Simpson was shot and killed in this incident, and his last words were "Fight! Fight hard!" After they found they couldn't penetrate the log walls, the raiders tried to ignite a bundle of hay. Fortunately, a rain earlier in the day had dampened their matches, and they were unable to light the torch. This morning shower, no doubt, saved Gardner's life.

After Quantrill attacked Lawrence on August 21, 1863, he advanced southwest toward Lone Star. Some of his men reached Washington Creek ahead of him, and one of them rode into Lars Johanson's yard with the intention of harassing him. Johanson grabbed the ruffian's horse and called for someone in the barn to bring an ax and kill him. The raider quickly shot Johanson in the chest and rode away. At the J. S. Eckman farm, son Carl was shot and killed by one of Quantrill's men; the exact circumstances of the shooting were never known. At the corner of Johanson's farm, the guerrilla band turned south and rode directly for Lone Star.

Some free-state men riding ahead of Quantrill were able to warn the settlers of the possibility of a raid. John Metsker and his family sought refuge in the cornfield behind the house, and he and his son Martin led the horses to a bushy area where they hid them from sight. Metsker, while scouting along the road, heard Quantrill's men coming. They were discussing plans to burn his place to the ground, but they missed the road leading to his house. This oversight saved his farm. Two other families were not so lucky. The ruffians burned the Ulrichs' farmhouse and well-filled granaries, then committed another murder at the home of Abe Rothrock when they shot him and threw him into the cellar under his burning house. Quantrill finally rode away to the south.

Lars Johanson survived his chest wound, though not without considerable suffering. The Eckman boy died instantly. Abe Rothrock, who was snatched barely alive from the ruins of his house, lived only a few days. Jacob Ulrich, who was already ill when his farmstead was burned to the ground, lived a month before he died. Quantrill's ruthlessness left long-lasting scars on the people of the Lone Star community.[2]

No formal semblance of a town appeared before the mid-1870s. A steam sawmill was constructed in the 1860s, but it ceased operation when a violent fight broke out between the two owners. The survivor soon lost not only his money but also his interest in business and closed the mill, causing a hardship to the community.

In 1875 Silas Bond requested that a post office named Bond, Kansas, be established in his home. Later, the government opened a second post office named Gideon in 1883. Mail arrived semiweekly until delivery was discontinued in 1902.

By the mid-1880s there were several businesses in "Bond," including a blacksmith, a wagonmaker's shop, and a general store opened in 1885 by J. M. Flory. Within a few years the population reached twenty-five, and by the turn of the century the population had climbed to around fifty. Census figures are complicated by the fact that the Lone Star community lies in three townships—Clinton, Marion, and Willow Springs.

By 1900 the wagonmaker was gone, but a tannery and grist mill had opened. The Lone Star school was completed in 1896, and all eight grades were taught in a single room. The school served a community of approximately 300 people. The frame structure became a private residence, still occupied today. A shoemaker shop and cheese factory opened around 1900; the latter had been a creamery in the late 1890s. By 1908 the community supported two general stores, two blacksmiths, two feed mills, a meat market, a carpenter, and a doctor.

Between 1918 and 1920 Lone Star reached its zenith of development. It offered banking services, a post office, a school, church, a grocery store, a garage, a physician, and a veterinarian. The Lone Star community also promoted such special events as religious revivals, Chautauqua lectures with music and entertainment, band concerts by the Lone Star Brass Band, pie and box suppers, and baseball games. The school sponsored spelling bees, Christmas parties, recitations, and plays. Before the drought of the 1930s reduced Lone Star Lake to a mere puddle, there were ice skating parties in the winter on Washington Creek. These activities typified the country town in the years when Kansas was a primarily agrarian state. When the automobile became popular and long drives routine, the feel of the small town changed radically.

By the late 1930s drought and depression had settled over the community, but when the nation recovered and the wartime boom replaced the depression, Lone Star failed to make a comeback. The effects of the automobile, which at first had drawn the community together, inevitably undermined the town's base of existence, conveying goods and people to Lawrence or Topeka. One by one, businesses closed for lack of customers.[3]

The post office, store, school, and church held out the longest, but finally the post office closed in 1953. The wares in the Flory store were sold at auction in 1960, the same year the school was consolidated. Today only the church still functions. The current residents are either retired or drive to work elsewhere. The town consists of a few homes and a country church near a small, isolated lake. The days of Lone Star as a separate entity are over.

POTWIN PLACE/AUBURNDALE
Shawnee County

Listed among the thousands of Kansas ghost towns are a few that were located too close to a major urban area to maintain their identity as the city

Charles W. Potwin, developer of Potwin Place.

expanded. These communities became known as "annexations," and they comprise roughly 7 percent of all Kansas ghost towns.

Perhaps two of the more prominent annexation examples are Potwin Place and Auburndale, two affluent communities located west of Topeka when they were founded. As Topeka expanded westward, these places lost their fight to remain separate entities, and thus lost their identities.

Potwin Place, the larger of the two towns, was the dream of capitalist Charles W. Potwin, who purchased seventy acres of land west of Topeka in 1869. Potwin waited until the big land boom of the early 1880s to develop the property, but when he did, he lost no time in turning his grandiose plans into reality. He had the property platted in 1882 and divided it into eighty lots, each 122 by 205 feet. He provided circular parks at street intersections and planted about two thousand elm trees. After allowing the trees to mature, Potwin sold the first lots in the fall of 1885 only to those people who promised to build homes costing at least $2,000. The first six homes averaged $5,000 apiece. By 1888 Potwin had incorporated the town as a third-class city, partly to counteract efforts by the city of Topeka to annex it. By this time the western boundary of Topeka was within a few blocks of Potwin.

From 1888 to 1899 six men served as mayor of Potwin, several of whom were prominent physicians and lawyers. The *Topeka Daily Capital* of January 1, 1889, estimated that 600 people lived in the growing suburb. Interestingly, many well-to-do families rented their houses and were quite mobile moving from place to place in (and out of) Potwin as their fortunes improved. Some blocks in Potwin had only a house or two on them by the 1890s; other lots remained open fields. One tract of land owned by financier M. S. Keith became the site of Topeka's first golf course in 1899 and the site of the city's first golf tournament. Later the nine-hole course was called the Topeka Golf Club.[1]

By the late 1890s Topeka was too close for comfort. Several efforts were made to annex Potwin, and one finally succeeded in 1899. Today Potwin is still a well-preserved Victorian neighborhood with many beautiful nineteenth-century homes lining Greenwood, Elmwood, and Woodlawn streets. A neighborhood association and citywide interest in this section of Topeka has kept the community alive. In this case, annexation did not mean elimination.

A lesser-known community known as Auburndale developed just to the northwest of Potwin. On May 2, 1888, Topekans read about the establishment of Auburndale in the *Daily Capital*. The small one-or-two-line items about the town first appeared mingled with other news on the pages of the morning newspaper. That night, the readers were exposed to the same messages again, and the whole population of Topeka was wondering about this marvelous new "town." On May 3 the *Capital* ran the following article:

> After passing through Potwin east to west we reached a narrow strip of land yet unplatted, on the opposite side of which were a baker's dozen teams and twice as many men grading streets and clearing away underbrush. "That," said George F. Parmelee, agent of the Boston Syndicate, "is Auburndale."[2] . . . The managers of the Topeka Land and Development Company have arranged with Marshall's Military Band for a series of concerts to be given at Auburndale one evening each week. When all the improvements are perfected there will not be a more delightful pleasure resort, nor a more beautiful place to live in all the grand and growing west, than in "Our Auburndale."

Thus, Auburndale became one of several subdivisions that encircled To-peka. During the preceding two years, the local newspapers had been prof-iting from the developers' large advertisements describing the joys of subur-ban living in such retreats as Highland Park, Chicago Heights, Cottage Grove, and Boynton. While developers were building these subdivisions, George Parmelee was building his own empire.[3]

Parmelee, president of both the National Loan & Trust Company and the Topeka Land & Development Company, was a big man in Topeka busi-ness affairs. During the early months of 1887, he purchased more than a thousand acres of farm land located between Topeka's western boundary and "Martin's Hill." The other parties in the transactions were a group of investors known as the Boston Syndicate.

The syndicate's investments in the area came as a surprise to Topekans when they were announced in the *Capital* of May 4, 1887. Although at that time Auburndale was not mentioned, the syndicate's future planning in-cluded a large resort hotel, a manmade lake, a spacious park and botanical garden, a university, a cemetery, and a steam railway line that would serve the new community. The developers envisioned the transformation of To-peka into a "Boston of the West."[4]

The Boston Syndicate continued to prosper and grow until by the end of 1887 they had a reported capital of $2,000,000. Out of these funds Parmelee paid ap-proximately $45,000 for forty-five acres that he platted as Auburndale. Its west-ern boundary was several blocks east of the State Hospital grounds next to a fifty-acre tract known as the Sam Cross Addition. On old maps, the two addi-tions of Cross and Auburndale appear to be connected by one common thor-oughfare known as The Drive. Undoubtedly, the two additions were laid out by the same planner, Ernest William Bowditch of Boston.

Bowditch was an asset to Auburndale, although his fame as an architect was not taken seriously at the time. In snob appeal Auburndale could have easily ad-vanced over Potwin had some of the newspapers cited a few of the millionaires' country estates in the East designed by Bowditch, such as the estates of the Cor-nelius Vanderbilts, the Robert Goelets, and the Lorillards of Tuxedo Park. Bow-ditch also planned the resorts of Hot Springs and Warm Springs, Virginia, and the complete park system in Cleveland, Ohio. At that time, Auburndale was the only Bowditch-planned residential suburb west of the Mississippi.

Auburndale's grand opening was held on May 19, 1888, and over 1,000 people attended. A public auction of lots was held on June 9, and at the end of the first day the sales amounted to $23,000. Before the end of the second summer, the Topeka Land & Development Company informed the *Topeka Journal* that $112,000 had been invested in Auburndale during the last ninety days.[5] The price of lots had boomed. Rectangular lots were selling from $225 to $375 each, and buyers needed two or three for a homesite.

Auburndale was transformed into a major suburb, but water, gas, sewers, and fire protection were still unavailable. Talk of annexation threatened the town. Most residents opposed merging with Topeka, and they were seriously considering incorporating their suburb as a city of the third class in order to avoid it. The *Capital* of June 3, 1890, reported that "the people of Auburndale presented a petition for the incorporation of Auburndale as a third class city. The petition was slightly irregular, and the commissioners were in doubt as to their ability to act at an adjourned session . . . so the petition was laid aside."

In 1890 the population of Auburndale peaked at 475.[6] On July 24 of that year, Auburndale was included under the charter of Potwin Place, and for a few years the town remained there. In the mid-1890s the Boston Syndicate experienced a financial depression and never recovered economically.[7]

Early in 1896 a small group of civic-minded townspeople at Auburndale believed they could muster enough votes among "new" Potwin citizens to elect a mayor. Supporting the Auburndale ticket was, of all people, a resident of Potwin, W. P. Tomlinson, editor of the *Kansas Democrat*. When election day arrived in April 1896 the ticket showed J. B. Larimer running for mayor of Potwin and W. A. Meyers for mayor of Auburndale. Although Larimer won with 234 votes, Meyers was not far behind with 192. Potwin's victory was short-lived, however, for in the end, both Potwin and Auburndale faded away and were annexed to Topeka. Auburndale remains one of Topeka's best-designed neighborhoods, thanks to Ernest Bowditch and his less illustrious clients, the Boston Syndicate.[8]

WILLARD
Shawnee County

In the 1860s and 1870s Willard was not much of a town; in fact, it was little more than a ferrying point on the Kansas River. In 1883, however, the Rock Island Railroad laid tracks through the community, and from the 1880s through the 1920s Willard was a typical railroad town.

Lydia Rogers, a citizen of Willard, wrote the following about the town in its heyday:

[In] the town of Willard, no streets were ever named. It was a small peaceful community. Horse-drawn vehicles were the fashion. The Rock Island giving freight and passenger service and the only hotel serving boarders and transits was owned and operated by Mr. & Mrs. Nelson Gibson for many years. . . .

The town had two general stores, one by Mr. Blackburn on Main Street; the other owned by Mr. Douglas on the hill going south.

The brick school [was not] far from the store. Church services were also held there. . . . Fishing from the Kaw [Kansas River] good business. Ice taken from river during winter stored in a warehouse with saw dust.

. . . Vegetable gardens, fruit orchards plentiful. . . . After cars came to Willard, it was a big change. The population increased, more business. The town was incorporated, a mayor appointed.[1]

Until his recent death, Vitasco D. Jones, a local historian, owned and operated a museum in town. The building contained interesting relics and memorabilia of Willard, Topeka, and other nearby communities. Jones collected many of the items while he was an auctioneer. He saw Willard's economy rise and fall. During an interview in 1976, he showed me an empty field just south of town where many homes once stood. Jones explained that Willard was a wide-open town in the early 1900s, boasting a population of over 300 and having several saloons and taverns. Willard then was a major cattle shipping point for this region, and the local cowboys enjoyed spending their hard-earned money on women and liquor. Jones named from memory many of the town's former businesses, including the Willard Hotel one block south of the railroad depot, a livery stable, a brick factory, a long-lived post office, and a ferry that was in use through the late 1890s.

Willard had its share of disasters and setbacks. In a newspaper interview, H. S. Jones, a Willard pioneer, recalled the blizzard of 1886 as "the worst in my time." He froze his right ear while on a bobsled ride to school and noted that the ear remained "stiff" for the rest of his life. Some thirty years later, robbers held up the Willard Bank, the town's only financial center, on Independence Day, 1916, and shot Bob Best, a citizen of Willard. Again on September 12, 1924, the bank was robbed, but this time the robbers were caught in Topeka the same day. Less than a year later, on March 6, 1925, the bank closed its doors and moved to Dover.

Willard suffered several fires during its heyday. On May 19, 1921, the Lynde Brothers store burned down; and on January 19, 1924, the Ross Smith store followed suit. Meanwhile, Willard's lifeline, the railroad, caused its own share of problems. One memorable train wreck occurred on September 8, 1923, when an engine and five cars derailed and severely injured three people. On November 11, 1935, a Rock Island freight train left the track, causing eight gasoline- and oil-laden tank cars to pile up just a few yards from Main Street. Although the resulting fire threatened to spread flames over several store buildings and houses, the real danger lay in the oil tank cars located near the flames, ready to explode.

Frank Stone, Jr., son of the Topeka Chief of Police, and some other men with rifles and machine guns rushed to Willard and opened fire on the remaining tank cars. This prompt action allowed the contents to escape and burn naturally, thus averting a possible disaster. Stone's heroism was commended on an NBC radio program broadcast in early March, 1937—he was said to have "saved Willard, Kansas."[2]

During the 1930s many businesses closed. The railroad became less important as a shipper of agricultural products; however, the final chapter in Willard's history was written by the 1951 flood that destroyed most of the town. Water from the Kansas River came to "middle-door level" on most of the remaining businesses, including the doctor's office, Lloyd's dance hall, and David Stitt's general store. Many homes suffered major damage as well. But the biggest problem confronting Willard at the time was the bridge across the river that collapsed on July 5, completely isolating the town from St. Marys, Rossville, and Silver Lake, and causing even more businesses to close.[3]

Today Willard is a quiet rural hamlet with a few residences. But if Vitasco Jones were alive, he would tell you that Willard was the soul of the region for nearly six decades.

RICHLAND
Shawnee County

In 1872 John Helton platted the village of Richland on Camp Creek after the Lawrence, Leavenworth & Emporia Railroad established a depot there. As early as October 1854, however, Charles Matney had settled in the area. Several weeks later Harvey Matney, C.H. Buzzard, James Linn, and Samuel Thompson took up homesteads nearby. Many other families soon joined them. The Richland post office, established in the fall of 1856 a mile north of the townsite, moved after the town was laid out. W. C. Murray was the first postmaster.

Richland eventually became the center of a rich agricultural region, and its businesses included a bank, a barber shop, a church, two blacksmiths, two doctors, a pharmacy, several lodges, a hotel, and a large general store built by David and Albert Neese. In 1895 the population of Richland was between 200 and 250.[1] The town was located strategically on the Lawrence to Emporia rail line and on the eastern edge of the Carbondale coal mining district. Unfortunately, the railroad existed only briefly. Originally, the builders planned to run on down to Texas, but arguments arose between investors in Emporia and Lawrence, and the result was that the railroad failed to build past Emporia. When the Missouri Pacific laid track near that

A bird's-eye view of Richland, 1900. This entire townsite was bulldozed to make way for Clinton Reservoir.

town, the hopes of Richland ever getting a railroad were dashed.

After the railroad stopped running in 1894 Richland was "just an ordinary country town"—until August 1942, when the "Hooded Man" appeared, or so a fifteen-year-old farm boy claimed. The boy's mother called the Douglas County authorities on a Sunday and told them that a tall man in a cowboy hat with a hood over his face had held her son prisoner at gunpoint. The following Tuesday the family returned from an auction to find a note pinned to the door. It stated, "We're gunning for . . . ," using the boy's nickname. The FBI stepped in and concluded that the note writer was someone who knew the boy at Overbrook High School. That night some fifty neighbors armed with guns patrolled the farmhouse. Most of the residents stayed awake to see if a gunfight would develop, but no masked man appeared.

Two *Topeka State Journal* reporters went to Richland the next day. They were suspicious that the whole story might be a juvenile prank. After interviewing several boys, who were not particularly talkative, one told the reporters that he could explain the entire matter in two minutes. "But I ain't talkin'," he said. Residents in the area stayed close to their guns, but the "Hooded Man" failed to appear. Finally the boy confessed that he had dreamed the whole thing up because he "wanted some excitement." This was the end of the story, much to the relief of the Richland residents.[2]

Another dramatic incident occurred on March 16, 1954, when two B-47 jets collided over the town. One plane managed to land, but the other exploded four times in the air, dropping metal fragments all over the immediate area. Air Force investigators scanned the fields for weeks trying to pick up all the wreckage. They missed some pieces, and that spring several cows died after eating a large quantity of metal in the nearby pastures.

As early as the 1930s there was discussion of a Clinton reservoir in the

The main street of Richland, ca. 1900. At the extreme right stands the hotel building.

The Richland Creamery, with a customer, ca. 1900.

area. When the government announced specific plans in the early 1960s, the citizens were wary of investing in a town that was destined to end up at the bottom of a lake. Richland dwindled steadily after the 1970s, but even today former citizens seem filled with pride when they speak of the town. There was some talk of moving the little village to a crossroads known as "the corners" a mile north of the old business district. The "corners" included a restaurant, a tavern, and a service station that was not a part of the reservoir. However, nothing further developed.[3]

Fire! A building on Main Street in Richland goes up in flames.

Georgia Neese Clark Gray, former treasurer of the United States, is the last survivor of three generations of the Neese family of Richland. In August 1967 Mrs. Gray sold the old family store that had been a landmark for so many years. In its day the store handled everything from hair ribbons to fifty-dollar Stetson hats. "You didn't have to go anywhere else to buy whatever you wanted," Charles Allbaugh, an old Richland native, said. "They handled the best, or would order it for you." In the early 1900s, when the farmers in the valley were hard pressed for money, Albert Neese issued his own scrip in the form of a brass token, and it was good as gold anywhere in the area. Various federal and state restrictions now prohibit the use of tokens, but in the depression years of the 1930s this scrip saved the little town of Richland.

The store held many memories for Mrs. Gray. She was working there when President Harry Truman's secretary called to tell her that the president wanted her to be treasurer of the United States. Mrs. Gray remembered, "I thought a moment and recalled a woman never had been appointed to such a high office and told the President I could not afford not to accept." She served in Washington from 1949 to 1953. After she and her husband returned, they stayed in Richland "until the last" in the two-story white frame house Albert Neese built in 1892.[4] Many locals blame Gray for the "sellout" of the Richland townsite to the Corps of Engineers.

Some feel she should have made a greater effort to halt the reservoir construction. She has always maintained that sentiment cannot stand in the way of progress. The sad reality is that Richland never did end up at the bottom of Clinton Reservoir; the lake is miles away. Perhaps condemnation of the town was unnecessary.

Today the town is in ruins, and even if you had passed through the area in the old days you probably would have believed nothing ever happened there. It was the kind of place that prompted city slickers to ask, "What do you folks find to talk about, way out here in the sticks?" And the folks responded quickly: "We find plenty."[5]

110 MILE CREEK
Osage County

The Santa Fe Trail crossing at 110 Mile Creek in Osage County was one of the best-known and most colorful historic sites used by early travelers and freighters. One Hundred and Ten Mile Creek got its name in 1840—the Santa Fe Trail crossing at this point was exactly 110 miles from Sibley Landing east of Independence, Missouri. The trail came from the east, crossed the creek, and from its west bank split into two trails. One became a branch of the so-called Mormon Trail, which went northwest to the Kansas River valley and eventually west to Utah. The Santa Fe continued westward to the next stage stop at Switzer's Landing, then on to Council Grove. Since the trail split at 110 Mile Creek, the site was a natural place for development of a trading point.

The first white inhabitant of the area was a trader named Richardson who had married a Shawnee Indian woman. In the late 1840s he operated a farm and sold vegetables and other staples to freighters on the trail. This farm, located at the north end of the Sac & Fox Indian reservation, commanded much interest from Indians and white settlers alike. In 1849 Fry P. McGee and his family were returning from a trip to Oregon when they came upon Richardson's establishment. McGee immediately recognized the commercial potential of this trading post and offered Richardson a handsome sum for the place. In 1854 when the land was available for purchase, McGee became the new owner of "110."[1]

The McGee family figured prominently in the history of the territory. James, Fry's father, was a trapper, hunter, and trader, as well as one of the first white settlers of Kansas City, Missouri. He located in the heart of the city in 1828, taking a government patent on 320 acres of land that became regional headquarters for trappers and Indians for over twenty years. Fry immediately established a tavern and toll bridge on the trail and brought in his brother, Mobillon, to help with the operation. They aimed to make the site a city the size of Westport; they called this fledgling city "Washington."

Fry was proslavery, and he brought his slaves with him to the new site. In fact Fry was one of only two men in Osage County to own slaves. His tavern soon became headquarters for proslavery sympathizers, many of whom could be counted among the state's lawless element.[2] His proslavery affiliation gave McGee a bad reputation among the free-staters. On November 29, 1854, "110" 's voting precinct, one of only seventeen in the territory, caught the attention of New York editor Horace Greeley, who singled it out of all the Kansas polling places as a particularly egregious example of disregard for law and order. Proslavery forces, hoping to open the territory to slavery, had arrived the day before the election and had cast 587 fraudulent votes out of a total of 607. McGee himself was determined from the outset that no abolitionist should settle on "110."

Despite McGee's rough exterior and his political partisanship, however, most of the early settlers had found him to be kind-hearted and honest and had never known him to resort to bloodshed. The rumors and stories about McGee were often unfounded or embellished, but somehow they lasted for years. Many people thought that a traveler and his money often got no farther than McGee's crossing and that a secret tunnel ran from his tavern to the creek bank. As late as 1927 and 1928, Topeka and Kansas City newspaper stories reported that gold coins and human skeletons had been found on the site and that two boys had discovered the tunnel at the creek. Actually, if anyone was guilty of lawlessness, it was the free-staters. In 1856, a party of free-state men raided McGee's tavern, looting his store and taking $2,000 worth of goods as well as twenty horses and mules. McGee blamed John Brown's men, but no hard evidence of their identity exists.[3]

W. F. Eckart's father settled on a claim three miles from McGee's tavern. His reminiscences of McGee's claim provide insight into the 110 Mile Creek site:

McGee was living in a frame house built out of native lumber sawed on his premises with a horse-power mill. . . . McGee's house had 4 rooms with kitchen and dining room. At each end was a fireplace. The east room generally was occupied by travelers and in winter the floor was often filled with fellows sleeping before the fire in buffalo robes. . . . There was a toll bridge there at that time built of logs. The toll was 25 cents for wagons and the revenue amounted to $20 or $30 a day at times. In 1860 McGee built a new one and during the war only Santa Fe trains paid the toll.

The Santa Fe mail came twice a month carried in a coach that often held 12 to 14 passengers. The coach would always stop and feed overnight, the passengers rolled up on the floor before the fire for the night.

In 1857 Fry McGee had in his possession 3 slaves: a negro woman and child who helped Mrs. McGee in the kitchen; a boy about 14 years old and was a handy boy all around. Several times he would take them to Missouri on suspecting a raid from the Abolitionists and return them when things quieted down.[4]

By 1857 McGee had the makings of a typical Kansas trail town at 110 Mile Creek. Besides his tavern, he built a hotel and a supply store and established a post office known as "Richardson." The "Washington" site became just a memory. The tavern was popular with the local Sac and Fox Indians, who spent their annuity money there. Unfortunately, they did not know the value of a dollar and would pay for a three-bit drink with a five-dollar gold piece. Fry often failed to acquaint them with the change they had coming. McGee became a good friend of Chief Keokuk, the most famous of the Sac and Fox chiefs. Contemporaries often reported seeing old Keokuk wander into McGee's tavern, bearing buffalo tongues as a token of friendship and good will.

McGee's wife can best be described as a true partner. She was supposedly "patient and long-suffering," and like many women of the day, she wore her long black hair parted in the middle and drawn back and knotted on her neck. She became legendary along the Santa Fe Trail and was known as the "worst cusser." Once she defied a sheriff by attempting to free a murderer he was taking back to Wyandotte to stand trial. The man was the husband of Mrs. McGee's hotel companion. While Mrs. McGee entertained the sheriff with her cursing ability, the wife attempted, unsuccessfully, to slip her husband out the back way. In retaliation, the sheriff hanged his prisoner on the cottonwood tree in front of the tavern.[5] Indeed, many cottonwoods around the tavern are said to have operated as gallows during territorial days. Some graves found in the early 1900s were attributed to that violent period in the history of 110 Mile Creek.

Fry McGee was proprietor of the Richardson site until he died in September 1861. William Harris, his son-in-law and partner, then continued most of the operations. McGee's name lived on in print for a few more years—when the officials organized what is now Cherokee County, they first named it McGee County in his honor.

During the Civil War, William Harris kept most of the businesses and the toll bridge operational, but few settlers used the site, then known as Harris Stage Station. Harris added a stone annex to the hotel, using fine walnut in the flooring, and he improved the toll bridge by putting stone in the abutments. A ford also existed a short distance from the bridge, and many wagon trains used it to avoid paying a fee to cross the bridge. According to local gossip, the bridge operator often went to the ford and dumped buckets of water on the banks, making them so slick that a wagon could not get down without slipping. Business at the bridge prospered after such underhanded arrangements. Harris also operated a blacksmith shop and a community store with a stock of "practically anything."

In the 1870s Harris quit the business, and the settlement disappeared when other towns in the immediate area, such as Overbrook and Scranton, became established communities. Some of the buildings remained standing for years. Although decrepit, the old hotel and the tavern were local landmarks through the 1920s. Both were considered haunted, but generally the strange noises that emanated from their walls were created by owls and other varmints. The orchard remained wild for decades and was the site of several graves of questionable origin. Until the old road was altered the toll bridge remained in existence;[6] no one chose to dump water on the new road.

Today the site lies in an empty pasture on private property, but you can see it from Highway 56. A Santa Fe Trail marker, a half mile from the area, is the only reminder of a once busy trail town that made history when the territory was young.

ARVONIA
Osage County

Arvonia was a Welsh colony with big plans for becoming a major railroad town in a rich agricultural region. But, in the words of one local historian, "Nothing ever worked out for them. It was a town that never really was."

The town was originally surveyed and platted by J. Mather Jones, head of a Welsh colony from Utica, New York, who found rich farmland at $2 an acre an attractive investment. By November 1869 the population, mostly of Welsh ancestry, had already reached 100. By 1875 this figure had grown to 400. They chose the name Arvonia because it meant "land of willows," an accurate description of the townsite.

Oddly enough, many families had the same last name. There were fifty families by the name of Jones, thirty-two named Williams, thirty-two named Lewis, and about twelve families named Griffith, Evans, and

Thomas. This preponderance of similar surnames resulted in much confusion for the settlers. When people referred to a member of a particular "Jones" family, for example, they usually identified them either by their first initials, by distinct mannerisms, or if all else failed, by different parts of the country. There was a Johnny "One-Eye" Jones, who had one eye; a Johnny "Butch" because he was a butcher; a "Little Johnny" because he was short; and a "Cattle" Jones, who raised cattle. Similarly, in the Williams family there was a Billy "White House" because he lived in a white house; a Billy "west of town," who lived west of Arvonia; and a William "Green Point," who lived on a big green hill.

Those early years saw the establishment of two general stores, the Dooley Hotel, a hardware store, a shoe store, a blacksmith shop, a cheese factory, a post office, and a hall called "Walnut Hall."[1]

The Reverend R. D. Thomas's *A History of the Welsh in America*, published in 1872, mentions the founding of Arvonia:

> In less than six months after the starting of the settlement, the great Temporary Hotel and about a dozen houses had been built in Arvonia, and over a score of accountable persons had bought land in the settlement. This is proof that our nation needs wise, learned, wealthy, and adventuresome leadership, that they trusted John Mather Jones, Esq., and that the district is a good and pleasant place to live in. . . . From the start to the present time they have been faithful and zealous for the cause of the Savior and of Welsh literature. Nothing is able to prevent success for men like this.

Arvonia's attempts to secure a railroad connection were unsuccessful and resulted in one of the town's most serious problems. By 1875 the town was booming, and the St. Louis Osage Company, Walnut Valley Railroad promised to lay track through the community. When the railroad was unable to secure the necessary right-of-way, however, the venture failed. Later the Texas & Orient Railroad attempted to bring track to Arvonia and went so far as to construct a depot in town, but the railroad never completed the route. The Santa Fe Railroad also promised to go through Arvonia, but they missed the town by four miles; their line went through Reading and Emporia.

Coal mining fever affected the colonists as much as farming and ranching. The coal boom that had an impact on the region in Osage County from Carbondale to Osage City soon spread to Arvonia. In the winter, farmers opened a few drift mines and extracted small quantities of coal. The

Most of the east-west streets in this 1887 town plat of Arvonia are named for presidents. The one exception is the northernmost street, apparently named for abolitionist Henry Ward Beecher.

more ambitious men secured teams and started open pit mines. After the men removed the coal, the open pits formed ponds for watering stock.[2]

The social and spiritual center of Arvonia was of course the church. Many of the Welsh settlers were Congregationalists and building a church was high on their list of priorities. They borrowed the money from a congregational fund in Topeka to build their first church. The brethren agreed that they would pay for the church according to membership, and they figured it would cost each member twenty-three cents a year. Sunday worship was usually a daylong affair. Members worshipped during the morning, then stayed for lunch and socialized the rest of the day.

At one time two churches were united, but a feud among the members split the two. The ill will began when the editor of the *Lebo Star* sponsored a contest in which the person who sold the most subscriptions to the newspaper would win a piano. The Christian Endeavor, a group of young church members, decided they would try to win the contest. They had everyone sell subscriptions and then credited one woman with all the sales. The woman won the piano; however, a dispute arose when the woman's mother-in-law thought that she should keep the piano for herself. The result was a drawn-out fight that split the congregation into two churches, the Calvinistic Methodist and the Presbyterian Congregational. What happened to the piano? It ended up in the Methodist church.

The biggest celebration of the year was St. David's Day. The whole town took on a festive air with balloons and banners on every corner. People came from miles around to hear the recitations, the oratory, and the beautiful singing. Through the years, as congregations at Arvonia became smaller, the Welsh colonists in nearby Emporia continued the tradition.[3]

By the turn of the century, Arvonia had begun to decline, as was apparent in dwindling church congregations as well as in reduced business activity. The primary cause was the lack of a railroad. Farmers shipped their goods and grain from other towns, and eventually they shipped themselves out as well. The early settlers also left the community, depriving the town of the leadership of such men as John Mather Jones. As the young people left for employment in larger cities, Arvonia slowly disappeared.

Today some old buildings and a few ruins remain in town. A church still stands; it has a small congregation, most of them descendants of the original Welsh colonists. Arvonia is well worth a visit, for it is one of the best-preserved old towns in the Osage County area.

FOSTORIA
Osage County

Fostoria, located just east of Burlingame, was first called Fosterville after William Foster, a coal miner. At the turn of the century, Fostoria, as it later became known, was a typical coal-mining camp that attracted many European emigrants. The different nationalities brought a relaxed, outgoing atmosphere to the town. The Italians sang beautifully, accompanying themselves on the mandolin, accordion, violin, and guitar. They also played bocci ball, a game played with large and small leather balls on an indoor court. A comradeship developed between these men from Italy, England, Ireland, and France, most likely because of their close association in a small town and their work together in the mines. Many of them had quaint nicknames, such as "Jumbo" Rieck, "Crocky" Parker, "Bingo" Dunn, "Hammer" Silotto, "Bear" Miller, "Timber" Morrison, "Bugger" Hall, and "Tarzan" Isaacs. At one time, fifteen mines operated in the Fostoria area. Three main ones lasted longer than the others—the Chappel Mine #6 worked by George Chappell, the Comet operated by George Elliott, and Bell #1 owned by John Bell and located on his farm near the railroad tracks.

George Chappell, who lived one mile north of Fostoria, bought a boarding house in Scranton and had it moved to his farm where he lodged many of the single miners. Chappell served two meals a day and packed his lodgers' midday meal. Some of the miners cleaned the rooms and did the laundry in exchange for their rent.

As the years went by there was less demand for coal, and the Fostoria mines gradually closed. During World War II and the early 1950s, many of the miners went to work at the Air Force Supply Depot at Pauline.[1]

In 1944 Clarence Helstrom began gathering some old buildings and moving them into a "corral" north of the old Fostoria site. His dream of grouping these buildings into some sort of merchant's district didn't materialize until his daughter Delores Helstrom Richman and her husband Norman took over in 1973 and completed the work. After they finished the project, the "corral" contained the Old Fostoria Corral, a private club; Sherry's Western Wear; T. J. Beauty Salon; Leo's King at Stud, a horse breeding service; Dean Prescott's barber shop; Fostoria Excavation; and Helstrom House Movers. Norman Richman did basement excavating while his wife Delores did the house moving. As Norman explained, "Usually when someone moves a house somebody has to be there to put a basement under it." Delores articulated their goals more fully:

> We are trying to restore old Fostoria. . . . Last year we had a small stable out here and the buildings were all deteriorated. We had a flash of what we would like it to be like and Norman and I had it all planned out in 48 hours. We wanted a western store here because we are western oriented. My brother-in-law Gary Richman got one of those Amtrak (train) cars out here and I decided a beauty shop would be good there, and then maybe my hair wouldn't be a mess all the time. It turned out to be quite a brainstorm to put the car on the railroad tracks. . . . Whenever an impulse hits—and I got lots of things in mind—that is when something will go in. This is where I hope to complete it."[2]

Unfortunately for the re-creation of the old town and the Helstrom's dreams, the Corral burned in 1983. Thus ended another era at Fostoria.

OLD STRAWN
Coffey County

The town of Strawn, founded sometime in the early 1870s, was named after Enos Strawn, a Kansas territorial official and one of the commissioners appointed to locate the county seat. He held the office of probate judge and also served as justice of the peace.

Strawn was the second largest shipping point on the Neosho division of the M. K. T. Railroad, and by 1910 it was booming. Hoover's grocery and Pennybaker's Hardware, a post office, a bank, two general stores, two res-

The Old Strawn railroad depot, 1957, shortly before construction of the John Redmond Dam, which inundated the townsite.

taurants, two barber shops, a blacksmith shop, a lumberyard, a hotel, two churches, a school, and an elevator—all were doing big business.

The town's success, however, made it the target of local criminals. On the night of October 14, 1921, burglars forcibly entered the Strawn bank, but the thieves didn't find enough money to pay them for their trouble. They dug a hole through the vault near the side door and broke open several tin containers and about twenty-five safety deposit boxes, but they didn't touch the bank safe. The intruders left no clues to their identity.

From 1904 to 1951 floods from the Neosho River plagued the townsite. After the settlers had cleared the timber and drained the fields, the river carried even more water, causing the floods to grow steadily worse. On July 13, 1951, all of Strawn was under water. Eighty-two year old "Sport" Kennedy was on the second floor of the hotel along with three dogs, two cats, and a pet raccoon. Since he had plenty of food, he said he planned to stay put. A Mrs. Baumgarner climbed up in the attic of her home, and she, too, refused to leave. She said she had fresh water and a bucket of cracked wheat that would last her until the flood receded. Both were fortunate—they survived the high water.

After 1951 the residents begged for flood control. They believed that if a dam could be built directly above Strawn, the town would remain intact and the flood waters could be controlled. The next year the government authorized a project known as the Strawn Dam. No sooner had they made their plans than they decided to move the Strawn Dam to a different site and to rename it the John Redman Dam. This change in location forced everyone to move. Old Strawn was largely made up of retired residents and farmers who lived within a few miles of their farms, and their resentment and bewilderment grew. No one knew whom to contact or where to turn. Howard Claycamp and M.C. Williamson proposed that they plan to move the whole town to a new location, which seemed like a good idea to many of the residents, and they immediately began to acquire the land the town of New Strawn now occupies.[1]

In 1961 Old Strawn moved to New Strawn. By 1972 only the grade school building was left standing on the old townsite. The transformation was complete.

MILLER
Lyon County

Miller was once a part of the Sac and Fox Indian Reservation. In the fall of 1846, a band of 2,000 Sac and Foxes and Kickapoos led by Chief Kennekuk settled along the Marais des Cygnes River; the west line of the reservation was a mile and a half west of the Miller site. Many of the Indians were either farmers or wild-game hunters, and they remained in the area until 1859, when the land was ceded back to the federal government. A half century later, Miller was established, becoming Lyon County's youngest community.

When the Missouri Pacific Railroad built through the region in 1886, a country post office was established to cater to local farmers and ranchers. W. W. Miller and H. B. Miller deeded a small tract of land to the Missouri Pacific with the understanding that the railroad would survey it into blocks, streets, alleys, and lots. However, no further development occurred until 1907, when William Schultz established the first store there.

The name Miller was derived from the Miller Ranch, the land surrounding the townsite. In 1910 a plat of the town was filed showing it to be an area two blocks wide and five blocks long lying north of the railroad. The main north-south street was called, appropriately enough, "Main Street," and it was flanked by Oak Street to the west and Walnut to the east. The east and west streets ranged from first through fifth, with the diagonal

The Missouri Pacific Railroad depot at Miller, a railroad town that originally catered to the adjacent sprawling Miller Ranch.

Miller Avenue on the south and Maple Street running parallel to the railroad and city park.[1]

The Miller Livestock Investment Corporation, formed in 1882, added men to the town's payrolls. The workers needed housing, and thus many of them lived in homes built in Miller. The corporation built the Miller Hardware and Supply Company in 1910, which led to the development of other business establishments. Jacob Crawford opened a general merchandise store; he was followed by the Edwards and Westmacott Lumber Company. Other businesses included another hardware store, a general store, a blacksmith shop, and an implement business. By 1915 Miller was in the midst of a boom. More general stores, a lunch counter, a barber shop, and a state bank opened, soon followed by a gasoline station, a canning factory, a hotel, a livery stable, and a railroad depot. What had started as a place designed for ranch hands alone had transformed into the biggest little town in Lyon County.[2]

Times were good during the 1910s and 1920s, but the 1930s and its accompanying agricultural depression had a severe impact on the economy of the community. A fire in 1929 destroyed quite a few buildings on Main Street, and many were simply never rebuilt. During the next twenty years there was no improvement—indeed, the state bank moved to Admire. In 1958 the Missouri Pacific removed its depot and disrupted all services, and several other businesses failed. Even the post office was discontinued and the community schools were closed in response to declining enrollments and consolidation. One of the oldest businesses, the Hoglund lumberyard, burned down in the 1960s, and the town records were lost in the flames.

By 1976 the town had only four businesses remaining, but it could point to one community improvement—a rural fire department. After flames had already destroyed much of the town over a fifty-year period, the residents formed the Miller Booster Club to keep Miller on the map and to ensure that fires would no longer be a severe threat. The club purchased several fire trucks and made their fire department one of the best in the state. By the late seventies the Miller Fire Department consisted of five expensive firefighting vehicles, including a fully equipped ambulance.[3]

Miller has had to confront water as well as fire, for flood control in the area has also been a problem. Elm Creek has inundated Main Street on several occasions. A particularly bad flood in 1946 dampened most of the stores in town. A few businesses have red lines painted on them indicating how high the water level was at that time.

Today Miller has about fifty people and contains several abandoned business buildings, which makes it a good choice for ghost town hunters. A bicentennial history of Lyon County offers the following apt description of Miller: "It never was incorporated, never has flourished, but has endured."

DUNLAP
Morris County

Dunlap's history reflects the all too frequent tale of racial strife. Although bloodshed and fighting between blacks and whites were infrequent, tensions beneath the surface revealed intolerance among both these groups.

For example, the following quotation appeared in a 1925 Council Grove historical booklet that briefly described nearby Dunlap:

> Dunlap almost crossed the color line irrevocably during its pioneer days when a colony of 500 Negroes arrived to settle in the village. The immigration resulted from the circulation of a rumor in the South that this section of Kansas desired colonists and that Uncle Sam would deed forty acres of land

and give a mule to every settler coming into the Kaw reservation. Only a part of these colored settlers remained long in Dunlap, but for many years those who stayed staged an Emancipation Day barbecue in September which drew hundreds of their brethren to Dunlap from Lawrence, Leavenworth and other dark belts of population. At one time a Negro academy with two teachers was maintained at Dunlap by the Presbyterian church, but the colored children showed themselves little more appreciative of "schooling" than had the Kaw Indians at the Mission in Council Grove a few decades previously.

During the mid-1920s such bigotry and ignorance was common among many white settlers, even to the point of involving the local Council Grove chapter of the Ku Klux Klan. A few charter members of this Klan came from the Dunlap vicinity, but whether they joined as a result of prejudice against their black neighbors is not known.[1]

Dunlap was established in 1875 and named for the Indian trader Joseph Dunlap, who was also the first postmaster. Before the town's founding, settlers in the area traded with the Kansa Indians, a tribe that lived on a reservation extending from Council Grove south to Dunlap. The main government trading post and mission, located four miles from Dunlap, conducted an experiment whereby they built stone houses for the Indians as a "civilizing process." This test procedure failed because most of the Indians preferred to live in their tepees and stable their horses in their new stone "barns." The government tried giving them plows, but they stuck them in the notches of trees and laughed at the authorities. A few years later, the Indians sold the windows, sashes, doors, and doorknobs from the stone houses for money to buy government whiskey.

The *Emporia Gazette* of May 3, 1962, described other activities of the Kansa Indians in those early days:

> There was a Methodist minister whom the Kaws liked and they never went off with his apples although they had the reputation of taking anything not nailed down and scaring the daylights out of women and children by peering in the windows. Occasionally if they saw the family at meals they could come in, squat down and begin the freeloading—which they delight in—especially if there were white biscuits and "hoggie meat" on the table.

By the late 1860s many settlers lived near Dunlap. At that time the town owed its existence to the Missouri, Kansas & Texas Railroad, whose policy was to establish a town every ten miles, but for some reason Dunlap had no depot, just a rough platform and a station agent. Nonetheless, stores and businesses began to spring up quickly after Sylvester Aldrich constructed a frame hotel. Leonard Still built the first general store; George Love established a hardware store; Mose Strickland and George Bennett started a blacksmith shop; and "Black" Stevenson built the first frame house. One of the stone buildings intended for the Indians was converted into a school, which later became a private academy for the local blacks. Dunlap had an undertaker, William Collins, who also established a furniture store in the growing city. Jerry Sheaffer operated the first meat market; Fred Bernard opened the first ice cream parlor; Dr. Soto was the first physician; and Dr. Sowers was the druggist. C. W. See built and operated a large sawmill.[2]

During the early 1880s several thousand blacks came West from the Deep South to find new homes in Kansas. About three hundred of them came first to Lyon and Morris counties, where irate citizens barred them from stopping in the towns of Emporia and Council Grove. After moving on to Dunlap and encountering little resistance, they established themselves about a mile north of the railroad. Some were unable to make a successful living and soon left, but others stayed on for several years. Though there was little outward show of animosity, many settlers were unhappy about having blacks in the neighborhood, and they segregated them as much as possible. Segregation, however, did not extend to the public school, where 247 black and white children attended classes together.

Fay Parsons built the first stone warehouse, and its second story became the social center of the town, a gathering place for dances, card parties, and other activities.[3] In a few months the town had a population of 1,000. Unfortunately, this boom was accompanied by trouble, as the following account of the "Dunlap Murder Trial" illustrates:

There are traditions of frontier times when life could be rough and tough. The murder trial of hotel keeper [Sylvester] Aldrich is a case in point. A hardened character named McDermit, worthy of those villains portrayed as coming into tangle with Matt Dillon of Gunsmoke, lived near Dunlap. It seemed that a neighbor's hogs got loose and trespassed on McDermit's land. These he promptly penned up and was prepared to keep them as his own. One day during his absence, the original owner—a man named Green—went over to McDermit's and drove his hogs home. Infuriated, McDermit went after the unfortunate man and beat him up with a pick handle, leaving a badly injured man.

The hotel keeper in Dunlap named Aldrich was the wounded man's

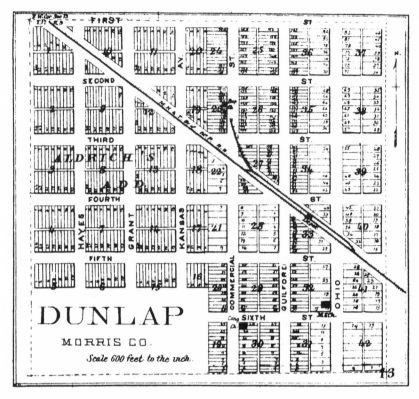

Dunlap was cut in half by the Missouri, Kansas & Texas Railroad in this 1887 layout of the town. Many black residents lived near the tracks in the southeast part of the city.

friend and took care of him in his hotel. This appeared to raise McDermit's anger even more and he perpetually threatened Aldrich hurling insults at him as he drove through town in his wagon carrying his pick handle or threatening with a gun. At that time work was being done on a bridge for the Katy railroad and workers were enjoying room and board at the Aldrich Hotel. These workers became indignant at the insults thrown out by McDermit and his threats of bodily mayhem.

It is reported that workers said, "If you kill McDermit we will load your gun with buckshot." There was a stone wall by the main road not far from the hotel and Aldrich took up his position behind it. As McDermit, riding his wagon and carrying his rifle, at the same time calling out threats against Aldrich, drove by the hotel, Aldrich rose up and let him have it. The horses ran away with the wounded and dying man lying in the wagon box. The runaways being stopped, McDermit was carried into a store, where he died. Then came the Aldrich murder trial but McDermit had so often acted with cruelty and had so frequently threatened Aldrich that people absolved him on the grounds of self-defense and he was freed.[4]

Dunlap was a major cattle shipping point until 1914. By that time the population had fallen to 333, but there were still quite a few stores open for business. The coming of the automobile spelled more trouble for the town. Bill Waters brought the first motor car to Dunlap; the car shook so much that everyone said it "caused the passengers' teeth to fall out after about ten miles." A short period of prosperity came in the 1920s, however, when W. H. Clark opened a theater and Charles Haucke and Win Bernard introduced the first radio sets to the town.

In the 1930s the depression hit the town hard. The railroad became unimportant to Dunlap when the farmers found it was cheaper to ship their cattle by truck to larger towns such as Council Grove. Consequently, many businesses closed. The coming of this new age found the small railroad town and its people unable to cope with these changes.[5]

Today Dunlap is a small community of about a hundred people, located nine miles southeast of Council Grove off Highway 56. It's worth the trip to visit this once-major cattle-shipping point and former home of many "exodusters."

SKIDDY
Morris County

When the Missouri, Kansas & Texas Railroad laid track through Morris County in 1869, some of the laborers who had bought farms nearby started a town and opened a post office in the Clark Creek Valley. Francis Skiddy, an official of the New York company that furnished money for the railroad, wanted the town named "Skiddy" after himself. In return he promised to build the settlers a town hall and other structures that would benefit the community. The offer sounded good to the settlers; they named their town Skiddy. The town hall, however, never materialized.

After a few years some of the town's leading citizens wanted the name changed because they found it embarrassing to be called "the gentlemen from Skiddy." They did change the name temporarily to Camden, but at that time there were twenty-three other Camdens in the United States, which caused too much confusion in the mail service. The name then reverted to Skiddy, and today it remains the only Skiddy in the United States.

Even letters from foreign countries addressed simply "Skiddy, U.S.A." arrive safely at their destination.

By 1871 there were four buildings in town: a small brown structure near the railroad where many settlers lived until they found permanent residences; the home of Stephen Willes; and two store buildings at the junction of Main and Front Streets. Joseph College and his nephew, Amos McDaniels, built the store on the north side of Main. One annoyance the storekeepers had to guard against was pilfering by local Indians. While a clerk waited on one Indian, others in his party would help themselves.

In the summer of 1871 many prospective buyers were considering land purchases around Skiddy, but these transactions were temporarily halted when a particularly destructive prairie fire swept into town from the west. All the male citizens fought the blaze under the leadership of Patrick Maloney, who was said to be "the best fire fighter in the state." While the women pumped the water, the young boys wet the sacks. One frightened couple in a buggy drove furiously toward Skiddy for sixty miles, just barely keeping ahead of the fire. When they finally reached town, both of their horses dropped dead from exhaustion.

More excitement occurred in town the day the two Farbridge girls disappeared. The girls had been sent to the butcher shop near the schoolhouse, but when heading home they took the north road instead of the west and wandered for several miles before coming to a corral and a farmhouse. They were shy and afraid to go to the door, so they sat out in the cow lot for a long time. Finally they summoned the courage to go to the house and ask for shelter. The girls learned the next morning that at least thirty men had been out all night searching for them. Their parents were afraid the Indians had taken them.

In fact the whites and Indians generally coexisted peacefully at Skiddy, and few real conflicts occurred. The Indians would leave their women and children at a nearby spring during their hunting trips. Once in a while, however, the Indians became hostile, and the frightened settlers fled to a stone house down by the creek or hurried to Fort Riley, if time permitted.

In 1880 Skiddy was a thriving railroad center with two general stores, two blacksmiths, a lumberyard, a grain elevator, a drugstore, and a harness and shoe shop. One of the earliest buildings was a seventeen-room hotel built by D. J. Shore.

During the 1880s area farmers shipped much of their wheat by rail from Skiddy to Texas and abroad. This wheat was a hard-grain variety raised by the Germans who had settled on Lyons Creek. During the winter of 1880–

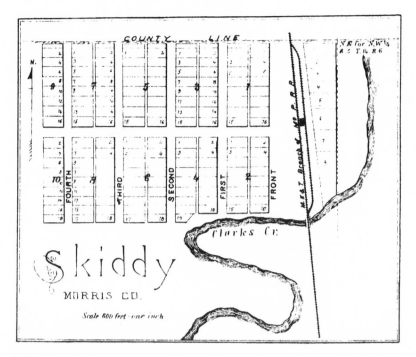

Skiddy was developed after the Missouri, Kansas & Texas Railroad built track through the community. This 1887 layout of the town shows a meandering Clarks Creek just south and east of town.

1881, long lines of wagons loaded with grain could be seen every day bound for Skiddy and the railroad.

When the Rock Island Railroad officials spoke of building through the town, the settlers had high hopes of further economic development at Skiddy. Unfortunately, the Rock Island built through White City instead. When Alta Vista, Dwight, Latimer, and Herington sprang up, most of Skiddy's residents left for these towns.

The county officials constructed a bridge at "Doyle's Crossing" several miles away. The new bridge meant that trade from the east would go to Junction City and White City instead of to Skiddy. "Doyle's Crossing" was a well known old ford where freighters from Fort Riley and Fort Dodge crossed the river in the 1860s. When the workmen laid the abutments for the bridge, they found saber hilts and Spanish coins at the site, lending credence to the legend that Coronado had crossed there. The ford accommodated another figure of legendary stature: in the 1870s General George Custer had crossed the ford and noted in his journal that he saw a young boy killing a large black snake over twelve feet long on the bank nearby.

Skiddy's contributions to Kansas have been considerable, but the reverse cannot be said. Today Skiddy is a rural hamlet in the Flint Hills, silent and undisturbed by outsiders.[1]

3

SOUTHEAST KANSAS

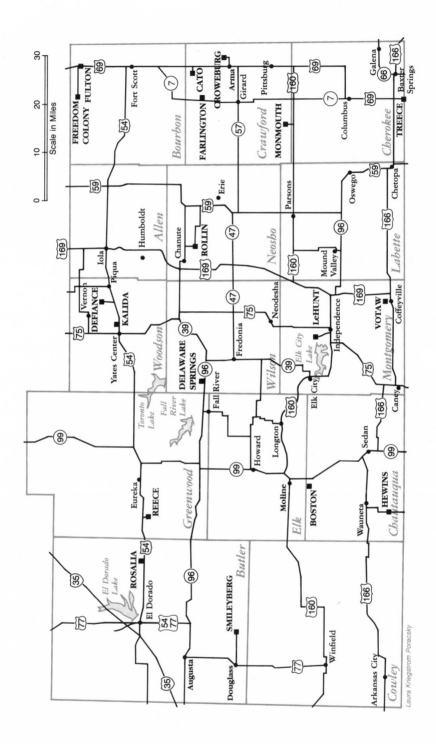

Scale in Miles

Laura Kriegstrom Poracsky

FREEDOM COLONY
Bourbon County

The experimental Freedom Colony was established on March 8, 1897, at the Howard brothers' farmhouse five miles west of Fulton in Bourbon County. The founders included Frank Cotton and E. Z. Ernest of Olathe, John Fitzgerald of Fort Scott, and James Howard and his brother John, owners of the farm.

Frank Cotton noted that "we adopted a constitution, elected officers, discussed business projects, and decided upon work to be done," and voted to locate the colony on land owned by the Howards. Their farm was ideal because of the "coal, oil, natural gas, and other natural deposits of value" found there. The location of the land in the heart of the state's mining district also made it an excellent site. By not having to pay a high price for the grounds, the colony saved money that could be used to build their utopia.

The colonists quickly constructed temporary housing (tarpaper shanties), started several industries, and planted crops. In the summer of 1898, John Howard asserted:

> We have raised a very good crop. Fitzgerald and us boys put in 15 acres of cane, and it looks nice—some is ready to make up. We have the mill ready to start making sorghum tomorrow. The boys and I have 10 acres of castor beans and 25 acres of corn on the land we rented. . . . We started a shaft to the coal the 4th of July and reached the coal day before yesterday. Have a good quality of coal in a vein 24 inches thick. . . . We really need more men who are able to work . . . but we have no place to board them.

Unlike the neighboring mining communities where everything was owned and operated by the company, private ownership flourished in Freedom Colony. Members owned their personal possessions, and most held title to their own lots and leased additional agricultural property on a long-term basis. The town's "utilities" were municipally owned, and its largest industry, a coal mine, was a cooperative venture.

Freedom reached its peak in 1901, when the experimental colony achieved some publicity in eastern newspapers. The town, however, received most of its publicity from an unusual factory, one that was supposed to build flying machines! In the winter of 1900 Carl Browne, the "Chief Marshal" in the Army of Jacob S. Coxey, joined the colony. Browne and his wife Mame quickly set about to perfect a commercial flying machine based on "The Carl Dryden Browne patent-applied-for principle of rotary winged wheels," and within a few months he had constructed a wooden model of his invention. Browne's general plans were to build a flying machine factory, one that would provide "employment to all those needing jobs in the Middle-West," and to sell these machines "so cheap as to soon supercede the bicycle for home use."

On a bright, crisp Sunday in October 1900, nearly a thousand people jammed the colony grounds to witness the laying of the cornerstone for this flying machine factory. Success for Browne's project, however, was not to be. He built a small factory but did not construct a single flying machine. Browne couldn't perfect his model, and the money he needed, always in short supply at Freedom, never materialized for the venture. Browne and his wife left the colony in 1902.

The collapse of the flying machine enterprise was the beginning of the end for the settlement. In 1902 strife among the colonists began to tear them apart. The Howard brothers and several other colony members became embroiled in a fight over the ownership of the property, a conflict that resulted in expensive and lengthy litigation. In the same year, external problems also arose. Nonresidents charged that the colonists practiced "free love" or were at least guilty of sexual promiscuity. They continually refuted the charges. "I emphatically deny that any persons now living in Freedom Colony are immoral or breakers of the law," wrote Frank Cotton to the *Fort Scott Weekly Tribune*, "The accusation of Free Love practice—so called—is the work of malicious gossips whose small souls have been moved to petty spite over fancied grievances; and they have distorted and magnified innocent circumstances into an appearance of evil and have not hesitated to brace up their statements by unblushing falsehoods."

This statement by Cotton only exacerbated the gossiping of outsiders. The county attorney who investigated the case turned up nothing to substantiate the accusations. Although the charges made by the outsiders may have been false, the colony was continually in trouble with the law. The area newspapers, who had initially dubbed the colonists "dreamers," "eccentrics," or "men of good hope," now labeled them "troublemakers" and "threats to society."

After 1901 new colonists ceased to arrive at Freedom, and some of those who were already there left. Today no records exist concerning the colony from 1903 to 1905. Local papers ignored the settlement, and their own newspaper ceased publication in 1903. A census in 1905 showed that all members of the colony had drifted away except the Howards, Cottons, and Fitzgeralds. The only material relating to the death of Freedom Colony was found in the "Kansas Magazine" for 1949. Wayne Delavan wrote the following:

> Then one dark night in 1905 every cabin burst out in flames. All were destroyed but one. . . . Although the fire was believed to have had a human origin, the real cause was never determined. One colonist nicknamed "Cotton" had stepped outside before going to bed. He discovered the fire and saved his own cabin. He found that the pine boards on one side of his house—the side next to the wind—were soaked with kerosene. The county authorities were not too interested in the case.

Freedom Colony was just one of the many unsuccessful experiments by early settlers to start a labor reform settlement in the depression era of the 1890s.[1]

ROLLIN
Neosho County

The town of Rollin, established on October 23, 1890, was of little importance economically until 1896, when the Santa Fe Railroad erected a station there. The depot was a converted boxcar left standing alongside the rails. The local "jokers" termed the town "Roll-in" in deference to this solitary piece of railroad stock on the siding.[1] According to Tom Evans, one of the last owners of the Rollin townsite, Delos Johnson founded the town, which had a grocery store, a post office, an oil refinery, a doctor, a schoolhouse, and a church.[2]

In 1902 Rollin made the headlines. An article in the *Erie Record* of June 20 related how the town became an "odd" religious colony:

> A number of people of the "Restitution Faith" organized under the name "Church of God" met at Shaw [Kansas] last week to discuss the project of establishing a colony of that faith in Rollin. These people have no creed but the Bible, but they believe it teaches only the complete mortality of man, conditional immortality and future reign of Christ on earth under the 12 tribes of Israel and finally over the whole earth. . . .
>
> . . . [A] town company was formed and over $2,000 subscribed for the purchase of the townsite now held by members of that faith. Next fall when the crops are off, the land will be surveyed and the town incorporated. After this the intention of these people is to develop gas for the use of their town and establish industries that will give employment to the poor of the church.

As stated by the *Record*, the incorporators proposed to:

> make the colony a model of morality and accomplish much good for humanity. In the deed conveying the property it is stipulated that no intoxicants or tobacco in any form whether chewing or smoking shall be permitted sold on the townsite. Any member of the colony who barters or sells liquors or tobacco forfeits his rights in the colony and he is expelled from the colony and his property shall revert back to the company together with all improvements.

Lewis Taylor, a local resident, remembered that the religious group was commonly known as the "Soul Sleepers." These people believed that the body and soul are not separated at death, but that the soul is buried with the body and will sleep there until resurrection. Taylor added that Delos Johnson "was the greatest man who ever lived in Neosho County. There wasn't a human being so bad that Delos didn't help him." Taylor noted that every year Johnson would build two or three houses for the poor families in the area. He also recalled the start of an oil refinery in 1906 and its demise sometime after 1909, and he remembered future President Harry Truman coming to Rollin on business matters concerning the refinery.[3]

In a 1903 issue of the *Erie Record*, Johnson is noted as president of the colony; A. J. Eychane, vice-president; W. L. Crowe, secretary; and A. D. Dewey, treasurer. In later years, the *Record* welcomed the Rollin Manufacturing Company, a business known for building "Heriff Stoves." In 1909 the newspaper mentioned that the oil refinery was still going strong, which was one of the few bits of recorded information found about the refinery in which Truman was supposedly involved. Today there are a few people who believe that the refinery never existed, charging that Truman was behind the selling of shares in the company knowing full well that it would never be built.

Fulton Lewis, Jr., in his "Washington Report" of July 9, 1951, was extremely critical of Truman's involvement in Rollin's refining company:

> The Morgan Oil and Refining Company owned by President Harry S. Truman, D. H. Morgan, and W. H. Lynn of Kansas in 1916 cadged a lot of easy money by floating 60,000 shares of worthless oil stock.
> In large newspaper advertisements they welcomed a flock of suckers by extolling the virtues of the company, mentioned its rich holdings and its oil refinery in Rollin, Kansas. . . .
> I never thought I'd get lost in Kansas looking for an oil refinery. Nor that

I'd get lost looking for Rollin, Kansas. Both have vanished. In fact, as far as I can find out, the refinery never existed and Rollin at best was a store, an outhouse and a wide spot in the road. I've practically had to disinter old-timers to find someone who remembers Rollin. Only Mr. Truman's buddy, Morgan, remembers the refinery. And he's hazy about details. In fact, he's wrong. If there was anything at Rollin it was an oil skimming plant not a refinery.

Mr. C. D. Black of the National Supply Company at Chanute remembers Rollin. His best recollection is that the so-called Truman-Morgan refinery went out of existence in 1911 or 12. That was 4 years before Truman and Morgan were touting it as a choice bit of property they were willing to share with a few thousand investors. . . .

Nothing is left of the Rollin plant, not even rusty iron scrap. Thirty-five years isn't such a long time for a big plant to be in operation. Apparently none of the Kansas citizens who purchased shares in the Truman-Morgan oil company ever journeyed to Rollin. They might have started hollering for their money sooner; some of them are wondering right now if they might not be able to collect.[4]

Lewis mentioned neither the town's religious foundation nor its founder Delos Johnson, nor did he write an accurate description of Rollin's appearance. He stereotyped all towns in one geographical location as "oil boom towns." Fortunately, no other newspaper treated Rollin so harshly. Anything else Lewis stated against Truman should be viewed with a suspicious eye. Chances are, as later interviews have noted, Rollin did have an oil refinery, albeit short-lived.

Rollin struggled for its life until Johnson's death in 1921. Still standing today is the former Johnson home, built before 1890. There are no stores, no school, no church, no sign to announce where you are—just a few houses along a country road. Rollin's controversial past seems relatively unimportant, as the peaceful site lies amid scattered gravestones and abundant prairie grass.

CATO
Crawford County

Crawford County's earliest settlement was the small town of Cato established in 1858 by E. J. Boring, who named the town after Judge Sterling G. Cato of the Kansas Territorial Supreme Court. The Cato post office was the first in the county. When the mail arrived, the postmaster dumped it on a table, and customers picked out their own letters. At this time, the entire town consisted of the post office, one general store, and a few log cabins.

On October 27, 1860, the Cherokee Indian agent, with the aid of the U.S. Army, began driving the settlers out of the Cherokee Neutral Lands. The Indians had complained to President James Buchanan that the white settlers were taking their lands from them, although their complaint was actually a ploy to get the government to purchase their land. The government officials, however, were not interested, and so the president had no choice but to order the settlers removed from the area. The Army burned nearly a hundred of their homes in an effort to drive them out. At Cato, the evicted townspeople discussed the problem with the government agents, who agreed to give them a month's grace. After the troops left the area, the settlers repossessed their land.

When the Civil War erupted, most of the men in Cato enlisted in the Union Army, including John, Francis, and Bill Coonrod; John Coonrod, Sr.; John Rogers; and Peter Smith. These men were involved in the Battle of Drywood Creek near the town of Nevada, Missouri. After the battle, Bill and Francis Coonrod and a few others defected to the Confederate Army. Some of the Union Army's horses and mules disappeared at the same time, and the Army suspected that these men were responsible. Back at home in Cato, the Coonrod family, who had sons on both sides during the war, received threats of violence from both the proslavery and free-state forces, which prompted the eldest male Coonrod to leave for Denver until the end of the hostilities.

Cato witnessed several violent incidents during the war. On one occasion in 1863, Captain John Rogers, after being called to the door of his cabin, was shot and killed by Confederates. On October 22, 1864, a guerrilla band led by Allen Mathews, another Confederate, killed a settler named Simons. The Civil War did not, however, hinder the settlement of Cato. John Hale, Sr., Jacob Workman, and H. B. Brown homesteaded near the village in 1862. Chad, Ezekiel, and I. K. Brown arrived in 1865 along with George and Peter Fowler, William and Sam Endicott, and Dr. C. H. Strong, who came from Illinois hoping to improve his health. The move to a different climate must have worked, for he later noted that "the gentle zephyrs and dry and healthy atmosphere of Kansas, the change of water and diet, venison, and prairie chicken, were a great help, and in a few months time I began to gain strength and an appetite, and have not had a week's sickness since."

In 1866 Peter Smith built a new brick building at Cato. The structure served as store, post office, and home of the Smiths and is still standing today. William Shamblin constructed a blacksmith shop, rivaling another es-

A painting depicting Isreal Brown's log cabin in Cato in the late 1850s.

The Peter Smith store and residence at Cato. This building is now listed on the National Register of Historic Places.

tablished earlier by Hilman Coonrod. In 1867 a steam grist mill built by E. B. Robbins was a huge success. When it opened, nearly a hundred farmers in wagons were waiting in line to have their grain ground. In fact, some of them waited as long as three days for their turn.

In 1867 when Cherokee County was divided into Cherokee and Crawford counties, the biggest problem for the early settlers was to obtain and keep title to their land. "Claim jumping" in southeast Kansas was sometimes a frequent activity. At least one attempt at claim jumping occurred near Cato in 1866. A man moved onto the property of Riley Dalton, proclaiming it his own. Since there was no land organization at the time, the settlers formed a committee to settle the dispute, and they decided the land rightfully belonged to Dalton. They ordered the other man to vacate.

In 1867 the Cherokee Neutral Lands were sold by the Secretary of the Interior, James Harlan, to the American Emigrant Company. After Harlan resigned, his successor, O. H. Brown, declared that the sale was fraudulent, and he sold the land to James F. Joy. This action worried the settlers, for they had hoped to purchase their land from the government. The situation was further complicated when Joy entered into a purchase agreement with the Missouri River, Fort Scott, & Gulf Railroad. On November 17, 1868, the railroad officials told the settlers that if they could prove they had settled on the land before June 10, 1868, they would be allowed to purchase 160 acres for two to five dollars per acre. The government established a land office at Fort Scott in order to record these sales and register the deeds.

This proposition infuriated the settlers, and they formed an organization known as the Land League. According to this group, the sale of the land by the Secretary of the Interior to James Joy was not valid, and they vowed to resist. The members mobbed the land office at Fort Scott in protest, burned the *Girard Press* because it had taken an anti-Land League stance, and harassed the railroad building crews. The governor called in the U.S. troops to try to ease the situation. The Leaguers warned that anyone who accepted a patent (deed) from the government for lands purchased by Joy would be killed. When I. K. Brown went to the Cato post office to pick up a letter containing a patent for his land, however, some Land Leaguers were present and asked to see his patent, which they examined and returned to him without causing any trouble.

When the Missouri River, Fort Scott, & Gulf Railroad attempted to lay tracks through Cato in 1869, the Land Leaguers pulled up the stakes and caused so much trouble that the railroad was constructed through Farlington instead. The League managed to insure that Cato would have no railroad, and the settlers would either have to buy land from Joy or move on. The ultimate effect of the Land League on the town was negative.

In 1891 the Missouri Pacific built a rail line several miles east of Cato, which meant the town's growth would be limited. People began moving away, and on July 31, 1905, the post office closed. After World War I the community ceased to exist. At its peak Cato had about 300 citizens; in 1910 the population had dropped to 112, and by the 1920s it was below 50. The chances of Cato developing from a pioneer community into a permanent town faded away completely when the railroad was rerouted through Farlington.[1]

FARLINGTON
Crawford County

Farlington's beginning dates back to 1870 when the Kansas City, Fort Scott & Gulf Railroad laid track south from Fort Scott. Here the railroad built a small wooden platform and a water tank for the locomotives. For many years local railroaders referred to the site affectionately as "Tank." In addition to the platform, the crew constructed a section house and a store to provide food for the men working on the right-of-way. A local entrepreneur by the name of Farley operated the store and before long the place became known as "Farleyville." When the government opened a post office, it changed the name to Farlington because another town already existed with almost the same name.

A colony of Swedes settled nearby, and they discovered a large quantity of coal on their claims between 1870 and 1874. Overnight Farlington became a mining town. The coal provided cheap, accessible fuel for the railroad company, who shipped out thousands of tons during those years. Most of the Swedish colonists were skilled craftsmen with stone, and those who did not work in the mining industry found gainful employment constructing stone buildings in the Pittsburg/Fort Scott area.

The settlers constructed several buildings on Main Street: a town hall, a lumberyard, and several hardware and general merchandise stores. Most of these early buildings were made of stone as a protection against prairie fires, common in the summer and autumn months. The region around Farlington was especially vulnerable to fire because of the thick grass, sometimes higher than a man's head, that grew wild there. On at least two occasions, prairie fires nearly destroyed Farlington and threatened lives as well as property.

As in many early country communities, railroad service was disrupted

Main street of Farlington around the turn of the century.

during the depression years of the 1930s, and local residents began shopping in other larger communities. Farlington narrowly missed a major highway, but the town was far enough away that the businesses did not benefit. To-day Farlington is nearly gone except for a couple of old stone buildings.[1]

CROWEBURG
Crawford County

In the colorful Cherokee-Crawford County coal-mining region, dozens of small mining camps were established to house and service the thousands of miners who worked in the shafts in the late nineteenth and early twentieth centuries. Most of these "camps" were short-lived, however, as their existence was based upon the mining shafts and the companies that operated the mines. The "company" houses built for the workers were often temporary "shotgun houses." These structures had a front door, three or four rooms linked one after the other all the way to the back room, and a back door. In theory, the miners called them "shotgun houses" because a man with a shotgun could stand at the front door and fire, and the shells would go straight out the back door.

Croweburg is a fairly typical example of the mining towns that existed in this region, but in some ways it outshines the others. It was larger than most of the other towns, having a population of nearly 1,500 at its peak.

Shotgun houses dominate the background of this street scene in Croweburg, ca. 1915.

This mining boomtown also existed several decades longer than other communities in the area.

Croweburg was established in 1907 during a period of feverish coal-mining activity in northeast Crawford County. The residents named the town for the company that owned the land and built most of the town, the Crowe Coal Company. As in most mining camps, the company established Croweburg along a section road that preceded the town or, in this case, where two section roads came together. The town was unique in that it quickly became a motley collection of coal camps joined together, which added immensely to the total population. The Crowe Coal Company platted the town on July 31 and quickly began building houses and constructing a long main street that was soon filled with stores. Most of Croweburg's streets were oriented to the basic directions of the compass and ran parallel to the section roads. At its peak the town sported several grocery stores, a restaurant, laundry, two blacksmith shops, two hotels, a lumberyard, a drugstore, and a collection of other short-lived businesses. The largest building in Croweburg was the Trianon, a two-story false-fronted building used as a community center. For years popular regional bands came from all over the midwest and played for dances held in the building. This structure caught fire and burned to the ground in the 1930s.

In the 1920s and 1930s, Croweburg was a typical coal company town—and not without its problems. As the market for coal dropped and the mines began to decrease in productivity, the company hired black laborers to work the mines because they could pay them markedly less money. The

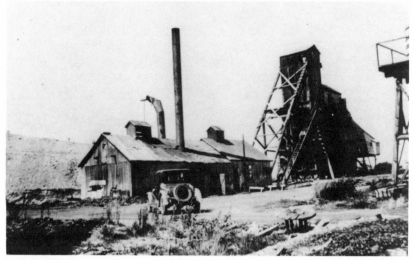

Photographs of early mining communities are rare, but we have several good images of Croweburg. Pictured here is a typical mine shaft near Main Street, ca. 1930.

white workers became resentful, and the result was a clash between the two working groups. Many blacks were forced to leave town, and the other miners lived in fear that violence would escalate into bloodshed. The fears were never realized; only minor disturbances were recorded during this time.

The depression of the 1930s had a devastating impact on the entire coal mining district, not just Croweburg. Dozens of camps closed down, their buildings sold or moved to other parts of the region. Although Croweburg's depopulation began during this period, the town was fortunate enough to survive long after its neighbors had become empty fields.

Today Croweburg still has a few shotgun houses, ruins of other structures, and traces of streets and foundations where buildings once stood. Most of the mines are completely gone now due to the strip mining that became popular after the shafts closed. Any visitors interested in exploring the coal-mining region around Pittsburg will find Croweburg an inviting detour.[1]

MONMOUTH
Crawford County

In 1866 the citizens of Monmouth witnessed the first murder and hanging in Crawford County, for their town hosted the trial of the locally notorious Tippie brothers. The two men were sent to the gallows.

In February 1866 Joe and Sam Tippie made a business deal with Ralph Warner concerning the purchase of some cattle. After they reached a monetary agreement, the two brothers promised Warner they would come back in the spring with their other two brothers to get the cattle. Their scheme was to return as planned and pay for the cattle, and then the other brothers were to hold up the seller at gunpoint and demand their money back. A friend of Warner's heard of the plot and told Warner, who immediately summoned his neighbors to help him catch the robbers upon their return.

When the Tippies came back late in April, Warner was ready. Although he had taken all the proper precautions and hoped to capture the Tippies without a fight, word of the ambush reached the brothers just before they arrived to pay for the cattle. When the men completed their business and were ready to leave, two of the brothers drew guns and fired, killing one of Warner's men. The Tippies then rode away, but a posse caught up with them in a nearby cabin and took them back to Monmouth for trial. A jury of twelve men under Judge Jacob Miller found the two men guilty, and although they denied any wrongdoing, the verdict was hanging until dead.

After a minister offered a prayer for the souls of the doomed men, Joe Tippie confessed, and Sam cursed his brother for weakening. The hanging was supposed to take place the next day, but an angry mob took the Tippie brothers from the jail to the cemetery and hanged them from the limb of an oak tree. The next morning, the sheriff took the bodies down and buried them under the same tree. For years stories circulated in Monmouth that the tree died soon after the hanging and that the ghosts of the men could sometimes be seen on a windy night swinging from the old tree.[1]

Although the Tippie brothers' hanging occurred in 1866, the community of Monmouth was actually settled as early as 1857 by squatters trespassing on Indian grounds. The U.S. troops from Fort Scott had to be called out to remove these people from the region. Not until 1865 did the government open the area for settlement.[2]

Southeastern Kansas was not an ideal place to live before the Civil War, as the settlers in Monmouth soon discovered. In August 1861 a band of 200 Missouri ruffians rode into the area and fired on the defenseless citizens, capturing and killing some of the men. Another raid occurred two weeks later. No one really knew how many people the ruffians killed in that attack, but several eyewitnesses claimed there were at least a dozen.

Lafayette Manlove, a county commissioner, laid out Monmouth in 1866 and named it after his home town in Illinois. In 1869 A. N. Chadsey of

Among the streets in this 1887 plat of Monmouth is a short street called "Hooker Street." Was this named after an individual or the most popular profession there?

Cherokee established a general store. The first Sunday school in Crawford County was organized at Monmouth by the Reverend Isaac Thorp. At that time, the townspeople at Monmouth were filled with religious fervor, and every Sunday they held three different church services: Methodist, Presbyterian, and Christian. The citizens built a schoolhouse in the summer of 1870, but within a few years it burned down, and they constructed a second one in 1880. The post office opened in 1879, and a carrier brought the mail from Fort Scott on horseback until the railroad built a narrow gauge track from Cherokee to Parsons through Monmouth. A society of the Ancient Order of United Workmen was organized in 1882, and a post of the Grand Army of the Republic was formed in 1883.[3] By the mid 1880s there were 400 people in town and five large businesses.[4]

In the early days Monmouth had a large grist mill, but now all that remains are fragments of the foundation and the old pond where the water collected for the steam engine. No exact date exists for the mill's construction, but it was probably around 1867, and it was either torn down or burned down in the late 1890s. The mill was a three-story building, operated by steam, and it had a large number of feed burrs. Other big businesses in the 1890s had forced the mill out of operation.[5]

By 1910 the town was going slowly downhill. The population had dwindled to 179, and the only businesses were an elevator, a store, a few churches, a school, a telegraph office, a post office, and a few residences.[6] The population declined further through the years, and the post office closed on September 30, 1955. Today Monmouth is a semi–ghost town located in the coal section of Crawford County, barely existing, bereft of all industry, including coal.

TREECE
Cherokee County

In the famous "Tri-State District" of Missouri, Kansas, and Oklahoma, many towns went from boom to bust mining for lead and zinc. Some had colorful names such as Badger, Bloomington, Bonanza, Peacock, Empire City, Crestline, Teapot, and Treece, the newest of these towns.[1] The earliest mention of Treece in the local newspapers was in 1917, when the government established a post office there. Today huge chat piles surround Treece, some as high as 500 feet. In those early years children attended school in the shadows of these white mounds and played on their dusty slopes after school hours.[2]

An incident occurred in 1935 that has affected the attitude of the people in the area to this day. The lead company employees, seeking recognition of their Mine, Mill, and Smelter Workers International Union, were locked out by nonunion employees who had created their own local union.[3] During a Mine, Mill and Smelter Workers strike, the union members ceased work in the lead and zinc fields. They were replaced by these nonunion workers who had organized the Tri-State Metal, Mine and Smelter Workers Union, also known as the Blue Card Union. The resentment between the striking workers and the Blue Card unionists smoldered for two years, then burst into flame when the Committee for Industrial Organization (CIO) undertook to eliminate the Tri-State Metal, Mine, and Smelter Workers Union. On April 10, 1937, several men distributing leaflets for the CIO at a smelter in Joplin, Missouri, were seized and severely beaten by Blue Card unionists. On the following day, about 5,000 members of the Blue Card Union met at Picher, Oklahoma. After arming themselves with clubs, they dispersed a meeting of CIO organizers and wrecked the hall of the Mine, Mill, and Smelter Workers.

The following week about 500 Blue Card unionists traveled to Treece and demolished another hall of the CIO union.[4] During the peak period of dissension, Governor Alfred Landon sent troops to protect the men who had replaced the striking workers. To help prevent violence, strings of electric lights illuminated the chat piles around Treece for several weeks.[5] Until recently the hostility between union and non-union workers actually divided the town into two geographical areas—the union men lived on one side of Main Street and the non-union men in a section on the other side known as "Scabtown."

Air pollution as well as labor violence threatened the miners in Treece. The high rate of silicosis seeded the region with tuberculosis, and the infec-

Treece was a major lead and zinc mining center (shown here in the 1960s) before declining prices and unionization affected the industry.

tion appeared not only among miners but also among their families and other non-mining residents as well. In 1936 a tuberculin testing program found an alarming 36 percent positive reaction among all age groups, and those over twenty years of age had a reaction of 54 percent.[6] Another government survey taken in 1929 showed that silicosis afflicted 21 percent of the workers in this region, and 43 percent of the men who worked where the dust hazard was highest ultimately contracted the disease. The symptoms of silicosis are similar to those of tuberculosis, and death is caused by the formation of scar tissue on the lungs. According to a 1930s survey by the State Board of Health, about one-third of the children living in the mining region had tuberculosis induced by silica dust in the air.[7]

By 1930 Treece had a population of 749, most of whom were miners. Within ten years, however, a gradual decline in lead and zinc output brought progress to a halt in the community. Increased production during World War II and shortly thereafter kept the town alive, but during the 1950s production again slackened noticeably.

A visit in 1950 to the Eagle Picher West Side Mine near Treece would have revealed the ideal in modern mining procedure. The ore was mined at the

428-foot level. A huge mined-out gallery near the shaft with a 125-foot ceiling contained a tool shed and blacksmith shop, which made the mine a
self-contained unit underground. Nearby, but at a safe distance, was the
powder magazine. The miners stored the fuel for the vehicles in tanks near
the tool shed. Arrell Gibson, author of the *Wilderness Bonanza: The Tri-
State District of Missouri, Kansas, and Oklahoma*, describes the days when the
mines were operating:

> The preceding night, a huge bench had been blasted out of a slope in the
> west drift, and workmen were busy slusher-loading ore into diesel-powered
> ten-ton trailer trucks. Oxygen tanks were fitted to the motor manifolds,
> thereby minimizing the carbon monoxide fumes. These vehicles coursed
> along two-lane graveled roads leading to the skip pocket. A railroad, also op-
> erated by Eagle-Picher, carried the ore to the central mill at Commerce, Okla-
> homa, ten miles distant. A locomotive from the ore train was rented from
> the Frisco Railroad.[8]

Mining and milling of lead and zinc ores slowly declined until the 1960s,
when operations closed down. The lack of other industrial jobs to absorb
the unemployed miners caused a migration of many residents to other parts
of the country. This mass exodus nearly depopulated Picher, Oklahoma,
and Galena, Kansas; and Treece, nestled between both of them, became a
ghost town.[9]

LE HUNT
Montgomery County

The southeastern Kansas region was at its industrial peak when, at the turn
of the century, production of the lesser minerals such as natural gas, coal,
lead, and zinc elevated the area to national prominence. Another low-value
"mineral" that contributed to this boom was cement. Kansas, in fact,
ranked fourth among Portland cement-producing states before World War
I, exceeded only by Pennsylvania, Indiana, and California.

Around 1900 the largest and most productive cement mill was in the
planning stage five miles northwest of Independence near Table Mound.
This site offered some distinct advantages, including several gas wells nearby
and a rock quarry atop Table Mound where the gravel could be easily transported downhill by mules and wagons. Once the promoters had settled all
the preliminaries, they selected the Hunt Engineering Company to construct the plant. Its president, Leigh Hunt, had built other highly success-

Three generations of the Ringle family in front of the family residence in Le Hunt.

ful mills in both Michigan and Kansas. Construction began on October 20, 1905, and was completed ten months later. The plant became known as the Independence Portland Cement Company. Mr. Hunt, for whom the company town of Le Hunt was named, hired between 200 and 400 men, importing many workers from elsewhere. A local newspaper noted that "hundreds of tents and shanties" could be seen on any given day, giving rest and shelter "for the Grecians, the Italians, and the Negroes" employed at the plant.

Le Hunt's most notable resident was cowboy film star Tom Mix, who had served with Leigh Hunt in the Spanish-American War. When Hunt contracted to build the plant, Mix followed him to Independence as foreman in charge of labor. The local citizens remembered one particular incident involving Tom Mix. On most paydays a group of men described as gamblers and bootleggers descended upon the construction site with "money-grabbing" on their minds. Mix, who had recently been appointed deputy sheriff, single-handedly rounded up the troublemakers and booted them out of town, thus preserving law and order in Le Hunt.

In the early 1900s Le Hunt boomed along with the factory. The *Independence Daily Reporter* announced that "in addition to the plant itself, the company has built a town of 1,500 inhabitants with fine cottages, stores, hotels, schools—in fact, everything which goes to make a first class little city." Another article in the *Kansas City Star*, however, noted that the population never exceeded 150. In fact the actual population, although erratic, was somewhere in the middle.

The cement industry in Kansas between 1906 and 1909 shifted from expansion to consolidation. Wild speculation ended in 1908 when the industry experienced economic reversals due to overproduction. The solution seemed simple enough—control prices and demand through consolidation. In January 1908 the Le Hunt plant united with companies at Iola and Neodesha and was renamed the United Kansas Portland Cement Company. This combined arrangement had a total capitalization of $12.75 million.

The five years before World War I were unstable for the two Independence mills, whose only hope seemed to be further consolidation. One newspaper editor noted, "The plants have multiplied until they produce more cement than the market demands and those companies 'hard up for cash,' sell at cost and in some cases less than cost and that cripples the stronger companies." Railroads also contributed to the decline of the industry when they raised their freight rates during the prewar period. In June 1913 L. T. Sunderland, representing the Ash Grove Lime & Portland Cement Company, applied to the state for a review of the rates charged by four railroads. The state review revealed that unfair rates in Kansas were exacerbating the near disastrous conditions of the cement industry, already weakened by the depletion of once seemingly unlimited natural gas reserves.

This situation led to the closing of several cement plants, including the one at Le Hunt. On January 15, 1914, the Portland Cement Company filed an involuntary petition of bankruptcy. A local newspaper noted that "for four years the United Kansas Portland has been wobbly and most of the stockholders saw they had been plucked to benefit someone." Management had failed to overcome major economic problems, and indeed many of these controllers intended to sell securities only, not cement. The editor of the *South Kansas Tribune* noted that the stockholders were being misled by a "bunch of stock gamblers." The money lost in cement securities and investments in Kansas from 1912 to 1920 has been estimated at $8 million.

In May 1915 the Sunflower Portland Cement Company purchased the Le Hunt plant. After the sale, the *South Kansas Tribune* noted, "The water having all been squeezed out, and more too, the new people have it at a price that should make it a gold mine." George Nicholson, director of the new firm, planned to ready the plant for production within four months.

A limestone quarry at Le Hunt. The stone here was used in the production of cement.

The *Independence Daily Reporter* of September 11, 1915, remarked, "The past thirty days the houses at Le Hunt have been filling up and it is said that before the end of the month every house in the burg will be occupied." After hiring 300 men, the factory officially began production on September 12. During the first few weeks the average output was 1,500 barrels of cement a day.

In the early months of 1915, cement prices had fallen to a new low, forcing more companies into bankruptcy. Fortunately, the Le Hunt mill had reopened shortly after this period, when cement manufacturing was experiencing an upsurge in production. Cement prices increased steadily throughout 1916, and during the first seven months of 1917, they reached an all-time high of $1.35 a barrel. The American entry into World War I, however, forced prices down due to the shortage of fuel, labor, and vehicles, and by 1918 production had dropped 20 percent. The Sunflower Portland Cement Company at Le Hunt eventually fell victim to the war effort and was unable to compete with the larger companies. The mill was purchased in 1918 by the Western States Portland Cement Company, which was renamed the Atlas Cement Company and more recently the United States Steel Corporation.

Although the machinery at Le Hunt was sold, the site was still a good source of limestone for cement companies in Independence. The badly deteriorated shell of the cement factory, scattered foundations, an empty schoolhouse, and a huge smokestack are the only remains of Le Hunt today. Upon closer inspection one can still find old sidewalks, a tunnel that leads to nowhere, steps to homes that have vanished, a lone bank vault, and pickaxes, shovels, and parts of wheelbarrows embedded in the factory walls.

Le Hunt was a company town whose history parallels that of southeast Kansas during the first two decades of the twentieth century; it held a bright promise of industrial potential that was never fully realized.[1]

VOTAW
Montgomery County

An experimental colony known as Votaw, located two miles north of Cof- feyville, was a short-lived settlement started by blacks in southern Kansas. Although the town only lasted a short time, 12 percent of the current pop- ulation of Coffeyville are descendants of this colony.

Votaw was founded on June 1, 1881, on 160 acres of land deeded from E. P. Allen to Daniel Votaw, a Quaker humanitarian who conceived his pur- chase as a refuge in Kansas for southern blacks. With prompting from freed- man Paul Davis, a group of blacks from Shelby County, Texas, moved north to Votaw's new land. There's no doubt that Votaw established his colony for charitable reasons, but Davis's motives were not so noble. He stipulated that all the settlers in the colony vote for James A. Garfield for president. The list of black emigrants slated to come to Votaw that first year included Davis, Ancrum Goodwin, Martha Coleman, Abra Gudden, Wil- liam Gilbert, and fourteen others.

The colonists came to the settlement in ox-drawn covered wagons and a few horse-drawn vehicles. Some walked the entire route. Votaw gave each family eight acres of land. Paul Davis, the leader of the colony, was allotted sixteen acres.[1] Soon after their arrival, the settlers organized the colony and started a farming operation. Daniel McTaggert, owner of a nearby mill, in- stalled a cotton gin. Several cotton crops were produced during Votaw's existence, but the limited acreage did not allow for experimentation in the extensive growing of cotton on the prairie. The settlers eventually aban- doned the endeavor, but not before they had amply shown that cotton could be grown profitably in Kansas.

The winter of 1882 was hard on the new colonists who were not prepared for the cold weather. Since they had little time to construct adequate shel- ters, many suffered from frostbite. The following spring, however, brought babies and renewed hope. The colonists constructed many homes, but the largest belonged to Davis. It contained four downstairs rooms and an attic where the children slept. He used wood so hard that when the house was moved to Coffeyville in 1900, it was nearly impossible to drive nails into the frame. Other houses in the colony resembled the Davis home minus the attic.

Daily life meant work in the fields of corn, wheat, sorghum, and cotton. The settlers raised hogs for the meat portion of their diet. The Davis family also allotted a share of their land for an orchard. During the late summer, the fruit was cut into thin slices as it ripened and placed on a square of cloth suspended above the porch to dry. Davis hunted during the evening hours for fresh meat such as rabbit, opossum, and raccoon, which he slow-cooked all night. By adding biscuits to the meat, he created a nutritious meal that could be taken to the fields the next morning.

In the fall of 1883 both black and white children attended the same school, more than a mile's walk from the colony. In Votaw a community building housed the Mt. Canaan Baptist church, the center of social activity. There were quilting parties and square dances—a fiddler from town provided the music for the adults, and home freezers furnished ice cream for the children. The colonists celebrated their freedom from slavery at a big harvest event held in August. The "Jubilee Singers" led the festivities.

The colony existed until about the time of Davis's death in 1900. After her husband's passing, Mrs. Davis was the first to leave Votaw. She had their home divided into four sections, loaded on hayracks, and moved to Coffeyville. Shortly thereafter a devastating flood on the Verdigris River and Big Hill Creek caused the evacuation of the rest of the colonists from the Votaw site. Most of them moved to Coffeyville and Independence. The last vestige of Votaw disappeared in 1915 when a small shack burned down, claiming the life of the town's last occupant, Martha Coleman. She had held fast to her freedom colony, refusing to follow the others into new exile. She became the town martyr after all she owned turned to ashes.[2]

HEWINS
Chautauqua County

Early settlers in the Big Caney River Valley considered their homesteads to be prime property, and many incidents of violence occurred when an influx of squatters and claim jumpers forced the settlers to defend their boundary lines. Fights between these two factions became so prevalent that the present location of Hewins was once known as "Hell's Bend." The conflicts with the claim jumpers, who were ignored by the local law officers, caused numerous injuries and several deaths. Fortunately, the establishment of the nearby village of Hart's Mill in 1870 and the early settlement of Elgin brought some justice to the region and an end to most of these problems.

Hewins became a community gathering place in the early 1870s. Some of the first settlers included the Holroyds, Kygars, Lemmerts, Ellises, and Boyers. The Hewins Ranch, one of the largest operations in the area, gave the community its name. Hewins was served by two cemeteries: the Brown cemetery to the northwest of Hewins and the Miller cemetery located east of town. Viola Miller, a daughter of C. W. Miller, was the first person buried there after a horse she was riding dragged her to death.

Hewins remained a small town until the 1880s, when the Santa Fe Railroad began laying track through the area. The railroad financed the Hewins Townsite Company and purchased a tract of land from Peter Durland for the construction of a cattle-shipping operation. The town of Hewins was laid out and lots were sold to the public in 1886 when the railroad reached the town. After the small village of Hart's Mill missed the Santa Fe by two miles and a disastrous flood on the Big Caney ravaged the town, the settlers had no choice but to leave. Most of the stores and the post office moved to Hewins.

From its advantageous position, Hewins rapidly became a trade center that extended into the Osage Reservation in Indian Territory (now Oklahoma). By the turn of the century, the town had become the second largest cattle-shipping point in the world (behind Elgin), and often the railroad shipped as many as 36,000 head of cattle from the Hewins stock yards in one week. This would be equivalent to thirty trains, averaging fifty cars each.

During the 1890s Hewins experienced its largest boom. A large hotel constructed by Joseph C. Ellis was well known around the state and considered one of the best places to eat in Kansas. Included among the names on the hotel guest register were Alfred M. Landon and his father, John M. Landon. Many stores and saloons were built one after another, but unfortunately disorder and violence accompanied this prosperity.

Gunfights were quite frequent in Hewins; I will limit myself to a description of two of the more dramatic ones. One concerned Ben Graven, a local outlaw who robbed the Hopper and Tweedle General Store on three separate occasions. Miraculously, Graven managed to escape serious injury all three times, but he was killed a few years later during a robbery in Oklahoma. In another gunfight, three local businessmen defended the town. Jim Pope, R. W. Akin, and Walter Bennett recognized and accosted two bandits known as Chadburn and Matigan in front of the post office. In response to their command to surrender, one of the bandits fired his revolver and shot Pope in the foot. This brought gunfire from Akin and Bennett that ended abruptly with the death of both outlaws. On that particular day, justice prevailed.

The outlaws were well known in the area and wanted for shooting a man in Winfield and stealing horses at Cedar Vale. Before the Hewins incident, they tried to cut the telephone lines leading into Hewins, but in their haste they mistakenly cut a rural line instead. This blunder enabled the authorities at Cedar Vale to notify the Hewins townspeople well ahead of the duo's fatal visit.

The cattle boom began to decline around 1910, and Hewins's importance as a cattle-shipping town diminished significantly after Oklahoma became a state and major railroad points emerged south of the Kansas border. Hewins was not on a main branch of the Santa Fe, and in 1938 the railroad removed the existing track and closed the depot. In the 1930s the lack of a major highway through town crippled the economy further, and many residents drove to Sedan, the county seat, for their groceries and other necessities.[1]

Like many towns in southeast Kansas during the 1920s, Hewins was a major Ku Klux Klan center. Burning crosses were a common sight in the area for many years, and only the depression of the 1930s and the lack of extra cash for membership fees stifled local Klan activities. Klan membership cards and other memorabilia dating from the 1920s still lie among the ruins of some of the roofless old buildings. Today a few other markers of the old town remain: some old buildings, a few occupied homes, and a post office in a small store on Main Street that contains a number of old-fashioned mailboxes.

Hewins is located on a county road northwest of Elgin, although a more scenic route to the townsite might be along the Wilderness Trail, a beautiful stretch of road that is a paradise for nature lovers and bird watchers. A word of warning—these county roads have "low-water bridges" across some of the small streams. Drive these crossings with care after a hard rain.

BOSTON
Chautauqua County

In August 1871 a party of seven young bachelors from the Osage Indian Mission established the town of Boston in Howard County, four miles southwest of present Moline. These men were Dr. Robert Brogan, John Brogan,

Pat Nulty, Dodd Cartwright, Thomas Cunningham, J. L. Mattingly, and J. A. Oliphant.

A major problem for the first settlers was finding a reliable source of water. A spring just west of town supplied enough water for about a dozen families, but the rest of the population had to collect their water in rain barrels. The public well in the center of town was often dry and had to be filled by volunteers who, under the cover of darkness, hauled water from a nearby stream and poured it into the well. This was a well-kept secret, for the citizens knew that if word of a water shortage leaked out, it could curtail their chances of becoming the county seat.

Thomas Thompson, editor of the *Howard Courant* from 1881 until his death in 1935, lived in Boston before moving to the town of Howard. His first impressions of the town were as follows:

The first time I ever saw Boston was about a year after its first building was erected, perhaps in Sept. 1872. There was not a tree on the townsite but the half-dozen or so store buildings were . . . mostly two-story in height and looked clean and neat in construction. . . . One county seat election had already been held with no permanent results. By this time, August 1873—a newspaper had moved in, the Howard County Messenger, which had been published a year at Howard City and had been taken over by A. B. Hicks and moved to Boston. . . . Hicks was poor, not very honest and had little ability as a writer.

At the peak of Boston's prosperity, the town had a population of nearly 200 and about fifty homes and businesses. Many bachelors were still in the area, along with a few small families. During the early 1870s, the business section was composed of two stores, a hotel, and a post office established on August 28, 1871, and discontinued eight years later on September 1, 1879.

At a county seat election held early in 1872, the town of Peru won, but Boston did not participate. The first election in which Boston took part was held on September 10, 1872, but the voting was discovered to be so fraudulent that the election board refused to canvass the results or pay their officials. The voters circulated petitions for another election, which was held on August 12, 1873. This time Boston triumphed over Elk Falls. The election officials at the Boston precinct failed to certify their books properly, and the votes had to be thrown out; however, there was no charge of dishonesty in the vote tabulations. When another election was held between Peru and Elk Falls, the latter won. After Boston appealed to the courts, the judge rendered a decision stating that the August 12 election should be counted, and the recent vote electing Elk Falls should be declared null and void. The county commissioners ordered a final election to be held November 17, 1873, between Elk Falls and Boston. The campaigning by both towns was highly competitive, but Boston won by a majority of 235 votes. When the commission announced the results, the entire population of nearby Longton and Howard City flocked to Boston to celebrate with a big supper and dance. However, Elk Falls was dissatisfied with the results of the election and appealed to the courts again; they succeeded in securing an injunction against moving the county records to Boston. Unfortunately, the night the votes were counted, Frank Clark, the county clerk, had already moved his office but not the records.

It soon became apparent to all concerned that Elk Falls was not going to give up the county seat without a fight. After the newspapers revealed that Judge W. P. Campbell owned lots in Elk Falls, Boston promoters tried to present him with town lots in Boston so as to insure an ''impartial'' decision, but Judge Campbell would not accept a ''bribe.'' The townspeople, now desperate, planned a march on Elk Falls to take the county records by force, if necessary. What had been mere talk of a raid escalated into a war party, and nearly 150 armed men in twenty-four wagons headed for Elk Falls, arriving there about 10 o'clock in the morning. The attack took the Elk Falls citizens by surprise, and they offered little resistance. In less than thirty minutes, the ''raiders'' loaded all the county records and furniture on the wagons and returned to Boston. They placed the county property under guard and had the road from Elk Falls watched by riders who were to ring the school bell should the rival town make a suspicious move.

The first night and the following day armed men filled the town, but no one sounded the alarm. The second day a sentinel rode in and reported that the sheriff and a large posse of armed men were approaching. When they heard the school bell, 200 men in Boston began building defenses with lumber and boxes. Sheriff Eli Titus led the posse to the outskirts of town, where he was told he could come in and serve his papers but must leave the posse outside the city limits. Sheriff Titus and his deputy Joe Vannoy rode into town, ordered the arrest of the men who stole the county records, and asked for the immediate return of all the property. All he received for his demands was a sharp warning to stay at least 300 yards away from the buildings where they kept the records.

After three weeks the town began to resemble a guerrilla camp. The four buildings housing the records and furniture were under constant guard, and the town was patrolled twenty-four hours a day. Since the guards allowed no one to come or go without being searched, the citizens began to relax. One evening a warning did sound during a dance. While the men, who all wore guns, were waltzing, someone ran in, shouting "Elk Falls is coming!" It turned out to be a false alarm. Before long, however, the Boston townspeople realized that the law would eventually prevail. Once again, they loaded the county records into the wagons and took them to the Cowley County seat, where they hid them pending a satisfactory negotiation of terms.

In late February 1874 the sheriff swore out a warrant against every man in Boston. The men had been warned of this move, and some of them agreed to hide out while others gave themselves up. There were no jails in Elk Falls, and many Elk Falls men had to be sworn in to guard the prisoners. Sheriff Titus asked Governor Thomas Osborne and his adjutant general to review the situation. When the governor arrived in Elk Falls, the sheriff warned him against going to Boston without an armed escort. Heeding this advice, Osborne ordered the enlistment of several hundred men to serve as a militia, and they made preparations to move against Boston. Fortunately, they encountered little resistance and soon reached an agreement—Elk Falls was to cooperate with Boston, and the courts were to decide the legality of the elections. In the meantime, the Boston men were to return the records in exchange for their freedom.

While the supreme court was deciding the case, the regular county business was in utter chaos. By December only half the taxes had been collected, and the county treasurer then embezzled the other half by paying two Boston men to destroy the tax records. The sheriff arrested these two men, and the commissioners appointed Robert A. Mattingly the new county treasurer. No one could determine the exact amount of money embezzled, however, for the first county treasurer was never seen again.

The summer of 1874 brought a drought and hot temperatures to Boston. In August there was an invasion of grasshoppers that was both unexpected and catastrophic. A man passing through town told a sensational story about the swarms of grasshoppers he had seen the day before, but nobody believed him. Suddenly the atmosphere became hazy, and occasionally a lone grasshopper came drifting down. This strange phenomenon persisted for several days until all at once, in one day and a night, grasshoppers descended in hundreds of thousands and devastated the entire area. Thomas Thompson, editor of the *Howard Courant*, described the onslaught:

One afternoon we drove to Independence and it began to rain grasshoppers and the next day when we drove back to Boston we could observe how they had destroyed things. For miles the fields and prairies would be as brown as in December and then for a few miles they would apparently skip a space and things would be about as green as usual but in some neighborhoods the only green thing that could be seen were occasional fields of castor beans.

The main political issue in the fall of 1874 was whether or not to split Howard County, the second largest in the state, into two separate counties. After all the trouble between Boston and Elk Falls, many citizens approved of the split. The campaign was hot and bitter: one of the candidates for county commissioner, Ed Jaquins, favored dividing the county; the other, T. B. Rice, favored keeping Howard County intact. Although Boston and Elk Falls campaigned vigorously for Rice, Jaquins won, and with his election a bill was passed in January 1875 dividing Howard County into Elk and Chautauqua counties. The Boston townspeople tried to denounce this bill before its passing, but to no avail. On Christmas Day 1874 the men drank their fill of whiskey and started to fight among themselves. The day was long remembered as a "rip-roaring, frontier battle royal," but, happily, no blood was shed. Editor Thompson reflected that, "Instead of peace on earth, good will toward men, it was almost a Wild West roundup with the lid off." During the many fights that day, seven men tried to take on the town heavyweight, Pat Nulty. Only the snap of a pistol by a sober bystander saved Nulty and his adversaries from an all-out drunken brawl.

In its prime, Boston had three general stores, a grocery and hardware store, two hotels, a drugstore, three doctors, two office buildings, a shoe shop, two blacksmiths, two carpenters, a livery stable, a weekly newspaper, and the saloon operated by Nulty. In addition, six attorneys operated as real estate agents.

For several years, Nulty held a monopoly on the saloon business. One "quiet, little chap" decided to open another saloon and laid in a stock of liquor, a keg of beer, and a jug of blackberry wine. He fixed up a pine-board bar and stood ready and waiting for the thirsty customers. Nulty locked his tavern, gathered up all the "boys" and bought drinks for everybody at the new saloon. As evening approached and the regular trade discovered Nulty's place was closed, they all went over to the other saloon and proceeded to celebrate. They drank all the stock of liquors, largely on credit, then threw the bar fixtures out in the street and hinted to the new proprietor that Boston was not big enough for two saloons. He took the hint and never opened the bar again.

The state bill that divided Howard County took effect on June 1, 1875, making Sedan the Chautauqua County seat, and Howard City the county seat of Elk County. Almost immediately the exodus from Boston began, and by July most of the townspeople had moved away, either out of state or to Sedan.

Thompson recalled the Boston townsite a few years later:

About ten years after I left Boston, I went back to the old townsite. Not a single house remained. I drove around and tried to identify the various locations of the old town but I couldn't accurately locate a single spot. As I drove around two jackrabbits sat unafraid by the roadside which had once been main street of the busy, hopeful little town. The elimination, depopulation, and desolation of Boston was complete.[1]

DELAWARE SPRINGS
Wilson County

In the early days, before the advent of the pioneers, many Indian tribes camped at the "Springs"; however, the first recorded history of their using the grounds was when the settlers discovered human and animal bones on the site. During a period from 1861–1865, thousands of Indians, including the Creek, Seminole, Wichita, Chickasaw, and Delaware, moved into southeast Kansas to escape the Civil War. Several years after the Indians left, the local settlers dug up their graves looking for treasures that might have been buried there.

The first pioneers to occupy the Delaware Springs area were Joseph and Esther Smith, who purchased the land from the federal government in 1869. At that time the land was not heavily timbered, and Smith had to build his house and outbuildings with lumber shipped by team and wagon from a mill in Humboldt, fifty miles away.

After Smith's death at the turn of the century, the Springs became popular with the nearby residents, and until the 1920s, Delaware Springs was their favorite spot for Sunday outings and holiday celebrations. Soon people were coming from all around the region to enjoy the scenery, the hot baths, the water, and the dance hall. Mrs. Smith had the spring water bottled and shipped all over the United States. In 1909 she exhibited samples of the water at the World's Fair in St. Louis and won first prize.

In 1914 a tornado narrowly missed Delaware Springs and destroyed many outbuildings. Thereafter the Springs declined in popularity. Because Esther Smith, Joseph's widow, was getting too old to maintain the site, she sold the Springs in 1917 to the Blakely family. Mr. Blakely raised crops and traveled extensively selling the bottled water. Even during the drought of 1935, the Springs always had a steady flow of water.

In 1939 the property was sold to Dr. John R. Brinkley, three-time gubernatorial candidate and well-known radio personality, and then in 1942 to E.
F. Weaver, a Wichita nurseryman who built a house, outbuildings, and a
greenhouse. When the Worland Blankinships of Fredonia purchased the
land in 1960, they raised thousands of chrysanthemums and hundreds of
trees, including weeping willow, magnolia, cypress, Scotch broom, and
oak. The owners kept two deep spring-fed ponds stocked with bass, blue-
gill, and bullfrogs. Quail, deer, and other game were plentiful. The chrysan-
themum gardens were Kansas's largest, and Kansas State University purchased these flowers for experimental propagation.[1]

Delaware Springs is located about ten miles northwest of Fredonia on
Highway 96. Despite the years of use and hundreds of people who came to
the Springs, it was still a beautiful, pleasant place to visit as late as the 1960s.
Today Delaware Springs, or what is left of it, is no longer on the map.

KALIDA
Woodson County

Hale T. Chellis platted a townsite on his own land in January 1869 and
named the fledgling community "Chellis," after himself. After a year and a
half of very little growth, Chellis sold most of the site to Thomas Davidson
in September 1870. Davidson changed the name of the town to Kalida, a
Greek word meaning "beautiful." The town prospered, and by 1873 it had
several merchandise stores, a drugstore, billiard hall, a dry goods store, three
grocery stores, two hotels (the Kalida House and the Iola House), a blacksmith shop, an attorney, a physician, a real estate agent, a magistrate judge,
a post office, a public school, and a newspaper, the *Woodson County Advocate*. The population of Kalida then was well over 300. The largest store in
town was the Wells & Dryden general merchandise store, which advertised
as "dealers in dry goods, groceries, boots and shoes, hats and caps, gents
furnishing goods, Yankee notions, hardware, tinware, and queensware."
Kalida also had a fairgrounds located a half mile from town; at least one free
fair was held there in the fall of 1872.[1]

Promotion was always the heart of townsite speculation and growth. Besides advertising in their newspaper, the town promoters printed a circular
that they sent to anyone with even the slightest notion of settling there.
The circular described the town glowingly:

Kalida is situated on the proposed route of the Humboldt and Arkansas
River Railroad, in the geographical center of Woodson County in the most

beautiful and productive part of Southern Kansas. A railroad is contemplated from Topeka south through the center of this county . . . and (our town) is destined at an early date to become the county seat. . . . Persons seeking locations for business are requested to visit us before investing elsewhere.

Kalida's best chance at real prosperity came in October 1873, when county officials began to discuss an election to locate a permanent county seat. Until then, Neosho Falls had served as county seat, but in this election the Falls was not even in the running. The officials scheduled an election for November 3, and the two towns competing for the title were Defiance, a new town located on Owl Creek, and Kalida. A committee was organized to examine both townsites. On October 27 the committee visited Kalida, taking note of all its advantages and inducements. On October 28 they visited the townsite of Defiance. The next day their report, published in the *Advocate*, gave a considerable advantage to Kalida.[2]

The fight for the county seat generated its share of mudslinging; both towns appointed committees and county officers charged with the sole purpose of inducing the rest of the county to vote for them as county seat. The *Advocate* reported on the progress of the Defiance committee at the first county convention:

> About noon an ox team drawing a wagon containing three kegs of beer arrived on the grounds and the beer was dispensed with a free and liberal hand to anyone, men or boys, who would shout Defiance.
>
> It was claimed the beer was spiked, mixed with whiskey, and its effects soon began to be shown. . . . Drunken yells and blasphemous calls were heard above the voice of the speaker. . . . The best men of the county stood back disgusted, dismayed and astonished to find that a drunken, hooting, yelping, cursing rabble could succeed in breaking up a convention in Woodson County. The farmers, seeing that the control of affairs had been taken from their hands and that things were being run by a drunken mob, withdrew in a body.[3]

The second convention was held in Kalida, and despite the presence of free beer, this gathering was quiet and the meeting proceeded without incident. On election day Kalida narrowly defeated Defiance by a vote of 530 to 506, thus becoming the second county seat of Woodson County. The commissioners moved the county records from Neosho Falls to Kalida's newly built courthouse. But this election was barely over before the residents of Neosho Falls and Defiance were scheduling the next election.[4]

Thomas Davidson had planned for Kalida to be a temperance community. During the election campaign, however, a saloon opened. The *Woodson County Post*, Neosho Falls, related the story in their February 18, 1873, issue:

> When the saloon first started at Kalida the temperance people . . . protested vigorously and demanded that the institution leave at once. . . . The saloon men rallied their forces and succeeded in convincing the temperance folks that the success of Kalida in the county seat contest depended to a great measure on keeping the drunk shop. We are reliably informed that the temperance people then signed a paper pledging themselves that Prutzman (the owner of the saloon) might go on dealing out death and hell in the interest of Kalida and in violation of law without being prosecuted.

The next county seat election was held on February 11, 1874, and Defiance beat Kalida by 643 votes to 491. Although Davidson insisted that many of the votes were fraudulent, the election was not officially contested. This marked the beginning of the end for Kalida, the county seat of Woodson County for only three months.

One of the town's main disadvantages was the lack of water on the site. During a large Independence Day celebration in 1874, Kalida literally ran out of water! There was no water to quench the thirst of the hundreds of people who attended the festivities. In fact, Kalida had only three good wells in the whole town. Within a few years, the residents abandoned the town, many of them moving to nearby Yates Center, which eventually won the county seat from both Defiance and Neosho Falls. In 1883 the county commissioners officially vacated the Kalida townsite: a public square and eleven streets and alleys.[5]

Today the site is known as the Kalida farm. Visitors are greeted by two large stone entrances and a stone castle-like cellar, both proclaiming the name "Kalida"; James Davidson had this stonework done several years after the town was abandoned. The townsite is located about two miles southeast of Yates Center just off U.S. Highway 54.

•———————————— **DEFIANCE** ————————————•
Woodson County

Defiance was founded on October 13, 1873. The settlers dug wells and brought in lumber from Humboldt to build the first public building. Although Defiance lost the county seat to Kalida a month later, the town company pleaded to the county commission for another election.

During the month of November, the following headlines and articles appeared in the *Woodson County Post* at Neosho Falls about Defiance:

> Defiance has plenty of water so that when a meeting is held here, it will not be necessary to send beer from Neosho Falls.
>
> Defiance men are catching it hot all over the county. Defiance is a lively town. Buildings are going up and they are confident that inside of 60 days the county seat will be located here.
>
> [The] Courthouse at Defiance blew down during the high winds last week, but it is all right and ready for the roof. In the election of Feb. 25, 1874, Defiance won over Kalida.
>
> A beautiful flag waves over the courthouse at Defiance, in full view of Kalida. How is that for Defiance!

On March 4, 1874, the *Post* remarked: "The county seat was all taken from Kalida to Defiance Monday morning. The people of Kalida turned out and fired an anvil salute. Everything went harmoniously. Mike Reedy and Dave Phillips of the Defiance Town Company were at Kalida Saturday and were feeling just about as happy as a little boy with his first pair of pants."

The first hotel in Defiance was the Harvey House, and J. A. Freer was the landlord and keeper. A post office opened on May 1, 1874, with Isaac Jones as the postmaster.

In June 1874 the town's first trial, an assault case, was held in the nearly completed courthouse before Justice Freer. The trial concerned two German Methodists, the Kluckhuhns, who were visiting a camp meeting on Owl Creek near Defiance. One Sunday, they were attending the church services when Mrs. Kluckhuhn, being rather high strung, gave way to her religious fervor by "shouting." Her husband was so embarrassed and agitated by her actions that he beat her harshly, bruising her face and mouth. She swore out a warrant for his arrest, and Justice Freer fined him $5.00 and court costs. After the trial, Mrs. Kluckhuhn took their child and went to the home of Peter Smith to stay until their marital difficulties could be resolved. The Kluckhuhns later reunited.

After Defiance had been the county seat for about a year, the commission held another election in August 1875 to relocate the county seat. This election was a three-cornered race between Defiance, Neosho Falls, and Yates Center. Yates Center received 335 votes, Neosho Falls 301, and Defiance

235. On January 29, 1876, David Phillips petitioned the election board to re-consider their actions and order another election for the location of the county seat. The board examined the petitions presented and compared them with the assessment rolls of 1875. They found that ninety-nine names on the petitions were not names of legal voters.

On September 4, 1876, a special meeting was called for the purpose of canvassing the vote cast at the public election held on August 18, 1875. The board discovered that the poll books of several voting precincts had been stolen from the office of the county clerk before September 1, 1876; further-more, the duplicate poll books returned by the township trustees had also been stolen. The board proceeded to canvass the vote by using the ballots cast at the election and found that the towns involved had recorded the fol-lowing votes: Yates Center 335, Neosho Falls 301, Defiance 235, the same as previously counted. Since none of the towns received a large enough share of the votes, the court ordered a second election for the relocation of the county seat of Woodson County to be held on September 12, 1876. The voting was to be between Yates Center and Neosho Falls, the two places having the highest number of votes. On September 16, 1876, Yates Center received the most votes and became the permanent seat of Woodson County.

Losing the county seat was a blow to Defiance; the legislature vacated the townsite in August 1878. The courthouse and most of the houses moved to Yates Center that year. One of the hotels was left at the site and used as a residence. The post office closed on May 21, 1886.[1]

Although the town was "defiant" to the last, the loss of the election was definitely the end of Defiance.

REECE
Greenwood County

In the post–Civil War period, settlement of the vast grassy regions south of Emporia along the valleys of Spring Creek, Burnt Creek, and Silver Creek began in earnest. Stock raising, particularly sheep and cattle, and farming were the primary occupations of these landowners. Some ranchers estab-lished spreads of 1,000–2,000 acres. Starting in 1868, the area was served by a stage line that ran from El Dorado to Eureka.

In 1870 William Smith Reece arrived from England and established the Burnt Creek Ranch, which was composed of 1,500 acres. John Whitticar Bean joined Reece in 1871, and the two men built a large complex that in-cluded a ranch house; stone dairy and poultry houses; a good granary; sev-

A postcard showing several buildings in Reece: (clockwise from top left) Christian church, public school, Presbyterian church, general store, railroad depot, and state bank.

eral horse barns, stables, and sheds; extensive stone corrals; several miles of stone walls; a fruitful orchard; and a handsome catalpa grove. Reece kept many fine horses and often rode around the countryside in an elegant English coach.

In late 1882 Reece donated a portion of his land for the construction of a townsite. The St. Louis, Fort Scott & Wichita Railroad, a division of the Missouri Pacific, was building through the area, and company officers were looking for a good place to establish section equipment. The railroad men found a site they liked next to Burnt Creek, and Reece agreed to give them some land for a right-of-way. On January 22, 1883, the town of Reece was platted. During that year, the railroad built a turntable, a roundhouse, and machine and car shops, and they brought in a relay of engines. They employed scores of mechanics and crew men to work on the freight trains in need of repair. All trains going west stopped at Reece for meals furnished by the railroad hotel, known as the Sunflower. General officers of the company and friends of the railroad invested heavily in local real estate, and within a short time the town had over 350 people.

Reece attracted the attention of financier Jay Gould, who came to the community with his daughter Helen in the fall of 1885. They arrived in their own private railroad car, and they dined at the Sunflower with several local

The Missouri Pacific Railroad depot at Reece, taken shortly after a windstorm ripped off the roof, ca. 1908.

dignitaries. Gould was briefly interested in investing in the coal-mining operations in the area. After the miners dug two shafts, however, and found only small veins of coal, Gould changed his mind.

By 1885 Reece had nearly 600 people; by 1888, the number had increased to 1,200. Among the first businesses was D. H. Mitchell & Company, who constructed the first general merchandise store. H. H. Hubbard built a large hotel, a livery stable, and a lumberyard and employed several mechanics in his building and contracting company. Reece and A. W. Bell started a real estate business. Two drugstores, a blacksmith shop, a wagonmaker's shop, a bakery, a broom factory, a bank, and a flour mill were constructed during the 1880s. The town's newspaper, the *Sunflower*, lasted for five years.

The town started to decline in 1888, when the railroad moved its shops elsewhere, forcing several stores to close and leaving quite a few houses vacant. Two tornadoes, the first in 1909, also destroyed much of the early townsite.[1] The town's population dropped slowly, then revived in the 1920s by the discovery of oil. The oil boom that everyone expected would rejuvenate the community was offset, however, by the depression of the 1930s. Reece still exists, a shadow of its former self.

SMILEYBERG
Butler County

A rose by any other name . . . such was the story of Smileyberg. The town might have become Rock Center if not for the creativity of two business-men in 1908. This small town, fifteen miles southeast of Augusta, came into existence in 1904 when Barney Berg built a blacksmith shop there. Before that time, Berg had done his "smithy" work "under a spreading chestnut tree." Berg's business boomed due to its convenient location for the farmers in the area. About this time, a travelling salesman roaming through the area decided to settle down at Berg's place. His name was Thomas Smiley, and he was tired of plying his wares out of a covered wagon. He made a land deal with Berg and built a grocery store next to the blacksmith shop. Soon the place was drawing so many people Smiley and Berg decided the community needed a name. Rock Center was their first choice, since the place was in the center of Rock Township. After further thought, how-ever, they decided to name the town Smileyberg, a combination of their own two names!

Business at Smileyberg boomed, especially after the discovery of oil in the vicinity. The men constantly adjusted to the needs of their clientele. Smiley was a soft touch for children; he often dispensed free candy so the parents would come back to his store. When he took on a partner, Dave Welch, the store became known as Smiley & Welch. After Smiley died in 1919, Welch sold the store. Berg died on February 21, 1926. His son tried to take over the business for a time, but soon sold out, and the site of the orig-inal blacksmith shop became a gasoline station.

Today only a few structures can be seen in Smileyberg—in the early 1970s, a grocery store, a bait shop, and several houses remained. Barney Berg's house is gone, leaving only the storm cave. Though Smileyberg was never big, it served a purpose for the farmers who lived nearby. When Berg and Smiley died, most of the town died too.[1]

ROSALIA
Butler County

Readers love a good mystery, especially an unsolved one. One such mystery was the unexplained disappearance of a child from the neighborhood of Rosalia in 1889. El Dorado's *Walnut Valley Times* followed the story begin-ning September 27.

On the morning of September 17, George Dudley saddled his horse and rode three miles to Rosalia in order to hire Alonzo Edwards and his wife, Martha Jean, to help harvest his broom corn. On the road back, the group stopped at the farm of Elias Bloomer, Dudley's neighbor, and the two farmers made a deal to help each other with the harvest of their corn. The Bloomers' two-year-old daughter, Sadie, accompanied her parents to the Dudley farm, which they had decided to harvest first. As soon as the group arrived, the men went to the fields and began working. The two farm women went to dig potatoes and left Mrs. Edwards to fix supper and care for Sadie.

When Mrs. Dudley and Mrs. Bloomer returned two hours later, they discovered the little girl was missing. Mrs. Edwards said that Sadie started to cry and had followed the women to the potato patch. The women searched for the baby in the barnyard and in a nearby cornfield, but the child was nowhere to be found. A little later, when the men arrived for their supper, they were told of Sadie's disappearance. They went out searching but returned empty-handed. A neighboring search party formed to hunt for Sadie also turned up no clues. By this time everyone suspected that something terrible had happened to Sadie.

Tempers were mounting, and suspicion fell on the Edwards. They seemed too complacent, especially Martha, who had made no attempt to help find the child. By the second day, literally hundreds of people were searching the area, trampling through cornfields and dragging the nearby creek. Small boys even volunteered to crawl through the briar thickets. Still there was no trace of the child. After four days of hunting, most people believed that Sadie had disappeared forever. Several were outspoken in their belief that the Edwards were responsible for Sadie's disappearance. A mob formed and marched to the Dudley farm, where the Edwards were staying.

The local constable met the mob at the farm and accused Martha of murder and Alonzo of being an accessory. Martha's daughter revealed that her mother had hit Sadie on the head. Thereupon, Martha gave several versions of how she had killed the child. First she said she had knocked Sadie in the head because she wouldn't mind. Then she said she had thrown a stick of wood at a rat and hit the child by mistake, killing her instantly. Afterward she toted Sadie's body to the creek and threw her in the water. Alonzo Edwards then stated that he had thrown the child in the creek. The story varied with every telling. The creek was dragged repeatedly, but Sadie could not be found.

Frustrations grew, and the mob gathered again in Rosalia, where the constable was holding the Edwards. The mob pushed aside the guards and dragged the couple back to the creek on the Dudley farm, where they tried without success to force the Edwards to tell where Sadie's body was located. Finally, the men threw two ropes over a tree limb and pushed each of the Edwards into a noose. Twice they pulled the couple from the ground, and when their faces began to turn black, lowered them unconscious to the ground. At the last minute, help for the Edwards arrived, and the sheriff whisked them back to the county jail in El Dorado.

On Sunday evening, September 22, Val Piper, a young farmer living a mile from where Sadie had disappeared, gave up the search and returned to his home to find Sadie on his front porch, crying and trying to push the door open. She was wearing the same clothing she had worn when she disappeared, and it was still clean and untorn! Piper hurriedly sent word to El Dorado, and the Edwards were released. An attempt was made by the local authorities to punish the would-be executioners, but nothing came of it. Eventually the Edwards sued all the people of Rosalia Township and received an out-of-court settlement for $1,000.

Even after Sadie had been found, the Edwards continued to insist they had murdered her and were surprised to see her alive and well. What happened to her during that week remains a puzzle, and she was too young to give any clues. A few believed she was kidnapped by someone else, but no one ever solved the mystery. Fortunately, it all ended happily.[1]

The town of Rosalia was a railroad town founded in 1879, when the Missouri Pacific Railroad laid track through the township. But before the coming of the iron rail, the place was little more than a small collection of houses and buildings. When the railroad was completed in 1882, Rosalia became a major shipping point for cattle, and as many as four trains per day ran through town.

Just east of Rosalia was a hill known as the Summit, the highest point between St. Louis and Wichita. The railroad had to use pusher engines to get their trains over this hill. One story told of repair work being done to some railroad cars at the top of the hill, and since the train crew hadn't blocked the wheels, the cars started rolling downhill. Before they could be stopped, they had rolled through Rosalia and were on their way to Pontiac, just to the west. Fortunately, the depot agent at Pontiac quickly threw a switch, forcing the cars to derail.

Rosalia remained a small railroad town until 1903, when geologists began testing for oil in the vicinity. This was, in fact, significantly earlier than the El Dorado tests. A well was sunk on the D. R. Blankinship farm five miles southwest of Rosalia. This particular well turned out to be dry, but it was the first such test in Butler County and eventually led to the successful oil development a few years later known as the Blankinship Pool.[2]

The Missouri Pacific Railroad depot at Rosalia. Once an active shipping point, Rosalia today is merely a shadow along the rails.

Over the next fifteen years, Rosalia benefited from marked increases in oil leases. Workers came from all over the region to build the oil rigs, and the town's population reached a peak of 600. Businesses included two large merchandise stores; a large business building known as the J.C. Mooso Block that housed several small enterprises; the Ohio House Hotel, the Flesher Family Hotel, and the Henry Hammer Hotel; a barber shop; a livery barn; a dry goods store; and the Rosalia State Bank. On February 13, 1914, the town suffered its first major fire—the Piper Store caught fire and the flames spread to a drug store, clothing store, barber shop, and butcher shop, all on Main Street. The next day the butcher shop offered barbecued beef at a discount. A second lumberyard opened to take care of the building boom and to provide for transients and for families who needed apartments.

The largest oil concern in the vicinity was the Cattlemen's Oil Company, organized as a stock company in 1918, composed of Rosalia businessmen. Joe H. Liggett was president of the company and superintendent of drilling operations. By December their first well was producing 250 barrels of crude a day. The Cattlemen's Oil Company drilled a total of nine wells, and all nine were producers. This company remained active until 1958. Another important local company was the Liggett Oil Company, also operated by Joe Liggett. This corporation drilled sixteen wells in the area, all of them producers.

Liggett had other investments in Rosalia. He constructed the Liggett Hotel at a cost of $100,000; an additional $30,000 went into the furnishings. The three-story hotel had a lobby, dining room, barber shop, and the offices of the Liggett Oil Company. Liggett also built the Liggett Theatre next door to the hotel.[3]

Rosalia continued to be a prosperous town through the 1920s. In the 1930s Rosalia was visited by one of its most unusual residents, a man who brought the "Brinkley connection" to this Butler County oil town. In the spring of 1932, Dr. O. M. Owensby, chief surgeon for the Dr. John R. Brinkley Hospital in Milford, Kansas, traded 8,000 acres of undeveloped oil land in West Texas to Joe Liggett for the Liggett Hotel. Dr. Owensby then left the Brinkley Hospital and opened the Owensby Prostate Sanitarium in the hotel. Overnight, Dr. Owensby gave Dr. Brinkley, two-time gubernatorial candidate and famous "goat gland" doctor, a "run for his money." Dr. Owensby began advertising his hospital nationwide, and daily correspondence from patients all over the United States kept the Rosalia Post Office busy. Often it took at least three people to haul the mail to the hospital.

Dr. Brinkley was not to be outdone. In September 1933 he established the Brinkley Hospital in Rosalia in the former Mooso Hall. He hoped by offering lower prices he could lure patients who had planned to enter the Owensby Sanitarium. Advertisements in local papers and on the front door read, "New and improved Brinkley operation offered to you here for $250" and "Dr. Brinkley's Treatment here for Enlarged and Infected Prostates. Infection Cleared and Prostate Reduced. Visitors Welcome. $250." But the clinic failed to attract enough patients, and Dr. Brinkley left Rosalia early in 1934. In April a fire broke out in the Mooso Hall building, completely destroying the structure. In 1934 Dr. Owensby purchased Dr. Brinkley's old Milford hospital, closed his Rosalia sanitarium, and moved most of his equipment to Milford. Rosalia had two famous physicians, but within months they were both gone![4]

When the oil business began to dwindle in the 1930s, Rosalia also declined. Transient workers left for other fields. In addition, a major blacktop highway missed Rosalia by a half mile, diverting travelers away from town. This had a negative impact on the economy as automobile travel increased after World War II. In the 1950s most of the oil wells shut down, and Rosalia became little more than a small country community again. Today Rosalia still has a resident population, but nothing like in the oil boom days. Much of Main Street has been torn or burned down, and only a few buildings remain.

4

NORTH CENTRAL KANSAS

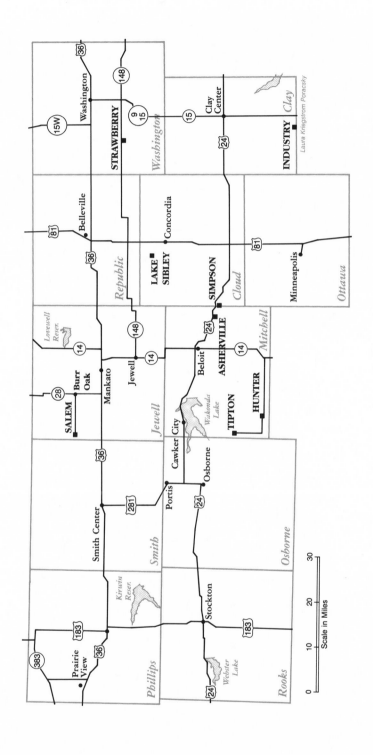

Laura Kriegstrom Poracsky

36
148
15W
Washington
STRAWBERRY
Washington
9
15
Clay
Center
15
24
INDUSTRY
Clay

81
Belleville
Concordia
81
Minneapolis
Ottawa
36
Republic
LAKE
SIBLEY
SIMPSON
Cloud

Lovewell
Reser.
14
148
14
Jewell
Mankato
24
Beloit
ASHERVILLE
14
Mitchell
28
Burr
Oak
SALEM
Jewell
Cawker City
Wakonda
Lake
TIPTON
HUNTER

36
Cawker City
Osborne
281
Portis
24
Smith Center
Smith
Osborne

Kirwin
Reser.
Stockton
30
183
183
20
183
383
Prairie
View
36
24
Webster
Lake
Phillips
Rooks
10
Scale in Miles
0

This hotel and store combination was one of the first structures in Strawberry.

STRAWBERRY
Washington County

This town's unusual name was derived from a large field of wild strawberries growing on Parson's Creek near the center of the township. John Gieber and John Millfelt first settled the area in May of 1861. They were soon followed by Peter Gieber and L. Meyers in 1863. Tracy Millfelt, daughter of the John Millfelts, was the town's first true native, born in April 1863. Seven years later, the town mourned its first death. Late one evening in 1870, Katherine Meyers started to herd the cattle home, when she became confused, lost her way, and wandered near Elk Creek. She stumbled on the doorstep of a nearby settler who, thinking she was a wolf, shot her. He didn't discover his mistake until the next morning when he found her body in the yard.

The government established a post office at Strawberry in 1868; Peter Gieber was the first postmaster. At this time the town's blacksmith shop, general store, hotel, and wagon shop served a population of 436. In 1878 the number increased to 934; and in 1880, to 1,258. A schoolhouse was built in 1876 across the road from the general store. In later years there was a skating rink and a dance pavillion, which attracted settlers from all over the county. People living near the site today still recall the fun they had in Strawberry.

The town no longer exists, but if you travel down Highway 148 you will see a lone monument, installed by a committee of caring people who remember Strawberry's early days. The plaque was dedicated on August 12, 1990, and I was proud to be asked to give an address. The lovely old townsite is located ten miles north and one mile east of Clifton.[1]

• ————————————— SALEM —————————————•
Jewell County

Located in the fertile valley of Rock Creek, Salem was first settled in 1871, when the founders of the community, M. W. George and H. L. Browning, started a steam sawmill, an important industry for the settlers. Browning, C. P. Miller, and George W. Smith laid out the townsite in 1872 by taking a strip of ground from each of their claims. In March 1872 Browning and Smith built the first store, a temporary one operated by the Wilson Brothers of Scandia. The first permanent store was opened in June 1872 by Wolbert & Parker, who freighted their goods from Hebron, Nebraska, some sixty miles away. Browning and George soon added a blacksmith shop to their lumber mill, and Joseph S. Miller installed a shingle-making machine.[1]

C. Clyde Myers, son of an early settler, recalls life in Salem:

The Salem community . . . had the usual Indian scares, buffalo hunts, a little deer and antelope hunting, droughts, grasshoppers, cyclones, prairie fires, and the hard times common to such western communities. Even as late as 1890 when the writer remembers playing about upon the prairies, he had seen countless buffalo bones and buffalo chips. The old buffalo wallows can still be seen in some places. The houses on the plains included dugouts and soddies.[2]

Myers describes an incident from the early 1870s, when the law was at the end of a rope:

For the most part Salem was a fine, law-abiding town. There occurred, however, one tragedy that Salem seldom speaks of today. Late one evening, in the early '70s a man and half-grown boy drove through the county headed toward the Northwest. They were driving a fine team of mules and a good buggy. It was soon learned that the mules had been stolen. A posse of citizens were rounded up and started in pursuit. The next day both man and boy were caught and hanged from the limb of an oak tree. It was later

learned that probably the boy was not actually guilty of stealing the mules
and that probably, so far as he was concerned, an injustice had been done.
But he had paid, just the same. Many a strange whisper has gone out about
this hanging. It was reported that many a man was haunted by fear the rest
of his days and the stump of the old oak tree is still a place evaded by playing
children.[3]

Harry Ross, in *What Price White Rock?*, offers a slightly different version
of the story:

Salem had been in its early days the scene of the Jewell County's only lynching. In 1871 Guy Whitmore and Jack Hanes, notorious horse thieves, were arrested at Grand Island, Nebraska. . . . They had 11 stolen horses in their possession when captured. The sheriff (William Stone) brought his prisoners as
far as his home, near Salem, and decided to remain there overnight with
them. Leaving them in custody of his deputy, Sheriff Stone went on an er-
rand from home, and during his absence a mob gathered, overpowered the
deputy and took the prisoners from him. They hanged the horse thieves
both from a tree nearby. Efforts to discover the perpetrators of the lynching
met with the usual results—the members of the mob were never identified.[4]

Salem continued to prosper throughout the 1870s, and by 1877 the town
had four stores, a hotel, and several private residences and was on the main
freight road from Cawker City to Hastings, Nebraska. Successful businessmen included Menzo W. Smith, postmaster and justice of the peace; J. H.
Crawford, proprietor of "Tavern's Home"; J. W. Crawford, hardware; L.
C. Mick, general merchandise; G. C. Ward, M.D., homeopathic physician
and surgeon; and L. P. Lytle, dealer in drugs, dry goods, groceries, boots,
and shoes.[5] Andreas, in his *History of Kansas,*, 1883, put the town's population at 300 and lauded its good schools and three religious organizations.
He also noted that the *Salem Chronicle,* started in Nelson, Nebraska, in 1879
by J. Wilkes More, moved to Salem in 1882.[6] Another newspaper followed
in 1883, the weekly *Salem Argus,* which ran for several years.
    Salem boasted its share of colorful characters, including one Hobart
Rabb, town musician and auctioneer, who advertised in the *Salem Argus* of
June 28, 1889, as "city barber, to buy or sell real estate or personal property
to be traded." Then there was Jason Dunton, a man who possessed a good
education although he had scarcely seen inside a schoolhouse; he scandalized fundamentalists in the area by asserting that his study of geology led

him to conclude that the world was at least fifteen million years old. And who can forget the story of the foot race, as related by C. Clyde Myers?

In her palmy days Salem was quite a sports town. Baseball, horse racing, and foot racing took the front. One day a stranger dropped in on "Joe" Burrow's stage. He shortly built up a substantial bet with the Salem sporting blood that he could outrun any man in town. John Adams was selected to run the race and as soon as the stakes were placed, the stranger stripped down to runner's trunks. The Salem boys then knew they had been taken in by a professional. But, good sports that they were, decided to do the best they could and try to save their money. As luck would have it, Adams was a real foot racer. So to his own amazement and to the surprise of the stranger, Adams was able to run fast enough to win the race. The stranger was "taken in," and begged his way out of town.

In "Historical Sketches of Smith and Jewell County and Old Salem," Ray Myers relates innumerable events and biographies of pioneers from that community, a few highlights of which follow:

The first store came into the hands of Lute Mick. . . . Mr. Mick may have become part owner; . . . They say he was a likeable, talented man, but apparently he became disheartened, for one day he lay down upon the counter and shot himself. He was buried in the Salem cemetery and today a monument [1935] stands over his grave. His widow, sometime later, married a clerk in the store. . . . This pair finally became the owners of the store, and were supposed to have gone broke; anyway, they disposed of the property and left the country. There is a story that Lute Mick met with foul play, but the rumor has never been substantiated. . . .

Menzo Smith was a dentist here in those days. He was in his day an artist in his profession, although today, he would be laughed to scorn. About two-thirds of the profane words in existence are credited to patients of the early "turnkey." The turnkey was a sort of arrangement, which, after the stout cord was fastened to the tooth, would commence winding the thing, thus pulling the tooth. . . .

Later a traveling dentist made this place, and he advertised his work as painless. He demonstrated on the streets. One time he had a lady as an exhibitor. He yanked out one tooth and asked if it hurt. She said, "No." He then pulled out another and inquired if it was unpleasant. "It didn't hurt as much as the other one," the woman replied.[7]

Merl Langley's print shop in Salem, 1912. The poster on the wall depicts his choice for president that year, Woodrow Wilson.

By the 1880s the town had not gained a railroad. The citizens hoped that the Rock Island would choose Salem as a future stopping point, but in 1888 the railroad missed Salem, building its track five miles to the south. This was a mortal blow to Salem, and many of the town's buildings were moved either to Esbon six miles southeast or to Lebanon eight miles southwest. The moving of people and buildings from Salem was described as an "exodus," and it was not uncommon to see two or three houses or store buildings being moved by wagons along the road to these towns. After the exodus was complete, the town had only one church, a schoolhouse, a store, and a part-time blacksmith shop.[8] The *Lebanon Criterion* of May 10, 1889, gave the following account of a quiet and peaceful Salem:

Upon invitation of S. P. Rickabaugh, we visited Salem last Monday morning—the staid old town of Salem, that for years, for an inland town, was one of the best and most enterprising in the West. For almost a year we had not seen her once busy, bustling streets, and the change is simply startling. A number of the old landmarks, like our flag, are still there, but an air of vacancy is noticeable on every hand, though the merchants remaining tell us their trade is fair. A. B. Phillips was at the old stand on the corner and still contended that the railroad surveyors were camped just below the town. . . . Today the streets are covered with fields of corn; nothing remains of a once great "city" on the Central Plains.

HUNTER
Mitchell County

Hunter was a comparative newcomer to Mitchell County; the townsite charter was issued in May 1915. The town company then elected officers, bought and platted the land, and sold town lots.

The town was named for Al Hunter, who came to Jewell County in 1879 and bought a forty-acre farm in Mitchell County. He traded a team and wagon for homestead rights on the land that later became the townsite, and he built a sod house that was his home for fifteen years. Hunter circulated a petition asking the postal department to establish a post office there, which they built in 1894 four miles west of the present town.

In 1915 the towns of Victor and Hunter tried to attract the Salina Northern Railroad, starting a feud between the two that lasted several months. In the end, however, Hunter gained the railroad, and Victor, seven miles away, had to be moved to Hunter. The move of Victor was total—everything on the main street, including the large bank building and a grain elevator, found suitable homes alongside the railroad at Hunter.[1]

The *Topeka Journal* of August 30, 1916, described Hunter's sudden boom:

> Miss Eula Thompson, a school teacher of Mitchell County, started the *Hunter Herald,* which made its first appearance last week. The newspaper is not much younger than the town. . . . Hunter bids fair to become an important town. A few months ago the site was nothing but prairie. Today there is a lumberyard, general store, hotel, hardware store, garage, barber shop, restaurant and newspaper, and the Victor State Bank soon will be moved here. Two elevators will be erected here soon. . . .

The boom continued through 1917. The *Topeka Journal* of May 23, 1917, noted a few additions:

> Hunter now has two elevators, two lumberyards, a bank, two general stores, hardware and implements, furniture, newspaper, two garages, cloth-

ing house, opera house, and about all other business avocations which go to make up a town. So much for a town less than a year old.

There is a rich country surrounding Hunter. Those who have invested money here, and others who are engaged in business, say they haven't made a mistake. Several of the business buildings are made of stone. At the present time Dr. H. A. Hope is erecting three brick business buildings, two stories high, each 25 by 80 feet. They will be occupied by a drug store, hotel office, and a merchandise house, while the upstairs will be finished for a modern hotel. The cost is about $20,000.

Dr. H. A. Hope actively promoted Hunter for the first few years. He not only sought an ice storage plant for the community but also concrete sidewalks, all-night electric light service, a city water service, and other modern civic improvements. Dr. Hope's goal was to make Hunter the "best little town in northwest Kansas."

Hunter's population rose to about 300, and it became an incorporated city of the third class in 1919. The town prospered for many years as a major railroad shipping point for cattle and grain.[2] As elsewhere, however, the depression years of the 1930s sapped the town's vitality, and many people left for employment elsewhere. Farmers began to ship their goods from other larger communities in the area, leaving Hunter with a dwindling economic base. The town's population has dropped to about 100 in the past twenty or thirty years. Although a few businesses are still open, and a small resident population remains, the boom years of the newest town in Mitchell County are over.

ASHERVILLE
Mitchell County

Asherville was one of the oldest communities in the Solomon River Valley. John Rees, an early resident, came to Asherville after he was discharged from the Civil War in 1866. The following year, he built the town's first grocery store. The village, however, attracted few people until the early 1870s, when the Indians ceased to be a problem and pioneers began to settle the valley.

Sarah Borgen, sister of John Rees, recounted her early days in the Asherville community in an article that appeared in the *Scott City Chronicle,* June 20, 1940:

We were the first settlers around (Asherville). . . . There was nothing in sight except grass and trees on the creeks and rivers. . . . The first thing to do was to care for the stock and gather brush for campfire to cook dinner. After the meal was over the men set two of the wagon boxes on the ground and stretched the wagon cover to make a tent until they could make dugouts in the creek bank.

We had been in camp only a few days when Indians paid us a visit. They came up to the end of the tent and said, "How! How!" All the men were out of the camp except my cousin, Tom, and of course he felt it was his responsibility, so he started for his gun. My sister said, "Tom, don't do that, they will kill us." She knew more about Indians than he did. The Indians hung around until they got all our dinner. We learned later that they killed a man three miles west of us by the name of Zimmerman.

It was some time before the settlers enjoyed improved living conditions, namely dugouts, and Borgen continued her story at this point:

By this time the men had the dugouts ready and we moved into them. A short time later, five hundred Indians came and set up tents on my brother John's homestead while he was gone to Glasco. That evening when he was coming home some Indians got after him but he had a good horse and outran them. . . . As my brother was nearing home he saw the Indian's campfire from away off. He could not see any lights at home and thought, "If all of the family has been killed, I just as well go too." But he came on home to the dugout and found us all right.

Borgen did not stay in the Asherville area long. The family could not stand the constant begging and harassment from the local Indian tribes. They eventually sought safety at nearby Glasco, and the men were hired by the railroad to grade the roadbed at Sand Springs west of Abilene.

Asherville became a local trading center beginning in the 1870s. Some of these enterprises included two general stores; a post office; two hardware stores, including one operated by Frank Rees; a doctor's office; a lumberyard owned by John Rees; the Funk Flour and Grist Mill on the Solomon River southwest of town; a barber shop; a meat market; and a sawmill. The town also had a school, Baptist and Christian churches, and later acquired the Asherville State Bank, which opened for business in November 1911. A rarity for a town of this size, Asherville's bank successfully weathered the 1930s.[1]

The *Beloit Weekly Record* of November 23, 1877, gave the following account of an Asherville citizen during the boom years:

The Union Pacific depot at Asherville boarded up in the 1950s.

Samuel Carter opened a general store here in 1871, which he has successfully conducted ever since. His trade is good and growing better; he owns a first class valley farm, has a good stock of humor, is a capital man, hails from the land of wooden nutmegs and is personally popular. My stay here was too short to form an extended acquaintance but if they are all like the gentlemen who sell goods here they will ''pass muster'' without any trouble.

In the 1880s the Union Pacific Railroad extended their line through Asherville, where they constructed a depot and appointed a station agent. This action guaranteed Asherville's existence for quite some time, as the town became a shipping point for cattle and grain. Despite all the construction, the town never incorporated, and a plat of Asherville was not registered until 1902.[2]

The depression years of the 1930s weighed heavily on the community. Many stores closed their doors, and rail service was limited and eventually terminated. The town slowly began to dwindle. Today Asherville is very small, with only a few original buildings left for the visitor to see.

TIPTON
Mitchell County

Tipton once competed with Pittsburg, Kansas, if in name only—the towns were settled one year apart and shared the same name. In 1872 W. A. Pitt, treasurer of the town company, gave his name to the Pittsburg in Mitchell County. Shortly thereafter, settlers in Crawford County named their own town Pittsburg after the coal company town in Pennsylvania, although in Kansas they dropped the final "h." A postmaster's nightmare ensued, which caused the Mitchell County residents to call themselves "Old Pittsburg" and their Crawford County rivals to call their town "New Pittsburg."[1]

In the early 1880s residents of New Pittsburg sent the town company of Old Pittsburg a $150 bribe to change their name. Two conflicting stories explain why the name was changed to Tipton. One story claims that the settlers named the town for Tipton, Iowa, the home of one of the first residents. Another theory is that Tipton spelled backwards is "Notpit," or "not Pittsburg."

Tipton developed into a community of 200 residents by 1910. Many settlers were German Catholics from wealthy families who had invested heavily in western lands and businesses that catered to the settlement of the central plains. They merged their resources in 1884 and built the beautiful St. Boniface Catholic church as a monument to the community. On the north side of the church, the settlers built a grotto out of stones from all parts of the world. The town also developed a two-school system. A Catholic parochial school, established in conjunction with St. Boniface church, was the largest in town; seven nuns taught first grade through high school. There was also a public grade school that was less popular and had only one teacher.[2]

The coming of the Santa Fe Railroad in 1915 brought trade and importance to Tipton. At that time, the Santa Fe was building several spur lines through the rich agricultural valleys in the Beloit vicinity, and Tipton was a lucky recipient of one of these railroad lines. Shortly after the arrival of the Santa Fe, the town's population grew to nearly 300 and stayed at this level for several years. That same year the town got its first newspaper, the *Tipton Times*, which lasted until its move to Cawker City in 1951. In 1916 the newly incorporated town held its first city council meeting, and within a month the wily council enacted their first tax laws.

Tipton had several community clubs and lodges: a Knights of Columbus organization with its own town band; an American Legion post; a St. Ann's Altar Society; a Daughters of Isabella group; and a 4-H Club. The legion sponsored a baseball team that played against other towns in the area. Local membership in the Knights of Columbus and other organizations was so successful that in 1951 they spearheaded the construction of a community building containing a large auditorium for dances, meetings, and

A 1970s view of the Tipton depot, one of the last buildings in town.

basketball games; a lobby; restrooms; and a clubroom. By this time, the
community had twenty-eight businesses and a lively main street.[3]

Tipton managed to survive the depression intact; however, the last
twenty years have not been kind to the town. Many residents have left for
better business opportunities in larger communities such as Beloit and
Cawker City. The Santa Fe line has cut back its activity, and the population
has declined. Several of the buildings on Main Street have burned down or
have been razed. Like many small Kansas communities, Tipton faces an uncertain future.

SIMPSON
Mitchell County

Simpson, the "biggest little town in Kansas," began as a gristmill site. In
1871 a settler known as "G" Beaver built mills in the newly settled area of
central Kansas. He had already constructed a thriving gristmill in Delphos
and was interested in building another mill farther up the Solomon River.
With the financial backing of the firm of Bilaner, Simpson & Shanks, Beaver erected a mill in the Simpson area to assist farmers in getting their corn
ground. As more and more settlers began using the mill, it became apparent that the site would make a good business center. A store was added,
and the little town of Brittsville was born. By 1879 other businessmen had
opened two general stores, a drugstore, a blacksmith shop, a post office,

Union Pacific station at Simpson in the 1950s.

and a stage station. The stage line that ran between Solomon City and Cawker City kept business booming in town.

In 1880 a railroad came through the area, narrowly missing Brittsville. The next year Alfred Simpson moved the town to land he owned adjoining the railroad and deeded it to the community. In return the residents changed the name of the town from Brittsville to Simpson in his honor. With a new railroad serving the community, Simpson boomed for many years. A hotel, a butcher shop, a barbershop, a doctor's office, a restaurant, a meat market, a harness shop, and lodge buildings had been added to the town's business directory by 1905. Electric lighting and waterworks were installed by 1915.[1]

Simpson began to decline in the 1930s. Today a few old structures and some residences are all that remain of this one-time railroad boomtown.

LAKE SIBLEY
Cloud County

Lake Sibley was an oxbow lake that formed north of the Republican River long before the white man came to Kansas.[1] In 1865 when the Indians were threatening settlers along the Little Blue River, the army established an important military station on the shores of the lake. Colonel H. E. Maynadier, 5th U.S. Volunteers, ordered Lt. Robert Jones to march Company A up the Republican River and set up camp at Lake Sibley. He was ordered to "keep constantly on the alert, frequently sending scouting parties to ascertain if there are any Indians in this section of the country, and reporting constantly to these headquarters any movement." Company A remained at Lake Sibley from May to July of 1865.[2]

In 1866 the Indian hostilities intensified. On September 16 Governor Samuel Crawford sent out a request for volunteers to help quiet the uprising, and after they had assembled at Salina, he sent one company to Lake Sibley in the Solomon Valley.[3] On August 14, 1867, a force of 200 Cheyenne, Arapaho, and Sioux attacked the settlers on the Solomon River. They killed thirteen men, destroyed their homes, and drove away their livestock. The company of volunteers stationed at Lake Sibley went into action but were only able to repel the Indians temporarily.[4] By 1868 the government had set up a small military post to guard the Solomon and Republican River valleys. This post was actually the beginning of a settlement on Lake Sibley, but by this time the Indians had driven out many of the settlers in the area.[5]

On May 21, 1869, about thirty or forty warriors armed with revolvers, spears, and bows and arrows struck a camp of farmers who were hunting buffalo on White Rock Creek. The Indians surprised four of the men while they were skinning the buffalo, and although the farmers tried to shoot their way to safety, the Indians killed them after they ran out of ammunition. Several of their comrades who witnessed the assault fled to a nearby settlement. A few days later, four hunters and several land speculators from Rose Creek, Nebraska, were killed by Indians on White Rock Creek near the Kansas-Nebraska border. A week later, six hunters from Waterville in Marshall County were killed after a two-day running battle with the Cheyenne. During this particular month, the Indians killed an estimated twenty settlers, ran off their stock, carried away provisions, and took about $1,000 in cash from their cabins.

After learning of this newest outbreak of hostilities, Captain B. C. Sanders gathered thirty men from nearby Lake Sibley and proceeded to the White Rock Creek area. As soon as the soldiers left, some of the Indians moved in closer, but since the Indians had never hesitated to strike Lake Sibley, a small military force remained there at all times to protect the settlement.[6] By 1870 the warfare with the Indians had calmed down a bit, and Lake Sibley prospered, though it did lose the county seat election to Concordia. Later that year, when the Indians again attacked the little settlement,[7] two companies of cavalry were camped there and helped quell any further conflict.[8]

Because of the hardships caused by the Indians and the loss of the county seat, Lake Sibley declined in population and importance. In February 1871 one of the settlers established a ferry just upstream from one at Concordia. An item in the May 24 *Concordia Empire* stated that the "Jenning's Ferry, two miles west of Lake Sibley, is now in good running condition. The boat is well made and competent men run it. Teams are charged 35 cents—other rates in proportion." The Lake Sibley Ferry Company started another ferry March 28, 1872, near Jenning's Ford; however, both companies went out of business before the 1880s.[9]

Lake Sibley's post office was discontinued in 1876, and one by one the other businesses closed. Today the town of Lake Sibley is gone. The lake, too, has completely disappeared.

INDUSTRY
Dickinson/Clay County Line

Grandma Amanda Knisely, accompanied by her six children, came to the Industry area from York County, Pennsylvania, in 1878. One of her children, Flo, married Professor Charles Menninger in 1885, and their two sons, Karl and Will, became world-famous psychiatrists and founders of the Menninger Foundation in Topeka. They spent most of their boyhood days on Grandma Knisley's farm south of Industry.

The first settlers of Industry came to the area in 1868 and platted the townsite under the name of Berlin. The main street of Berlin was the dividing line between Dickinson and Clay counties, which has caused considerable confusion in the recording of the town's history. That same spring, Christopher Kassebaum and John Bergman, millers by trade, homesteaded on Chapman Creek. In October 1869 Rudolph Berger built the first frame house on the northern boundary of Athelstane Township (Clay County). A post office was established in 1873 with R. Hamilton as postmaster, but in 1877 it was moved two miles south and the name changed to Industry by Christopher Kassebaum, the hard-working miller. The original families who homesteaded the area in and around Industry included the Robinetts, Steinbrucks, Buffmeiers, Walgasts, Schwandlers, Benfers, Elsassers, Bletschers, Iselis, Gottreaus, Backes, Benders, and Schenbergers.

One of Industry's early town characters was Dr. Robert Renner, who owned a fox terrier named Joe. When the dog died, Dr. Renner was so grief-stricken he decided to buy a casket and have a proper funeral. Howard Bender fashioned the casket and lined it with satin. The funeral went as

Barters Band playing for a town celebration in Industry, ca. 1916.

A street scene in Industry. In the center is the Brown shoe store, which burned to the ground in 1934.

The Industry roller mill. Notice the elaborate guttering system on the side of the building.

planned with Renner officiating. After Alva Ackus and Inez Gibbs sang a song, little Joe was appropriately sent on his way.[1]

In 1904 Industry was quite a bustling little burg, with the Industry Roller Mills, the Continental Skimming Station, three general stores, a drugstore, a butcher shop, a barbershop, a blacksmith and repair shop, a hotel and a livery stable, two physicians, a veterinarian, and a post office.[2] So little remains of Industry today, however, that the following poem written by an anonymous author seems appropriate:

I've reached the land of draught and heat;
Of cactus pies and gopher meat.
I got my land of Uncle Sam,
And I am beat, you bet I am.
When first I came to get my start,
The dog towns were not far apart.
Now all that I can get to eat
Is chinch bug pies and gopher meat.[3]

5

CENTRAL
KANSAS

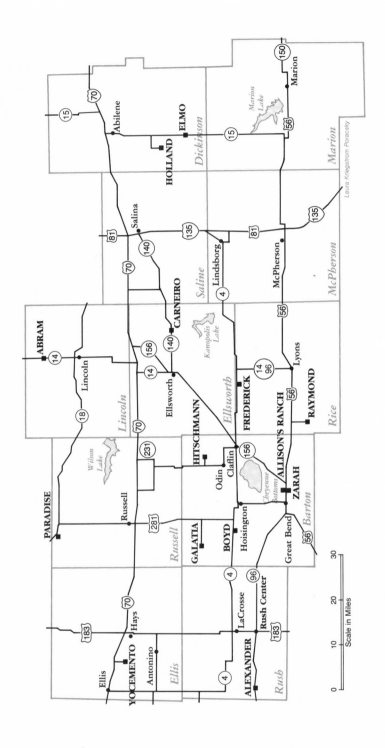

Laura Kriegstrom Poracsky

HOLLAND
Dickinson County

The exact date of the founding of the town of Holland, fifteen miles south-west of Abilene, is unknown, but sometime in 1872 thirty-seven Civil War veterans from Knoxville, Tennessee, occupied the area. Pioneer names familiar to the region included Bell, Anderson, Burkholder, Jones, Gibson, Lehman, Talbert, Harper, Biglow, Entriken, Hewitt, and Litts.

On July 20, 1888, W. T. W. Sterling started a creamery that produced the "finest butter" in Kansas. A few of the other businesses at that time included a gristmill, a post office, a store, a garage, the Holland State Bank, a blacksmith shop, a telephone office, a barbershop, a school, a doctor, and a dentist. The town grew slowly—indeed, it was surprising that it grew at all, since it was an inland town situated off both the railroad and the main highways. Holland's population peaked at seventy-eight residents.[1] Frank Myers, the town's "senior senior citizen," remembered when people from miles around filled the town on Saturdays—they only went to Abilene once every two or three months for items unavailable in Holland.

S. E. French had a large building moved from Carlton, Kansas, that housed the general store during Holland's early years. Many residents recalled the pickle, sugar, and bean barrels, and the ginger snaps that were stored in large containers. On rainy days and during the winter months, the men gathered around the store's pot-bellied stove to discuss politics and swap stories about local goings-on.

The school was also an important center for community activities. The students learned the usual subjects such as reading, writing, and "rithmetic," plus geography and history. These were quiet times when children walked or rode ponies to school. They played "black man" and "run sheep run," ate sack lunches, and rushed home after school to bring in the cows. On the last day of school as many as a hundred people came to eat dinner and to visit with old friends.

Holland had serious moments, too. In the fall of 1921 someone blasted the bank vault door open with nitroglycerine. Nothing was missing, but the reason for the crime and the robber's identity remains a mystery. Several citizens remembered a strange man watering his horses at various farms in the area and then disappearing when night came. Although the general store operator also reported some of his merchandise was stolen, the sheriff was never able to apprehend the culprit.

In May 1900 the townspeople organized the German Baptist Brethren church. It was a custom at that time for the men to sit on the south side of the church and the women on the north side. In order to encourage promptness, they built the church so that latecomers would have to enter facing the congregation. The last religious services were held in 1942, and the building is now a community hall and a center for local activities.[2]

Holland today consists of some empty business buildings and a few people whose interest in their community has not diminished. But as the "senior senior" citizen, Mr. Frank Myers, once said, "I think we've already vanished."[3]

ELMO
Dickinson County

When Elmo came into existence in 1866, it was known as Banner City and had a post office, a store, a brick kiln, a school, a United Brethren church, and several residences. But with the coming of the Missouri Pacific Railroad a half mile east, everything changed. J. J. Berry planned a new town and moved it to the railroad. He used brick from the Banner City brick plant to erect the first building in Elmo. Although Berry's move caused some opposition, others soon followed his lead, recognizing the need to be closer to the railroad.[1]

Elmo got its name in a most unusual manner, or so the story goes. In the early days of the settlement, a dugout graced a small hill near Banner City. A stranger came by one day, pointed to a tree near the dugout, and asked, "What kind of tree is that?" One of the settlers answered, "Elm." "Oh," replied the stranger. Thus the town became Elmo instead of Banner City.[2]

Elmer Bruce built the first house in Elmo; then came a hotel and other businesses including a lumberyard and hardware store. The post office and the school were moved from Banner City—the latter served as a center for community social activity. A Catholic church was erected soon after the founding of the town, and it is the only large structure still surviving.

By 1927 Elmo had a bank, a barbershop, a lumberyard, a blacksmith shop, two groceries, two garages, two churches, an implement business, a restaurant, two elevators, a town hall, a newspaper—the *Banner Register*—a millinery shop, a hardware store, and a depot.[3] Unfortunately, the depression and the growth of nearby Abilene had a negative effect on the little settlement. Today, except for the Catholic church and a few residences, the once-prosperous town of Elmo has disappeared into the surrounding flint hills.

ABRAM
Lincoln County

Founded in 1870, the town of Abram, sometimes known as Rocky Hill, was one of the first settlements in Lincoln County. After a November election, the new officials wanted to change the location of the county seat from where Lincoln now stands to the temporary site of Abram. In order to make the move legal, the county officers had to meet on the bare and bleak townsite one cold day in January 1871. They then made a motion to adjourn until February to the house of Ezra Hubbard, where they could conduct such important county business as granting a license permitting the sale of liquor, accepting petitions for county roads, instructing the county clerk to obtain seals for the probate judge and the register of deeds, and planning to advertise for proposals to build a courthouse. The bids on the courthouse were to be filed by April 1, and the courthouse completed by July 1, 1871.[1] The state legislature selected Judge James Canfield of Junction City to preside over the court, and the first session convened on November 6, 1871.[2]

Abram, the temporary county seat, was platted in April 1871, and Myron Green, the county attorney, was president of the town company.[3] The town seemed to go up overnight. The Graham Brother's flourmill was the first one in the county, and it generated a great deal of trade. A post office established on February 16, 1872, under the name of Rocky Hill, lasted only until December 5 of that year, but it was reestablished in 1873 and lasted ten more years.[4]

An election held in 1872 determined the location of the permanent county seat. Of the 153 votes cast, Abram received 75, Lincoln Center 58, and Elkhorn 10. The officials did not count the other ten votes because the voters did not write the words "county seat" on the ballots. In another election held on February 19 to relocate the county seat, 408 votes were cast, and Lincoln Center received 232 and Abram 176. This outcome caused a commotion because the townspeople had already constructed a temporary courthouse in Abram, and all the county records were there. The real turning point of the whole controversy, however, was the murder of Ezra Hubbard just before another election could be held.

A quarrel arose between Hubbard and John Haley concerning lumber Hubbard had taken to Haley's mill. The dispute grew violent. Hubbard seized a carbine and shot Haley. Hubbard, frightened and alone, eluded the law for several hours before giving himself up. Since Hubbard's son-in-law, John Cook, had seen the shooting, the sheriff arrested him as well. That night a mob of forty or fifty men surrounded the jail and began shooting at Hubbard through the window. Some even forced open the door and fired at him from the inside. After the mob left, the badly wounded Hubbard managed to climb up the slats on the wall to the loft. Realizing that he might recover, the mob again entered the building, placed a stone under the wounded man's head and beat his brains out with a mallet. A doctor had been summoned to take care of the wounded man, but he was not present when Hubbard's life was taken.

The trial resulting from the Hubbard episode cost Lincoln County $10,000 and aroused the indignation of the citizens. In fact, the county commissioners used "mob violence" as an argument in favor of changing the location of the county seat. At the trial the county attorney charged Ira C. Busick with Hubbard's murder, but the jury acquitted him due to lack of evidence. A few weeks later someone killed the guard who had been in charge of Hubbard the night he was murdered. The guard's body was thrown into a well and was not discovered until nearly three weeks after he disappeared. Supposedly this murder had no connection with the Haley-Hubbard affair.

After the last county seat election, the county clerk and the records moved to Lincoln Center. Many citizens soon followed, although some settlers stayed in the area, hoping that the coming of the Topeka, Salina & Western Railroad in February 1881 would help the town. Although the railroad did arrive, it did not benefit Abram. Most of the town was literally loaded on wheels and carted to Lincoln Center. One settler recalled the strange sight of the Gilpin family riding to the county seat inside their house, which later became a blacksmith shop.

A local newspaper editor was supposed to have written the following poem about Abrams's demise:

> If death should come with his cold, hasty kiss,
> Along the trench or in the battle strife,
> I'll ask of Death no greater boon than this:
> That it should be as wonderful as life.[5]

In July 1936 a monument was erected on the townsite. Its inscription reads: "Abram townsite, located here April 11, 1871, vacated Feb. 24, 1872. First county seat in Lincoln Co." Thus, as Andreas observes in the *History of Kansas*: "The fates which control the settlement of all new counties decided that this town should die—and it died."

CARNEIRO
Ellsworth County

A fascinating array of abandoned buildings greets the ghost town hunter at Carneiro. One perplexing problem, however, is the lack of worthwhile information about this town.

E. W. Wellington, a "Harvard man," platted Carneiro twelve miles east

The Carneiro school in 1900. Today this building is in ruins.

of Ellsworth. The town's checkered past may date back to the military and pioneer activity along the legendary Smoky Hill Trail. The townsite, located on the banks of Alum Creek, was a favorite campground of cavalry escorts in the 1860s. Originally, a small town was established on the east side of the creek and named "Alum"; it evidently lasted only until Wellington platted Carneiro on the west side.

Carneiro's proximity to the railroad transformed the village overnight into a bustling boomtown. At its peak, Carneiro had four grocery stores, two churches, a hotel, a school, a depot, and a huge stockyard where as many as 20,000 head of cattle waited to be shipped weekly. A large portion of the town's population were Mexican laborers who were left behind after the railroad laid track through the area. Few towns in Kansas had a similar ethnic mix.

Carneiro prospered for a few years but dwindled during the 1930s. The railroad terminated service; the stockyards and depot closed; the school unified with other districts; and the post office closed. The last grocery store shut its doors in 1942, leaving the town without a single important business.

Today approximately sixteen people still live in Carneiro, and the local

Methodist church is active. The town is now a collection of homes and abandoned buildings, including an old gas station, a grocery store, a feed store, and the school. Signs around town inform the visitor of the history of Carneiro, but actually offer little real information. The story of Carneiro is the tale of a community with a vague past and a certain future—oblivion.[1]

ALLISON'S RANCH
Barton County

In many sections of Kansas, the first white habitations tended to be ranches located on major trails or branches of trails. The owners of these ranches established trading posts offering a limited stock of goods. As these places became more popular, they often developed into small communities or even bustling towns, if the business trade continued. Others remained small places, often eventually abandoned by their owners.

Although they called these places "ranches," the owners made little effort to raise cattle or crops. They were trading posts designed to catch the attention of travellers and Indians, and the ranchers always kept a small stock of goods to trade or sell. As a necessary precaution against Indian attacks, the owners usually enclosed the area within walls or palisades. They spread the ranch buildings around inside the enclosure and left an open court or corral in the center to contain all the animals.

Allison's Ranch, located on the Walnut Creek crossing of the Santa Fe Trail, was one of the smaller places that never developed into a major town, but its history is no less exciting. The ranch was named for William Allison, a former Santa Fe mail contractor from Independence, Missouri, and the head of a party of traders who established permanent homes in this area. The earliest mention of Allison on the Walnut Creek crossing was a pictorial Kiowa Indian calendar history for the year 1845 that illustrated a trading post at the crossing. No further mention was made of the place until the mid-1850s, which leaves historians to conjecture that the 1845 Kiowa notation was far too early. James J. Webb writes in the *Adventures in the Santa Fe Trade* of finding "two men formerly conductors of the mail from Independence to Santa Fe. I think it was in 1854 or 1855 they went to Walnut Creek and built a small mud fort." The other man mentioned was a trader named Booth.

Newspapers at Lawrence, Independence, and Santa Fe ran articles on Allison's enterprise. On August 6, 1855, the Lawrence *Kansas Free State* noted that

Mr. William Allison and Booth, known as famed prairie men, have determined to make a settlement at Walnut Creek on the Santa Fe road. A short
time since . . . they started on an expedition to the gold region, their mules
and provisions dying out . . . they abandoned the idea and returned more
determined to settle on Walnut Creek. Booth left a month or so since and
Allison this week, and from last reports of Booth's progress he was busily engaged in building houses and corrals, etc. This is the first attempt at building
by citizens made west of Council Grove.

The *Santa Fe Gazette* of March 3, 1855, gave the following account of Allison's operations:

Walnut Creek Station. Allison and Booth Respectfully informs their friends,
and the public generally, that they have established a trading house and general depot at Walnut Creek, on the Santa Fe road; where they keep constantly on hand groceries, and provisions suitable for travellers. Also for forage. With corrals and Inclosures for the security of the animals. Prices
reasonable.

Allison constructed several structures over a large area, many of which we
know about today only from diaries and contemporary accounts, such as
A. E. Raymond's entry on May 5, 1859: "Allison's Ranch was built of poles
inclosed with sod. The roof is nearly flat one story high. The stone walls
and sods inclose about an acre of land. This affords a strong protection
against Indians. Here is a mail station, Tavern, Corn and Hay, etc."
Some accounts describe Allison's place as a "fort," and it probably did
resemble one. Buildings were offset with barricades, walls, and stockades.
By 1857 Allison's Ranch was definitely in full operation, busy catering to
freighters, emigrants, and Indians. Joseph Cracklin described the area in the
June 25, 1857, *Lawrence Republican*: "We continued on as far as Walnut
Creek, thirty miles beyond the bend and found a poor, miserable country.
Mr. Booth, at the Indian trading post, informed me that they had tried to
raise corn and could not. . . . There were at the post 80 Rappahoe Indians
. . . we obtained some very nice robes."[1]
Mr. Booth, Allison's partner, did not last long. In the fall of 1857 he was
attacked and killed by a Mexican freighter, who split his head open with an
ax. The murderer was arrested in New Mexico three weeks later.[2] Allison
had other associates, including John Adkins, as trading partners. A large
percentage of their trade was conducted with the Kiowa and other Indian
tribes. Most of their provisions such as harness, wagon repairs, ammuni-

tion, and firearms were reserved for travelers. Business with whites occupied Allison's attention in the winter, and in the spring and summer, he freighted robes and pelts to Independence, Missouri. He brought back to the ranch provisions and merchandise he had received in return for the furs and robes.

William Allison, described as a fearless man, had only one arm. This condition resulted from a gunfight with his stepfather. Two shots were fired. One hit Allison in the arm, causing the loss of that limb. The other shot cost the stepfather his life.[3]

Allison did not operate his ranch for very long, for in 1859 he suffered a fatal heart attack. Chris and Charlie Rath took over the ranch and operated it in partnership for a few months. George Peacock was the next proprietor, but he managed it for only a few weeks. He was killed on September 9, 1860, by Chief Satank of the Kiowas. In 1901 R. M. Wright described Peacock's death in an address he gave in Dodge City:

> Peacock and Satank were great friends, as Peacock knew the sign language well. He had quite a large ranch and traded with the Indians and kept them supplied with whiskey. In consequence, the soldiers were always after him. . . . One day Satank said to him, "Peacock, write me a letter that I can show to the wagon bosses and get all the chuck I want. Tell them I am the great war chief of the Kiowa, and ask them to give me the very best in the shop."
>
> Peacock said, "All right, Satank," and sat down and penned this epistle: "This is Satank, the biggest liar, beggar, and thief on the Plains. What he doesn't beg of you, he will steal. Kick him out of your camp, as he is a lazy good-for-nothing Indian."
>
> Satank presented his letter several times to passing trains and, of course, got a very cold reception, or a rather warm one. One wagon boss blacksnaked him, after which indignity he sought a friend who read it to him.
>
> The next morning Satank took some of his braves and rode to Peacock's ranch. He then shot Peacock full of holes. . . . Then they went into the (ranch) building and killed every man present, except one, a weak individual, who was lying in one of the rooms, gored through the leg by a buffalo.

The ranch was occupied sporadically for the next eight years. In 1868 raiding Cheyenne burned most of it to the ground. For many years afterwards the impressive ruins of the place were noted by dozens of freighters and emigrants heading to new homes in the region. The army constructed Fort Zarah either very near or actually on the Allison Ranch site, and when they abandoned that post, the ruins of the fort were also plainly visible. About 300 yards to the northeast was the old graveyard containing about eighteen or twenty graves; most of the dead had neither a stick nor a stone to mark their resting place.[4]

Today Allison's Ranch is part of the Fort Zarah site. Old mounds and depressions remain at the historic Walnut Creek crossing, and recent archeological excavations have unearthed new discoveries at the location. Allison and his ranch are remembered only by authors and historians, or by an occasional visitor to old Fort Zarah.

ZARAH
Barton County

Near the many fortifications that dotted the prairie in the early days are the remains of what were lovingly called "hog ranches." These "ranches" had nothing to do with hog raising but had a lot to do with drinking, gambling, and prostitution. They were towns established solely for the pleasure of the soldiers stationed in the camps or forts nearby. When the forts were abandoned so were the hog ranches.

Settlers built the town of Zarah to serve the soldiers at Fort Zarah and located it just far enough away from the post that the U.S. Army could not interfere with its activities, but close enough to have military protection in case of an Indian attack. Zarah, one mile east of Fort Zarah, was the largest town in Barton County in 1872. The town took its name from the fort, which in turn took its name from Major H. Zarah Curtis, who was killed during the Civil War in the Baxter Springs Massacre of 1863.[1]

The town was a stopping place for traders headed east with hides, bullion, and Spanish goods from Santa Fe, New Mexico, and wagon trains headed west with tools, cloth, flour, canned goods, and other manufactured items. Livery stables, stores, a post office, and many saloons fronted on the main street, and the owners had visions of Zarah becoming a prairie metropolis when and if a railroad arrived.

While the soldiers were at the fort, Zarah's businesses continued to prosper, but when the soldiers left in 1872, the settlers knew any chance for the town's survival was slim. After a surveyor for the Santa Fe Railroad planned to place the tracks a mile from the townsite, Zarah was doomed.

The railroad established a station at Great Bend, a small community three miles west of Zarah. Less than a year later, Zarah was vacated. Speculators in its town lots pocketed their pride and tried to recover their losses by moving ahead to the next town on the railroad. The townspeople removed the businesses and houses from Zarah in late 1872 and moved most of the buildings to Great Bend and Ellinwood.

In 1873 an artist for *Harper's Weekly* chanced to pass by the skeleton of the old town and noted several coyotes skulking in the shadows of what was once a busy street. This unknown artist's sketch gave Zarah immortality; it is the only significant record of the town's existence.[2]

GALATIA
Barton County

Talk about a place "going to the dogs"! That was what residents and visitors alike thought of Galatia in its formative years.

Galatia, originally called Four Corners, was founded in 1885 fifteen miles southwest of Russell at the intersection of two county roads. David C. Barrows laid out the townsite; it was only two blocks square. Barrows was followed by David Butler, who built a country store, and Henry G. Weber, who renamed the town Galatia in honor of his hometown in Illinois. This was not the first name suggested for the town. A few brave souls wanted to call the place Dog Trot. Weber found it amusing to see the large number of dogs accompanying their owners to Sunday morning church services. In fact, dogs outnumbered owners two to one. The citizens felt that this name would do nothing to promote the town, so they dropped the idea of Dog Trot.

Names, however elegant, do not ensure prosperity. Granted, Galatia developed for a short time, but it never became a boomtown. The first building constructed was a United Brethren church that later became the American Lutheran. Then the settlers built a small country school south of town in a pasture donated by a community-minded farmer. They replaced the school two times, once in 1916 and again in 1929. By 1972 student enrollment was too low to continue classes, so county officials closed the school indefinitely.

Galatia's biggest chance for prosperity came in 1916 when the Santa Fe Railroad laid track through town. Quickly the Farmer's Union built a grain elevator, which brought farmers to town from all around the area. Next came the Galatia State Bank, the Widgen lumberyard, two creameries, a movie theater, dance hall, the Odd Fellows and Modern Woodmen Lodges, two more grain elevators, three general stores, a hotel, and a blacksmith shop.

In 1920 two investors erected a brick building for a 250-barrel flour mill. They hired a man named Golden, who had been a miller, at the preposterous salary of $250 a month. Although Golden moved to Galatia, he never had a chance to earn the money promised him. The whole project was a disaster, and the investors left without installing any machinery. After a few years, the building was sold for taxes several times, and one of the buyers eventually tore it down and used the brick to build a house in Russell.

In 1921 the town's population reached 202. The citizens petitioned the county commission to make Galatia a third-class city, which they did on January 18. An election was held, and fifty-four residents voted for C. H. Milberger to be their first mayor. The 1920s, however, were not kind to Galatia. Better roads allowed residents greater mobility to travel to larger towns for supplies, and the population began to drop. By 1950 half of the townspeople were still there, but by 1980 only sixty residents remained. The bank was voluntarily liquidated in 1967, the post office closed, and two disastrous fires on Main Street left gaps where buildings once stood. A co-op elevator and a tavern were the last businesses left in Galatia in the 1980s.[1]

Because some young families still want to call a small town home, and because with youth comes opportunity and ambition, Galatia may yet see a comeback.

BOYD
Barton County

In 1886 the Missouri Pacific Railroad came through Barton County and built the town of Boyd. *Kansas—A Historical Survey* included the town in one of its volumes: "Boyd is a station on the Missouri Pacific Railroad, four miles west of Hoisington and twelve miles northwest of Great Bend. It has a money order post office, and is a trading and shipping point in the neighborhood. The population was 40 in 1910."[1]

Boyd, one of the smallest towns in Kansas, was not always located at its present site or known by its present name. The history of the town actually began in 1873 when Samuel Maher, a Civil War veteran, opened the first bank in Great Bend. When the bank failed, Maher became editor of the *Arkansas Valley* newspaper and changed its name to the *Barton County Progress*. Maher secured authorization for a post office to be established on the Great Bend-Russell stage route known as the Star Route. A dugout that served as a general store was its first location. Later the building, a popular stage stop, was expanded into a two-story stone structure. The townspeople, out of respect for Maher's hard work in obtaining the post office, named the town Maherville in his honor.

In 1890 the Missouri Pacific passed approximately one mile south of Maherville, so the settlers moved the post office to a new building closer to the railroad tracks. The town still went by Maherville, but because the name was too long, the railroad changed it to Boyd, and for nearly eighteen years the town went by two names—Maherville to the citizens and Boyd to the Missouri Pacific. Several farmers in the vicinity petitioned to have the name changed officially to Boyd. The government accepted the petition.[2]

An Englishman, E. J. Eveleigh, was the founder and patriarch of the family that owned and operated the Boyd general store until its closing. His young wife died of pneumonia soon after moving to Boyd, and Eveleigh raised his seven children alone. Eveleigh's granddaughter, Mrs. Elmer Tindall of Hoisington, remembered her grandfather telling stories of the Indians who lived near the town in the early years. "He told me if the Indians decided they wanted anything, you let them have it and were happy if they just left," she said.

Despite some setbacks, Eveleigh made money in his store. He couldn't read or write, but he drew pictures for his customers of what he'd sell on credit. "He was just a little fella," Ray Smith of Hoisington recalled. "He never enjoyed spending money; he only enjoyed making it." From the general store, Eveleigh expanded his operations to include farming and cattle raising. He kept the cattle on a tract of land he owned near what is now the Cheyenne Bottoms. "He finally bought a Model T to check his cattle in," explained Smith. "He would ride the caboose into Kansas City when he shipped cattle and he always took a supply of crackers and cheese with him. He told me this story," Smith continued. "He always wore his working clothes to Kansas City and one time the police picked him up at the stockyards for vagrancy. So he told them to take him to the Stockyards National Bank. The bank told the police he could probably buy the bank out."

Eveleigh bought wheat from the area farmers and built an elevator on the tracks just east of the train depot. In the early 1900s, the wheat was hauled in by wagon and team. Years later, Eveleigh installed gas pumps outside his general store. Eveleigh lived well into his eighties and died a wealthy man. "He was always busy with something," Mrs. Tindall said. "He had a white Spitz dog that he taught to sit up in a chair and wear glasses and pretend to read the paper."

The social life in Boyd was not especially lively. "But I don't think it was boring," added Mrs. Tindall. "The roads weren't very good, but we were always having get-togethers at the Olivette church just north of Boyd." According to Mrs. Tindall the town was just a flag stop on the Missouri Pacific line. "That was quite an occasion when someone stood out there flagging a train to get on," she said. One of the men would put the mail sacks on cranes outside the depot and as the train came by, someone would hook the sack and take it onto the train. "It fascinated me how they'd hardly ever drop it," Mrs. Tindall recalled.[3]

One by one, the families left Boyd. In the 1930s the store and elevator stopped operations. Other than the creaking of a piece of metal on the old elevator when the wind blows, Boyd is silent.

HITSCHMANN
Barton County

Occasionally, but not often, entire communities go up on the auction block. And often hardy, spirited families are more than eager to buy a piece of Americana. Such was the scene in September 1986 in the little town of Hitschmann, nine miles northwest of Claflin.

Frank Hoffman, owner of the Hitschmann townsite, decided to sell the place when he retired. The town held special memories for him, however, for he had operated the Hitschmann Cash Store there for nearly sixty years. In the early years his store was the only social center for miles around.

Hoffman acquired the store from his father-in-law in 1927, and during the first few years he owned it, making a living was especially difficult. In a newspaper interview September 27, 1986, Hoffman noted, "Those were the Depression years and it was hard to make a go. We had to give a lot of credit and we didn't know if it was going to come in. But most of our credit all came in. It took about ten years for some of it to be paid off." Hoffman struggled until the late 1930s, providing his customers with everything from beans, sugar, rice, and coffee to clothing and tools. During the wheat harvest, crews would work most of the day until it became too hot, then they would head to Hoffman's and play pool in the basement. Hoffman built an addition on one side of the store, to be used for dancing. Every weekend locals filled the building and danced to the jukebox. Since no beer could be sold near the dance floor, Hoffman cut a hole in the wall and sold beer from there. On weekday evenings men sat around the coal-burning furnace and talked or played cards.

The town grew rapidly during the 1940s after an oil company rented some of Hoffman's land and built some "shotgun" shacks for the workers. Later the company sold the houses back to Hoffman, who rented them to the local residents. A school built in 1948, two grain elevators, a lumberyard, and another grocery store comprised the buildings on Main Street for several years. Hitschmann was named after a member of the township board, and Hoffman often thought about changing it to "Hoffman." He didn't, however, so the town's name remained the same.

When the oil boom ended in the 1940s so did the town. The school closed, and the district bused the students to nearby Claflin. By the 1980s, the town was a shadow of its former self. The town's last hurrah rang out with the auctioneer's gavel in September 1986. Nothing was sacred—thousands of items ranging from julep fountains to pens and pencils to bowling pins and tractors went up for bid. The final bidding was for the town itself, forty lots containing several houses, the Hoffman store, and some outbuildings. It all went to a ghost-town lover who wanted to own a town. He got his wish: today the town is private property.[1] For those of you who wish to own your own place, don't give up—in Kansas, a new ghost town seems to be made, and sold, every year.

RAYMOND
Rice County

Raymond, named for Emmaus Raymond, a director of the Santa Fe Railroad, is the oldest town in Rice County to retain its original name. It was established in 1872, a year later than Lyons, which was then called Atlanta, then Sterling, then Peace.

Almost immediately, Raymond became a rip-roaring shipping point for cattle from the Oklahoma panhandle. The town brazenly flaunted open saloons along its sand-encrusted main street and offered cattlemen every vice they could afford. The Atchison, Topeka & Santa Fe Railroad building west toward Colorado temporarily stopped at Raymond, giving the community the distinction of being an end-of-track town for a few months. During that time the population boomed to nearly 500 people. In the early 1870s, Raymond was an inspection point for all panhandle cattle herded overland to the Union Pacific at Ellsworth for shipment. The town became a rendezvous for cattlemen, cowboys, gamblers, and the other restless wanderers who populated the outposts of civilization.

Raymond's business district was several blocks long and included a few two-story buildings. The town had two rival hotels and a huge lumberyard that provided all the building supplies for most of the town as well as some neighboring communities. The largest structure was the American House, a three-story hotel and the center of social and business activities. This building was often the target of boisterous cowboys who rode into town discharging their firearms; the hotel's lights were an easy mark. In later years the walls of the office and dining room were dotted with bits of tin

The Santa Fe depot at Raymond, 1931.

that covered the holes in the plaster made by .44 caliber bullets. One early
resident and the town postmaster, George R. Gill, noted in a newspaper article that he saw Raymond "shot up" quite often in the cattle days. He
said that more than once he had to drop to the ground fast and worm his
way behind the nearest shelter while drunken cowboys shot at glasses,
lamps, and other popular targets.

Raymond held an important position for a time as a purveyor of mail to
new counties. In the early 1870s the town was the central postal point for
Stafford County, responsible for relaying the mail to the settlers by pony
courier, a thirty-five mile trip across country. There were no roads, and it
was a two-day roundtrip.

As the settlers forced the cowboys farther west, Raymond lost its wild
and woolly reputation. One of the last reminders of those days was a saloon
that lasted, remarkably enough, past the beginning of prohibition and well
into the 1880s. When the saloon finally closed, the false-fronted building
still had a sign that read in bold black letters "SALOON."

In 1904 Raymond experienced several disastrous fires. The entire business district on the west side of the street consisted of frame stores that
burned down one by one with uncanny regularity. In 1905 the schoolhouse
and the Santa Fe depot were added to the list of fires in town, but no sus-
pects were ever arrested. As good sometimes follows bad, out of the confla-
gration arose a new brick business district.

At one time, Black Angus cattle bred at Raymond were well known all over the United States. The Parish & Schroeder Ranch was the largest breeder of Black Polled Angus stock, and they exhibited this Parish strain at nearly every western state fair, including the prestigious annual Chicago Livestock Show.[1]

Raymond continued to prosper into the twentieth century; however, as for many communities, the decade of the 1930s was difficult. Many small businesses closed, and the Santa Fe Railroad made less frequent stops. Ranchers began shipping their livestock from larger central Kansas towns, especially nearby Lyons and Great Bend. Since then, the population has slowly dropped. Today a few original buildings are left, and some residents still remain, but the town is very different from the rough and rowdy cattle shipping point that once scandalized the county.

FREDERICK
Rice County

Frederick is a ghost town with a lot of "ifs" attached to its history. *If* there had been enough water, it would have been a railroad division point with a roundhouse, offices, and a depot. *If* it had been a division point, the name would have been Golden City or Dacey. And *if* it hadn't been for a tornado in 1914, and a fire in 1934, Frederick still might be what it once was—the largest town in Rice County.

Frederick was founded in 1878 when the firm of Thomas & Turner decided to build a town there. They named it Golden City and nicknamed it Dacey. Nothing further developed on the site until 1887, when the Missouri Pacific Railroad built through the area and selected Dacey as their division point on the Great Colorado Short Line. The railroad needed a large well for its use near the tracks. As it turned out, water was scarce there but plentiful a mile west, so they moved the town west and renamed it "Frederic." They added the "k" later, probably out of respect for Frederick Litchfield, an early settler. The town was also a stop for wagon trains moving west through the area from Salina, Ellsworth, Hutchinson, and Great Bend.[1]

When the town became a railroad center, it boomed overnight. The population was estimated around 1,000 at its peak. There were three grain elevators, a bank, a three-story hotel, many stores, a flour mill, two blacksmith shops, a dentist, several doctors, a newspaper, some fraternal organizations, a lumberyard, a school, and a thirty-six member cornet band. This economic growth occurred when Frederick was the largest town in Rice County.

Two tragic events in the twentieth century caused the town's demise. First, a tornado struck the town in 1914. Though there was no loss of life, many of the businesses were destroyed and not rebuilt. Then, in 1934, at the height of the depression, a disastrous fire started in a wooden grain elevator and jumped from one building to another. When the blaze was finally brought under control, most of the structures on Main Street were gone.

One landmark that escaped the flames was Frederick's concrete jail, which still stands today. This jail was reportedly built during the 1880s, and it housed many cowboys who "shot up the town" during the days of the cattle drives. Other frequent occupants were townspeople arrested for being drunk and disorderly. Prisoners' children often appeared at the door of the jail and cried until even a strong man like the sheriff could do nothing but release the parent. The jail was used for the last time in the 1930s, when Marshal Fred Neilsen hit a drunk over the head and hauled him away to be locked up until sober. The jail's grated metal front door, rusty from exposure to the elements, still opens to admit visitors. The rear portion of the jail contains a broken metal cot that was once attached to the wall but now hangs loose on one end. Oddly enough, no one has attempted to tear down the old jail. Residents in town tried several times to blow up the bank vault, a similar structure, but were unsuccessful. Once, they set off eleven sticks of dynamite in an attempt to destroy it, but when the smoke cleared, the vault was still standing.[2]

Today Frederick is a quiet little country town of about twenty people. Only the jail and several miscellaneous buildings remain—a far cry from the days when Frederick catered lavishly to railroaders and settlers heading west.

PARADISE

Russell County

Paradise was so named by a group of explorers travelling through central Kansas. When they reached the region west of present Russell, they found freshly burned prairie and no feed for their horses. The group headed north and came to an area where the grass was green and lush. They called the place Paradise.

Its name notwithstanding, the region presented certain problems for the early homesteaders. On one occasion, a thief stole several horses from a neighbor of W. T. Houser, who with two other men rode out after him. The next day they brought the horses back, but not before they buried the thief, boots and all. In 1874 the settlers experienced a grasshopper invasion

The Union Pacific depot at Paradise around the turn of the century. Many of the town buildings in the background have since disappeared.

firsthand. On August 8 millions of "Minnesota hoppers" blotted out the sun. Terrified, the people seized their children and ran inside for cover. Soon a layer of crawling grasshoppers covered the ground. They ate the bark and leaves off the trees, they ate the corn, and sometimes they even ate the stalk. Although the settlers squashed them, crushed them under foot, clubbed and burned them, the fight was futile. They lived to return the next year.

Paradise actually came into existence with the coming of the railroad in 1889. At that time, the settlers renamed it Iva Mar, after a beautiful girl in the area. This name was still on the township records as late as 1909. Paradise boomed and had a hotel, a bank, a grocery store, two general stores, a barber shop, two grain elevators, a lumberyard, a hardware store, and a doctor's office. According to the *Russell Record* of December 18, 1897: "The only railroad stop in Paradise Township is Paradise. The population of the town can be written in two figures, but from a business standpoint it would be reckoned quite a town as it is the main shipping point for a large territory devoted almost exclusively to the livestock industry."

The Paradise State Bank opened in 1911, and within a year it had been robbed. The thief first cut the telephone lines and tied up the people in the bank, then he headed out of town with the money. Among those in the bank at the time was Bill Elliott, a man who walked on crutches. As the robber was tying his feet, he complained that the ropes were too tight, so the robber loosened them. This made it easy for him to get away first and go for the sheriff.

Another story covering the robbery features Tom Sparks, who was headed into town from the north when he met a man who was picking up "something" on the ground. When Tom asked him if he could help, the man said he was just picking up some nails that had fallen from his pocket. Later it was discovered that he was the thief, and he was picking up the money he had dropped accidentally. The sheriff's posse soon caught up with the robber and shot him.

In the 1930s fire destroyed several business buildings on Main Street, including the bank. The depression brought highs and lows to Paradise, however, for also in the 1930s Paradise's most historic landmark, the sixty-five foot limestone watertower, was built by the Works Projects Administration. Building the tower gave thirty-five men employment for about nine months during 1937. Each limestone block weighed about fifty pounds, and the workers lifted them from one to another until the tower reached twenty-five feet. Then, near the tower, they assembled an elevator powered by gasoline to lift the blocks the remaining forty feet. Great skill was needed to cut the limestone to the right size. When it was completed, the tower stored 65,000 gallons of water. The townspeople later learned that this watertower was the only one of its kind in the state.

Today most of the business district in Paradise is gone, the victim of the depression years. A small but loyal population remains, however. The town receives letters addressed simply to "City of Paradise" from folks around the country who are interested in knowing what Paradise is really like. Just ask the Angel family, descendants of one of the first families in Paradise.[1]

YOCEMENTO
Ellis County

"Yocemento," a combination of the words Yost and cement, was founded in 1906, the year that I. M. Yost and Professor Erasmus Haworth first met in Hays. Yost had come to Hays in the early 1880s and founded the Yost Milling Company. Haworth, a professor of the School of Geology and Mines at Kansas University, was revising and enlarging the first geological map of the state for his classes, and during the summer of 1906 he was busy making a survey of the Central Plains.

"I had heard of Ike Yost," Haworth said in later years, recounting his first meeting in the flour mill office with Mr. Yost. "I wanted to meet the man. I knew he had been in Hays many years and thought he would give me some pointers on topography of the country." After the geologist outlined the kind of information he wanted, the mill owner drove him to an area of outcroppings of different rock formations. About six miles west of Hays at a wide bend in Big Creek, the professor suggested they climb to the top of a high hill on the south bank. After carefully studying the rocks, he remarked that there was a thick bed of shale underlying the chalk cliff, and he was reasonably certain that cement could be made at the site "cheaper than anywhere else in Kansas." Yost was quite enthusiastic about such an enterprise, and in the next few weeks, the men began tentative plans for the project that would materialize within the next two years.

Before he left town, Haworth presented Yost with several rough drawings of the proposed plant and a cost estimate. He proposed that the cement mill be built within the proximity of a plentiful water supply and next to the Union Pacific Railroad right-of-way. Haworth pointed out that the rock could be quarried and placed on a chute, leaving gravity to do the work of transporting it down the side of the hill directly into the huge crushers. Vats for the mixture, furnaces for the finishing process, and barrel packing for the shipments could all be housed in the same plant, which would cut down on costs. Both men felt certain that the Union Pacific would be willing to help in developing the "largest" industrial enterprise in western Kansas and would build side tracks so the freight cars could back up to the loading docks.

In fact, Yost was the brains behind the project, and one day after their plans had progressed to a certain point he said:

> "See here Erasmus, we've got to enlarge the scope of our plans. We should have a town here. Maybe it will get larger than Hays. Why not buy out a townsite, start selling lots as well as stock in the mill? The Union Pacific will build a depot and we'll get them to stop with passengers as well as freight trains. There will be people coming here from all over the country because we're going to sell stock in the East as well as the West. We'll have a hotel, stores, office buildings, everything, even a newspaper.[1]

Haworth agreed.

They completed the plant in less than three years at a cost of $2 million.[2] Some handwritten papers from the early 1900s detail the events at Yocemento. The words are nearly obscured and the paper brown and fragile,

but the statements concerning the founding of Yocemento, "A New Industry for Ellis County," are clear:

> We understand the capital for this [plant] to be $750,000. So large an
> amount of money invested means much to Ellis County.
>
> It is said the work of constructing the plant will begin soon. It will employ
> not less than 500 men; it means a big payroll. It means a ready market for all
> sorts of other products; it means the advent of certain other enterprises
> which will bring large sums of money to our people.
>
> July 21, 1906—Mr. Yost and Mr. Woodworth, civil engineer of the Union
> Pacific Railroad, with two assistants went to Hogback [local name of the
> area] to lay out the ground for the cement plant and the side-track. . . .
>
> For the present the offices will be in Hays City. The mill is to be located at
> Hogback and a town will probably be started there and named "Yoce-
> mento." . . .
>
> March 23, 1907—The busiest place in all western Kansas at this time is the
> thriving town of Yocemento. An army of men is kept at work, in fact much
> trouble is experienced in getting laborers enough to do the work. The large
> cement piers on which the steel frame is to rest are now being put in. A 15-
> room hotel is built and is sheltering and feeding the workmen. A restaurant
> under the supervision of C. W. Bell is doing a good business.
>
> June 27, 1908—The first cement made by the U. S. Portland Cement Co.
> at Yocemento was brought to town by Clement Unrein on Wednesday. The
> cement will be used in the construction of a new flouring mill. J. H. Ward
> was given the first sack put out for which he paid $10. The cement mill is
> now working night and day.[3]

Within a short time, Yocemento became a town of 350 people and had a
depot, a post office, a forty-room hotel, a company store, a restaurant, and
an office building. A weekly newspaper, the *Yocemento Star*, was printed in
Lawrence, expressed to Ike Yost, and mailed from Hays.

When the mill was in full operation, more than 200 men were on the
payroll. Nearly all of them drove back and forth from Hays to their jobs;
some used horse and buggies and a few even walked the six miles each way
daily. Contractors used the cement produced there to build the Union Station in Kansas City and to pave the Denver Tramway. For several years the
mill showed a small margin of profit,[4] but by 1912 the cost of fuel became
prohibitive due to the fact that the furnaces were fired with coal shipped
from as far away as the Wyoming and Colorado coal mines. Then the
southeastern Kansas cement companies began cutting their prices below

market value, threatening Yocemento's economy. At the same time, the Boettcher Cement Company in Denver started expanding their operations and building new cement plants throughout Colorado. Their company officials flatly told the Union Pacific Railroad that they did not want competition from the Yocemento plant, which added to the problems that eventually broke the mill at Yocemento. When the plant began to lose money, the stockholders held Yost and Haworth at fault and forced them to relinquish control. A few years later the industry declared bankruptcy. When Boettcher, their Colorado competitor, proposed to buy the mill, the directors voted to take their offer, and the new owners promptly dismantled the plant. For years afterward the Boettcher estate retained ownership of this section of land.[5]

Handwritten letters from the 1900s told of the last years of Yocemento:

1918—It was sad to watch such a perfect dream die. The next general agreed and predicted Mr. Yost was about 30 years ahead of his time. When Western Kansas began coming into its own with a tremendous building boom in cities and towns, the construction of concrete highways, natural gas for the furnaces at low cost, the thrilling dream of Mr. Yost, along with those of the investors would all have come true.[6]

Although they came close to losing everything, Haworth and Yost did not go deeply in debt over the Yocemento failure. Yost turned all his attention to his flour mill and continued to prosper, and Haworth, who always had an interest in the circus business, bought race horses and had a large stable of trotters and pacers; they made the circuits throughout the Midwest during the racing season. Meanwhile he continued as the state geologist, a position he held for thirty years.

Today there are a few impressive foundations left on the site. Nearby are two large grain elevators, the only monuments to a town that slowly slipped into obscurity.[7]

ALEXANDER
Rush County

The town of Alexander occupies a unique place in the history of Rush County, for it is the oldest town in the county; it was established five years before the county was organized. In 1869 the site, first known as "Harvey's Ranch," was originally a trading post on the north bank of Walnut Creek built by Alexander Harvey, the namesake of the town. The place consisted of a log store building with a lookout above the portholes in the walls. Defenders could shoot or scare away any hostile Indians who might attempt to scale the stockade that surrounded the building. Later settlers used the stockade as a refuge during frequent Indian scares. The store was strategically located on the Fort Hays to Fort Dodge Military Road, and the owner sold supplies to the settlers, freighters, and military men passing through the area.

Occasionally when Harvey had to make a trip to Hays to replenish his stock of tobacco, meal, flour, bacon, whiskey, and hunter's supplies, he left his clerk in charge of the store. During one of his absences, someone looted the store and left the clerk for dead with a bullet hole in his body.

In 1872, after the first families began to arrive in the valley, W. R. S. King and Robert Stephens settled on the townsite. These men were followed in 1874 by settlers who changed the entire landscape of the valley. This second group forced Harvey to sell his holdings, then established the community of Alexander. Harvey remained in town for a few years teaching school and operating a store in his stockade. He even married one of King's daughters.

In 1874 the settlers experienced a serious grasshopper invasion—the insects stripped the leaves from the trees and devoured all other vegetation. This infestation was a discouraging setback, for it was difficult enough to grow anything in the hard Kansas soil.

Alexander remained a small community until 1886, when the Chicago, Kansas & Western Railroad came through the township, working its way up the north side of the Walnut River. Unfortunately, Alexander was on the south side. The railroad made attempts to resurvey, but in the end the town had to move to the north side of the river.

When the town was reestablished, businesses began to boom, led by Kepner Store. Mr. Kepner wanted to locate as close to the tracks as possible; however, he ended up too close. The railroad ordered him to move because they wanted to build a depot and stockyards. Kepner's store was right in the middle of the stockyards! W. R. S. King, the next merchant on the south side, literally moved his store building across the Walnut River to a prominent place in the new town. George Dickerson and Robert Waddle built a large two-story drug emporium and meeting hall. Alex Walker also built a store, and T. E. Ickes constructed a combination hardware and grocery store. Grant Kepner opened a small business where he supposedly sold "soft drinks," but some claimed that these drinks were not all that "soft." P. H. Kraft built a blacksmith shop, and next to it was a large stone creamery that later became a local landmark. The Ray Phillips House was the only hotel in town, and the owners moved it near the United Brethren

The Santa Fe depot at Alexander, 1931.

church from a farm three miles south of Alexander. The hotel finally went out of business when, according to gossip, Phillips's wife ran away with a handsome boarder.

After the arrival of the railroad, Alexander boomed for several years. By the turn of the century, the town had about 200 people, its peak population. The Alexander State Bank was soon established, and Dr. L. A. Latimer opened a unique hospital—the Ear, Eye, Nose, and Throat Hospital, the only one of its kind west of the Mississippi River. Dr. Latimer had a large practice and attracted patients from all over the United States. However, the hospital lasted only a few years, and little is known about it today.

Subsequent decades were not kind to Alexander. In time, railroad service became limited, and many residents moved elsewhere. As in other small country towns, the depression years of the 1930s had a devastating economic impact. Today Alexander is a small place, nothing like what it was in its heyday.[1]

6

SOUTH CENTRAL
KANSAS

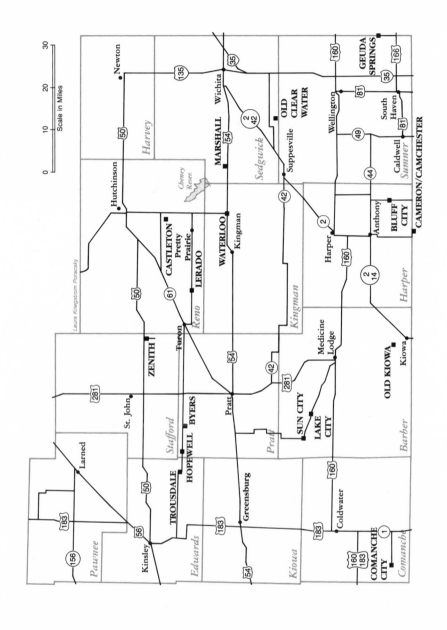

Scale in Miles
0   10   20   30

Laura Kriegstrom Poracsky

Newton

Harvey

50

135

35

160

GEUDA
SPRINGS

166

81

35

Wichita

2
42

OLD
CLEAR
WATER

South
Haven

81

MARSHALL

54

Suppesville

Wellington

49

81

Caldwell

Sumner

CAMERON/CAMCHESTER

Hutchinson

Cheney
Reser.

Sedgwick

42

44

CASTLETON

Pretty
Prairie

WATERLOO

Kingman

Anthony

BLUFF
CITY

LERADO

Reno

Kingman

Harper

160

61

50

Turon

ZENITH

54

Medicine
Lodge

2
14

Harper

281

St. John

Stafford

HOPEWELL   BYERS

Pratt

42

281

SUN CITY

LAKE
CITY

OLD KIOWA

Kiowa

Larned

TROUSDALE

50

Greensburg

Pratt

Barber

156

183

Edwards

183

160

Coldwater

56

Kinsley

Pawnee

54

Kiowa

183

COMANCHE
CITY

160
183

1

Comanche

GEUDA SPRINGS
Sumner County

Looking down the nearly deserted main street today, you'll find it hard to
visualize a town "so crowded with visitors that much more hotel room and
many more cottages were imperatively needed." But from 1880 to 1905,
Geuda Springs was the "health center of the Southwest." Its reputation
was established from a series of natural springs that flowed nearby. The water from the springs contained beneficial properties that supposedly cured
many ailments.[1]

The curative properties of the Geuda Springs's mineral waters were probably known to local Indian tribes for many years before white settlers built
homes there. The first mention of the springs comes from an 1857 account
written by a Dunkard missionary named Jacob Klepper, who visited the
Cherokee Nation encamped in the vicinity of Bartlesville, Oklahoma. Klepper met a white man, a Spanish Catholic, who was living with the Indians.
According to Klepper's account, a savage bull gored and critically wounded
Grey Eagle, one of the finest hunters of the tribe. He lay for weeks near
death. His sweetheart, Mona Lona, the daughter of the Spaniard, stayed
by his side, saying her rosary and caring for him. The Indians finally decided
to take Grey Eagle to a distant "fountain of life," where they believed the
healing waters could make the blind see, the lame walk, and the wounded
whole. The Indians placed the warrior on a litter swing between two ponies and started on their journey. After several days of travel, they reached
their destination of "Auawa Geuda," or "healing waters."[2]

At the springs, according to Klepper, were camped members of other Indian tribes—the Omaha, Cheyenne, and Comanche—all curious to see Grey
Eagle healed. The group gathered around the medicine men of the tribe
and drank the waters of the springs from buffalo horns, which were supposed to increase the potency of the waters. Twenty days later, Grey Eagle
was well, and his marriage to Mona Lona took place at the springs with all
the visiting tribes participating.

The first white settler in the immediate area was C. R. Mitchell. Mitchell
came from Indiana to practice law, and history credits him with being the
first man to recognize the moneymaking possibilities of the springs. In 1880
he walled up the springs so that they were neat and easily accessible, then
he built a large hotel and bath house nearby. Mitchell also started a newspaper on the second floor of a brick building that he constructed on the west
side of the main street.[3] Just north of the springs Mitchell created an artifi-
cial lake called Lake Juanita, which was fed by nearby Salt Creek. An arte-

This promotional advertisement lured prospective tourists to the town mineral baths and made Geuda Springs one of the most popular health resorts in the state.

The Geuda Springs bath house, now an impressive ruin, was a beautiful building when it was first constructed.

sian well was also constructed on the southeast corner of the business district.

Mitchell placed his hotel under the management of Joe Buckwalter, who served family-style meals. The hotel flourished year-round. The bath house was a popular spot with people suffering from all kinds of ailments. One story was told of a patient whose entire body was covered with eczema sores. After three weeks of treatment that included baths and internal consumption of the spring waters, her sores were completely gone. Another tale was told of a group of old men who sat hour after hour with their feet in mud mixed from spring water for treatment of their corns—and it worked! As an added attraction, the owner brought a water buffalo to Geuda Springs and tethered it in a field nearby. The animal was reportedly very tame and aroused much interest among the visitors, especially the children. On another occasion Mitchell diverted his customers with a Siberian bear.

During the 1880s and early 1890s, the springs boomed to the point of gaining worldwide fame. Visitors from all over the United States and from England were not uncommon. The bottled water was shipped overseas. New hotels dotted the landscape—one fancy hotel-sanitarium called the Mockingbird Lodge treated nearly 400 nonsurgical patients a day. The town offered a gun club and a bath house that had a dance pavilion on the second floor. Most residences had rooms for rent; a few smaller private cottages were built by rich easterners. Excursion trains from as far away as St.

A Kansas & Southwestern locomotive in Geuda Springs, ca. 1910.

Louis brought in hundreds of people who came to drink the water and stay in the hotels. Four physicians set up practice in town, and during an active season they were extremely busy diagnosing illnesses.[4]

Geuda Springs published a promotional pamphlet that circulated all over the United States. The brochure described the springs to prospective guests:

> [The bath house] is one of the finest structures in the state. It is built of brick and stone and veneered with pressed brick, contains 66 rooms with complete arrangements for giving all kinds of baths including Turkish, Russian, Shower, Douche, Sitz, Pack, Vapor, and common baths and is believed to be the largest and best arranged Bath House in the United States. . . .
>
> These springs are a sure cure for Diseases of the Kidney, Rheumatism, Sciatica, Ulceration of the Uterus, and female weakness, as well as Dyspepsia, blood and skin diseases and Salt Rheum. . . . The mineral springs are seven in number and bubble up in the crystal pure air within a space of less than 20 feet square.[5]

One of Geuda's more famous patients was Luke Short, a famous gunslinger and gambler who was best known for his association with Wyatt

Earp and Bat Masterson. He also operated the Long Branch Saloon in Dodge City in the early 1880s. After disagreements with the city over how he managed the gambling parlors, Short left Dodge City for Texas, where he stayed for a few years. In 1893, at the age of thirty-nine, he suddenly found himself terminally ill, and as a last resort he came back to Kansas to Geuda Springs and the plush Gilbert Hotel. Ironically, Short came and went in this town virtually unnoticed. At the time the area was teeming with thousands of homeseekers awaiting the opening of the Cherokee Strip.[6] On the morning of September 8, eight days before the land rush, Short died of "dropsy" at the hotel. The town's newspaper, the *Geuda Springs Herald*, wrote the obituary. The paper reported that he was embalmed by W. A. Repp, a Geuda Springs undertaker, and that his body was sent to Fort Worth, Texas. The *Herald* also mentioned that Short's wife and two brothers accompanied the body to Texas.

A week later, when the Cherokee Strip run began, Geuda Springs lost a large percentage of its population, and the town's decline can probably be traced back to this single event. Nevertheless, patients kept coming to the springs until after the turn of the century. In 1904 a sample of the town's water was entered in a competition at the Louisiana Exhibition in St. Louis. In this world contest, this particular sample won second place![7]

The next three years, however, were disastrous. A series of fires ravaged the community, destroying many of the hotels, bath houses, cottages, and other improvements. Most of these structures were never rebuilt. The Gilbert Hotel was one of these casualties. Schemes to revitalize the springs have met with limited success. Dr. John R. Brinkley, the famous "goat gland" doctor and Kansas gubernatorial candidate, attempted to bottle the spring water and sell it in grocery stores all over the state. His efforts were genuine enough, but the evaporation process used in bottling the water removed most of the chemical contents that made it healthy in the first place. Federal food and drug agents intervened and stopped production. In December 1947, a group of Wichita businessmen organized the Geuda Springs Development Company. These men drew up extensive plans to rehabilitate the springs, bottle the water for commercial purposes, build a 48-room hotel, and erect a sanitarium. The enterprise was about to get under way when one of its largest financial backers died unexpectedly, and the project died with him. A few years later, the town had hopes of getting the government to build a Veterans Administration Hospital there, but these hopes were dashed when the hospital was constructed in Wichita.[8]

Today nearly all the original structures are gone, as well as Lake Juanita.

Resort ruins in Geuda Springs, 1956.

If the springs are still running, they are well hidden under a dense growth of trees and brush.

One of the town's leading citizens, James Tuttle, once argued with the city over the construction of his large home overlooking the townsite. His plans required that an alley be vacated, which the city refused to do. In disgust, Tuttle remarked, "Go to hell. I will build up on the hill and watch your damned town die!" His prophesy came true. Tuttle's beautiful home long outlasted most everything else in this one-time health resort.

BLUFF CITY
Harper County

There were two Bluff Cities in the history of Harper County. The first was a fraud from the beginning. The second Bluff City was a one-time boom-town whose economy collapsed after the Cherokee Strip Run in 1893.

The story of the first Bluff City is commonly entitled the "buffalo skull swindle." It was a scheme created by two soldiers of fortune—George Boyd and William Horner of Baxter Springs. During the winter of 1872–73, the state legislature laid out several counties in preparation for settlement. Boyd and Horner saw an opportunity to make some money in this new

Main street of Bluff City during its heyday, ca. 1910.

land. Early in March 1873 they made the acquaintance of N. W. Wiggins, a grocer in Barter's general merchandise store in Baxter Springs. Since business was slow, they easily persuaded Wiggins to stock a wagon with provisions and head west with them to organize one of the new counties. Wiggins supplied the groceries, Boyd and Horner supplied the team and wagon—and a city directory of Cincinnati, Ohio.

A month later the trio arrived in Harper County. They found only one man in the entire area—George Lutz, a trapper whom they employed as a hunter for the group. First the men built a one-room log house on Bluff Creek and gave it the imposing name of "Bluff City." Then they gathered several large buffalo skulls, which were to represent county officials. They lined these skulls up in front of the cabin and etched fictitious names and their offices in the bones. "Daniel Holson" was county clerk; "H. H. Weaver," "H. P. Fields," and "Samuel Smith" were the buffalo skull county commissioners. A more impressive government could not be found anywhere!

Boyd, Horner, and Wiggins drew up a petition with signatures of forty persons taken from the Cincinnati directory. The petition declared the formation of a temporary county government with Bluff City as county seat. They also proclaimed Bluff City the largest trading center in the county. The petition reached Governor Thomas Osborn on July 13, 1873. Boyd and Horner had mailed it in Hutchinson, then a community consisting of a dozen houses on the Santa Fe Railroad. As per their request, the state appointed the county officers named in the petition without any investigation.

Then "John Davis" (another skull) took a county census out of the Cincinnati directory and reported that there were 641 inhabitants in the county. The report of this "census taker" was approved by three more "skulls"—T. J. Jones, J. D. Main, and J. G. Howe. The state approved the organization of the county and ordered an election to decide on the county seat, elect the officers, and vote on the bond issues.

The county "residents" were anxious to vote the bonds—$25,000 for a courthouse and $15,000 for other improvements. A St. Louis bonding house sold the bonds to innocent purchasers who, unfortunately for Boyd, Horner, and Wiggins, came to Bluff City in September to collect the interest on their "investments." At this point, the state decided to conduct an investigation and discovered the swindle. By then, however, Wiggins, Boyd, Horner, and the money were nowhere to be found. Horner was known to have used the same scam at least one more time, when he helped create Comanche County and the town of Smallwood, and again vanished before the fraud was discovered.

It was 1876 and 1877 before the first real settlers arrived in Harper County. Many saw the remains of the log house at "Bluff City" with the buffalo skulls in front, but they thought nothing of it. Unfortunately, Harper County residents eventually had to pay for this bizarre swindle. The con artists reappeared years later to tell their story, but by that time, the statute of limitations had expired and prosecution was impossible.[1]

The second Bluff City began in 1886, when the Borderline Town and Land Company was assisting in the construction of the St. Louis, Kansas & Southwestern Railroad. The town promoters sent James Glover from Arkansas City to the area to work for their interests. Glover pitched his tent on the present Bluff City site on October 6, 1886, and when he found the location favorable for building, he had the town platted on November 20. Within a month, the town company sold $35,000 worth of lots, and nearly 200 men had moved their families there.[2]

One of the first businesses in town was the newspaper office. On December 30 the *Bluff City Tribune*, with Will C. Barnes as editor, began printing newspapers in an uncompleted building. The *Tribune* was just one in a long line of Bluff City newspapers that included the *Herald*, the *Independent*, the *Messenger*, and the *News*. The first issue of the *Tribune* offered these insights into the fledgling town:

> There are forty buildings on the townsite in process of erection, but one of which is completed and that not fully. The buildings are all large and commodious. A 30 room hotel, complete in all its apportionments is being

The Bluff City State Bank shortly after completion in 1902.

erected by the company and is to be completed by January 20. Several large stocks of goods are now being opened by and within ten days Bluff City will be doing a rushing business in all lines of trade. All this has been done in the space of four weeks. . . . The plans for the (railroad) round house, freight house, and car shops are now complete. . . . The selection of the site for Bluff City was most happily made, both as a healthful place of residence and as regards of beauty, fertility and scope of the country tributary to it.

The town planners set aside eleven acres in Bluff City for a park, first named Walnut Grove, later Glover Park. The park became famous nationally as one of the most beautiful in the United States. For a time, it held the title of the largest per capita park in the world.

Between 1886 and 1890 the town grew rapidly, and by 1891 the community had over 1,500 residents. Stores and businesses of all kinds were represented, including not one but two pastry shops! Unlike other communities, Bluff City never earned a reputation for lawlessness. It was primarily a railroad and farming community and never even had a saloon.

In 1887 the town founders incorporated Bluff City and elected James Glover their first mayor; he served in this capacity for sixteen years. During this time, the boomtown was the terminal point for the St. Louis & San Francisco Railroad and earned much of its trade catering to visitors who disembarked there. In order to make these guests more comfortable, local

The "Anthony Boosters" with their motorcars on parade down the main street of Bluff City, ca. 1917.

businessmen constructed the commodious Chillocco Hotel. This hotel's dining room was large enough to accommodate an entire train crew at one time. Engraved silverware graced the tables at every meal, and the proprietor had a young daughter who entertained the guests with ballet performances. Unfortunately, in later years the hotel burned down.[3]

The opening of the Cherokee Strip in 1893 signaled the beginning of the end for the town's economy. Many residents had built only temporary homes in anticipation of the run, and after it was over they packed up and left. Most of the vacant frame buildings were moved across the border where they became readymade housing in Waketa, Oklahoma. As much as 75 percent of the town's population left within a year after the opening of the Cherokee Strip, and the town never fully recovered from the loss.

In 1905 the railroad that was expected in Bluff City built into Anthony, and with it went the railroad shops and the round house. James Glover came to the rescue by briefly luring another railroad into town, the Kansas Southwestern out of Arkansas City. Associated with the Santa Fe, the railroad brought some extra jobs and prestige, albeit small and temporary. During this period several fires destroyed most of the frame buildings on Main Street, leaving only the brick stores intact. The depression of the 1930s dealt Bluff City a hard blow, especially after the local bank closed and moved to the Citizens National Bank of Anthony. In the late 1960s and early 1970s, the loss of the grade and high schools to consolidation of the

Bluff City State Bank in ruins, 1985. This was the last impressive structure left on Main Street.

school districts was a devastating blow to the town's morale. In the last few years the demolition of the impressive bank building on Main Street has left the community with few reminders of the town's nineteenth-century boom. Although the building long stood empty, it had become a town monument. Another old landmark, Glover Park, still exists, but it has seen years of neglect and decay. Recent attempts to revive interest in the park have been only intermittently successful, and it stands as a four-block memorial to the early civic planners.[4]

Bluff City now has about eighty residents, all with great civic pride. But time has not been kind to the century-old town, and the future promises little relief. A few old structures, an antique store, and Glover Park are still there, however, and weekend travelers in southern Kansas should definitely consider making a visit.

CAMERON/CAMCHESTER
Harper County

The days prior to the opening of the Cherokee Strip in the early 1890s were exciting for the people of southern Kansas. The settlers who populated the small border towns in anticipation of securing land claims in Indian Territory on a "first come, first served" basis brought temporary prosperity to many of these communities. Once the Cherokee Strip was opened, however, the boom ended, and many towns like Cameron in Harper County faced total economic collapse.

We know Cameron began as a trading post in the late 1880s, but only scant information exists about the town before the early 1890s. Ten miles west of Bluff City where the Big Sandy Creek crosses the state line, Cameron was undoubtedly little more than a rest stop for travelers.[1] The *Anthony Journal*, March 31, 1893, described progress at the new townsite:

> So many inquiries concerning our new Town of Cameron, Kansas, are coming to the office of the company that we find it impossible to answer them as fully as they deserve. The State Line Town Company charter . . . was filed with the Kansas Secretary of State on Feb. 18, 1893. . . . By a glance at the map it will at once be noticed that Cameron is the only town lying directly on the dividing line between Kansas and the Cherokee Strip. . . .
>
> Cameron is the present terminus of the Hutchinson & Southern R.R. By April 1st, trains will be running regularly to the new town. Over 200 people from Wichita, Hutchinson, Kingman, Harper, and Anthony looked the town over and many bought lots on the ground. Four lumber firms have purchased lots for yards. One man is now building a good storeroom. . . . The H. & S. road will immediately put in a good depot. One or two elevators are soon to be built and a flouring mill is the latest project.
>
> There is no better point for investment than Cameron. With the opening of the strip there will be a great demand for supplies, lumber, coal, dry goods, groceries, etc. There is no doubt that as soon as the new lands are thrown open for settlement, Cameron will extend her limits across the line and much building will at once follow. . . .
>
> The company invites you to visit Cameron. We do not wish to boom the town. It will grow without booming. But we want all who are thinking of the new country to visit the ''Empress of the Border.''

The *Anthony Weekly Bulletin*, May 19, 1893, noted that: ''Cameron is to have a newspaper. It will be named the Cameron Journal and the initial number will appear in 2 or 3 weeks. J. M. Simmons will be the editor.''

During that summer Cameron's population zoomed to over 300, and the town had a saloon, a gambling house, a lumberyard, a drugstore, a blacksmith shop, and three grocery stores.[2] By late summer Cameron was bursting with activity, and the townspeople were awaiting the opening of the Cherokee Strip. The *Anthony Republican*, September 15, 1893, detailed their industriousness:

> A ten mile drive in the cool morning air last Monday brought us to the city of Cameron on the border of the ''boomers.'' The roads leading to the state

line were crowded with vehicles of every kind and description, from the ox cart to the trail wagon. . . .

The government booth is located on the hundred-foot strip just south of town and here was a scene long to be remembered. In the booth, which is simply an army tent with open front, were three government clerks filling out blanks while a fourth was stationed nearby handing out blanks to the waiting multitude. In line in front of the booth were, by actual count at 7:30 a.m., 883 men and women waiting their turn to be registered and receive a certificate giving them a right to enter in the great race to be called at high noon on the 16th inst.

Hundreds of these parties had formed in line at 8 o'clock Sunday evening, and slept upon the ground in front of the booth so as not to lose their places in line. . . .

Charley Golladay was at Cameron this week. He stood in line 11 hours before he could register. John and Sam Brown went to Cameron to register Wednesday and say that there were 1,400 ahead of them.

At nearby Harper, the *Sentinel* described the scene in Cameron on September 15:

At the booth at Cameron the line formed for registration Sunday evening, and men and women lay in line all night. Also all night Monday. Each booth can register about 1,000 a day and as there are nine booths, in the five and one-half days they are open, 50,000 can be registered. . . . No such rush for land has ever been known, and the scene tomorrow will be one in which a great many will be injured and killed.

Finally the day arrived. The *Anthony Journal*, September 22, 1893, gave this account:

The Cherokee Strip 56 miles from north to south and 400 miles from east to west lay before the wandering eyes as a grand and glorious panorama. Along the line as far as the eye could reach were horsemen ready for the race, sulkies, buggies, carriages, and covered wagons ready to follow as soon as possible. It was a sight never to be forgotten. At 12 o'clock noon the signal shots rang out along the line and a cavalry charge swept over the prairies . . . It was a grand sight to see the homestead flags staked upon claim after claim.

About this time, for some undetermined reason, Cameron was moved one-half mile south across the Kansas border into Oklahoma. The *Bluff City*

Independent, October 6, 1893, commented on the move: "The town of Cameron now occupies both sides of the state line, a new town of the same name having started just across the line on the 16th."

While surveyors were busy at the new townsite, work was also proceeding on another site just south of Cameron known as Manchester, Oklahoma. From the start, these two towns were strong competitors. In fact, the *Anthony Republican* noted on October 20 that "the *Cameron Journal* has moved to Manchester just across the line and is no longer a Harper County enterprise. It is reported that several of the buildings at Cameron have been moved across the line to the new town of Manchester."

The main reason for the competition between the two towns was the railroad, which favored Cameron for a time and ignored Manchester. There were nine businesses listed in Cameron in 1894 and twelve in 1900. The town had stockyards, a post office, a lumberyard, a department store, a grocery store, two livery stables, a schoolhouse, a Methodist church, and three saloons.[3]

On February 2, 1900, the Cameron post office closed, then reopened as "Camchester," the railroad designation for the town and the name of the depot located halfway between Cameron and Manchester. The feuding between the two towns continued, and several of Camchester's businesses and dwellings were burned by suspected arsonists from Manchester.

On April 6, 1900, the *Anthony Republican* reported that

Cameron is no more. Without a sign or moan the old town of Cameron passed out of existence, but Camchester is here in her stead, active, aggressive, and progressive. For the benefit of those who are a little confused in their minds about "where we are at" we will say you are at Camchester, this being the name of the town, post office, and R. R. station.

As time passed, Manchester became more prosperous and, one by one, the Camchester citizens moved their buildings to the Oklahoma town. The post office moved in 1903, a drug store in 1904, and finally in 1925 the local school closed. Today little remains of Camchester and almost nothing of Cameron. Only the railroad endures as a grim reminder of the life and death of these southern Kansas towns.

OLD CLEAR WATER
Sedgwick County

In 1868 Edward Murry settled on the north bank of the Ninnescah River and established a trading post for the Texas cattlemen. In 1871 the post be-

Tavernier's famous western scene, Halting Place on the Ninnescah River, *illustrates old Clear Water in 1873.*

came known as the Ninnescah Ranch, a meeting place for cattlemen coming up Chisholm Creek on their way to Wichita. In fact, there were two Clearwaters—the first settlement was known as Clear Water, a village about a mile southeast of the present town of Clearwater, which is still on Kansas maps. The name Clear Water is the English translation of the Indian word "Ninnescah."

The John G. Dunscombe store was the first store at Old Clear Water, on the Cheyenne Trail from Wichita to Fort Sill in Indian Territory. The promoters believed Clear Water would become a boomtown because of its proximity to the trail.[1]

In 1874 the settlers in the area were frightened by the Indians:

Aspey's brickyard near the old Santa Fe depot in Clear Water, 1886.

Tuesday evening the report came that the Indians were close upon us, burning everything and scalping everyone as they came. . . . It was but a little
while until all the neighbors were gathered together. . . . Some wanted to go
to Wichita. But I thought that if they were coming they would catch us on
the road, for we would have to go on the old trail that the Indians knew
about. . . . The boys thought it best to send all the women and children
away, so we packed all our trunks and lit out for Wichita, arriving at sundown at Mr. McCormick's, a friend of ours, who lived a short distance from
town. We had been there but a short time when news came that the Indians
had burnt Clear Water and were coming on as fast as they could. I never saw
such a rush; wagons full of people with their trunks piled in, coming as fast
as their horses could go. . . . We left Mr. McCormick's at midnight frightened almost to death. At daylight scouts were coming. We all returned to
Mr. McCormick's and waited and watched until word came that the Indians
had not been there. We were very glad to hear that and the next morning
started for home, all having a laugh at our big fright. The scouts came in yes-
terday and reported no Indians nearer than seventy miles.

Most of the early homes at Clear Water were frame buildings except for
those of the local Swedish colonists, who built some log and sod houses.
Otto Kopplin constructed a dugout that had the distinction of being, for a
short time, the house farthest west in Sedgwick County.
By the summer of 1876 the Cheyenne cattle trail was gradually declining

in use, and old Clear Water was at an economic standstill. But in 1884 the Missouri Pacific railroad built a line to Clear Water, and the town officials incorporated the little settlement as a city. The town began to boom. Businesses sprang up overnight, and by 1885 the town had over 2,000 inhabitants. In the 1890s, however, the boom subsided, a depression prevailed, and most of the buildings moved either to the newly established town of Clearwater or to Wichita. When the Presbyterian church and the schoolhouse burned, the townspeople wanted the school rebuilt in the new town of Clearwater. The old town slowly disappeared. The last mention of old Clear Water was in February 1894 when the post office moved to Clearwater.[2]

MARSHALL
Sedgwick County

The history of Marshall can be traced back to David Moore, the first settler in Grand River Township of Sedgwick County. In the fall of 1872 he started the Lone Tree Ranch, named for a single cottonwood tree located near the present Riverview Station on the Ninnescah River. The tree was well known to hunters and freighters because it was the only tree between Wichita and Kingman.

In 1872 Marshall and Bridgeport were platted a mile apart west of the river. Marsh Murdock was the namesake of Marshall and founder of the *Wichita Eagle*. Hiram Witten established Bridgeport when he opened a general store two miles west of the river and north of present Brandis Station on State Highway 54. A post office opened in the summer of 1874 at Marshall, and David Moore was the postmaster.

Soon rivalry developed between the two towns, as each tried to outdo the other in catering to the stagecoach and freight-line haulers. Finally some settlers from Bridgeport made a three-week trip with oxen and horse-drawn wagons to Medicine Lodge to get pilings for a bridge across the Ninnescah. They were hoping this would help Bridgeport economically, but the settlers at Marshall platted their town first. Leaders from both communities held a meeting and decided to support just one town—Marshall. Thus Marshall got the bridge and Bridgeport became a ghost town. The bridge was an important factor in the building of a road through the settlement. This road, later known as the Kingman Trail, was a regular stop for the Cannonball Green Stage lines. Within the last fifty years the original road became a part of Highway 54.

William Hays and James Fager built a water mill just north of the bridge, and businessmen moved several stores into the town. Some community backers included John Bowes, blacksmith; F. Brown, meat market; W. B. Day & Co., grist mill; James Ellis, hotel and feed stable; John Gadies, flour mill and saloon; E. W. Joslyn, drugs; F. Kuhl, hotel; T. H. Shannon and C. Taylor, physicians; and Samuel Whitehead, grocer.[1]

During the early 1880s Marshall became a flourishing trading post; the only missing factor was a railroad. In 1883 the Santa Fe Railroad was building the Wichita & Western branch from Wichita to Kingman, leaving Marshall about two miles north of the tracks. Marshall, with a population of over 100, was doomed. A new town, named Cheney in honor of B. P. Cheney, an official of the railroad, sprang up next to the railroad line.

Late in August 1883 the entire town of Marshall moved to Cheney. Most of the buildings moved to the first street west of Main, which the towns-people named Marshall Street. By September the official post office register noted that the Marshall post office had closed.[2]

O. H. Bentley, editor of the *History of Wichita and Sedgwick County*, wrote an epitaph for Marshall.

Marshall has dwindled away; its mill moved away and only a fine grove of cottonwood trees marks the spot of a once flourishing village. It was the evolution of the town. From the prairie sod, the favorite feeding ground of the buffalo, then a town with its streets and mill, its business houses and its hopes of the future, now back to the buffalo sod. When Marshall was in its prime, the patriotic citizens projected a fourth of July celebration. The morning opened with the usual firing of anvils and fire crackers and all the incidentals of such a celebration in the country. A young lawyer from Wichita was the orator of the day and stood upon a wagon in a grove of cotton-wood trees and made his speech. The trees were so small that the bald head of the orator stuck out above the tree tops. Today some of those trees are more than 100 feet high. Marshall has gone. It is only a memory, but the grove is there as a landmark; a few scattered cellars and small excavations mark the spot of the early village (1910), the village of Marshall beside the softly flowing river.[3]

WATERLOO
Kingman County

In 1880 Waterloo was just a way station, a place where two major trails came together—the Wichita to Medicine Lodge state road and the Hutchinson to Medicine Lodge road. Every day during the early 1880s, new settlers passed through the region on their way westward. In 1879 five promoters, including John H. Bromley and L. D. Biddle of Stanford, settled in the area and organized the Waterloo Town Company. Bromley was elected president of the company, and he presided over early lot sales and town organizational moves. In 1881 shares in the townsite sold from $2.00 to $10.00 a share, and through most of the decade these shares sold briskly and exchanged hands several times.

Railroad promotion began early, mostly through the sale of railroad stock. The Hutchinson, Waterloo & Southwestern Railroad made plans to lay track, but due to a lack of funds, the company eventually dropped the whole project. The *Kingman Citizen* of January 16, 1880, stated that the railroad corporation was "busted by thunder."

By 1885 business was brisk in Waterloo. The February 27, 1885, *Kingman Courier* listed Waterloo as a thriving little town with a hotel, three general stores, a post office, a blacksmith shop, a wagon shop, and a hardware store. The town also had a large new Catholic church, but the local schoolhouse had to suffice as a place of worship for other denominations.

In the early 1880s John Bromley, one of the town's founders, ran a livery stable; he also started a broom factory in the stable's loft. A half mile north of town Hugh McBride raised twenty acres of broom corn, which supplied Bromley with the material he needed for his factory. Earl Brown was the proprietor of the town's first general store. In July 1880 he ran an ad in the *Kingman Courier*: "I have just received a full line of muslines, domestics and prints, besides a general stock of groceries, flour and feed for the lowest CASH price anywhere." He was followed by no fewer than ten other grocers within the next ten years.

Another colorful early entrepreneur was Mike McCool, a large heavyset man weighing over 200 pounds. He drove a mule hitched to a wagon from which he sold Indian herb medicines and eyeglasses. Although McCool always appeared to do a thriving business, his friends couldn't find any of his money to pay for his burial. They made an intensive search of all his belongings and finally found $1,800 in a sack of oats that he kept on hand for his mule.

Several early residents of Waterloo were fervent Democrats and held many spirited rallies in the schoolhouse. Most of the township justices of the peace were Democrats in a strictly Republican area, but they did what they could to keep the peace. These justices were also responsible for registering early marriages, many of which were performed in the settler's homes. Later, when the couples went to the courthouse at Kingman for their nuptials, the justices could easily record the marriages, but once in a while they forgot, and it was not uncommon for a couple to have their first child before their marriage was officially registered.

Keeping the peace was not always easy. One day in the early 1880s, a man named Davis got into an altercation with a man by the name of Kerr. Davis used a large hawkbill pruning knife on Kerr and slashed him across the abdomen, causing a deep, severe wound. When Dr. Yancy of Kingman arrived, he did what he could to save Kerr's life, but his diagnosis was definite—the man was dying. The doctor dispatched a courier to Wichita to buy a coffin so it would be available before the man died. Suddenly, however, Kerr began to improve, and indeed he survived. Later when Kerr moved to Iowa, he took his coffin with him, for it represented a major investment. That coffin cost him over a hundred dollars!

By 1889 Waterloo had 200 people, three churches, a triweekly stage, three general stores, a land agent, a wagonmaker, three blacksmith shops, a hotel, a handful of livestock investors, and several other businesses. This was Waterloo at its peak. Over the next twenty years, the population declined to about seventy-five, and finally in 1912 the town lost its post office.[1]

Unfortunately, Waterloo lost most of what it needed to succeed. First, the county seat went to Kingman by a narrow margin. Second, a major road through the area missed the town by a mile. Third, the regional railroad went through Murdock instead of through Waterloo. All these things combined forced the town into a decline.

Today Waterloo sits between two major highways—Highway 17 passes a half mile to the east, and Highway 54 passes a half mile to the south. About all that is left of the town is a Catholic church, a few homes, a community hall, a ball diamond, an oil well, and the cemetery.[2]

CASTLETON
Reno County

The town of Castleton would have faded into obscurity sooner had the movie *Wait till the Sun Shines, Nellie* not been filmed there in 1951. Although the motion picture put Castleton on the map, it could not keep the town's business district from faltering. When the film crew left the community, the townspeople's spirits were high, but the publicity generated by the movie could not support the town's already sagging economy.

Castleton's history goes back to June 1872, when W. E. and C.C. Hutchinson laid out the townsite. In July William Wallace built the first store—he was the town's chief promoter, land salesman, postmaster, and owner of the first hotel.[1] A young Castleton weathered several disasters in the 1870s.

The year 1873 brought an agricultural and business depression as well as a severe winter blizzard that took a heavy toll on cattle and settlers alike. An Indian scare in 1874 that became a full-blown panic had Castleton residents hitching their horses and oxen to wagons and driving to Hutchinson and Wichita to escape the threat of a massacre. A company of nearly 100 volunteer cavalrymen rode into the area and routed any Indians who happened to be in the vicinity. Settlers reported two deaths west of Medicine Lodge; a band of Cheyenne had killed a local rancher and his son.

Castleton remained a small rural stage stop until 1889, when the Santa Fe Railroad built south from Hutchinson. The railroad missed the town by a half mile, so the town moved to its present location a half mile northwest of the stage site.

Castleton boomed overnight, and by 1910 the population exceeded 400. At its peak, the town contained three general stores, a lumberyard, a meat market, a restaurant, a blacksmith shop, two hotels, a bank, a post office, a lodge hall, a doctor's office, and the Santa Fe depot. W. R. Spillman operated one of the hotels until the mid-1920s, when the coming of the automobile caused his business to slacken.[2]

The dwindling of small town businesses due to the advent of the automobile was repeated in many little towns across Kansas, and Castleton was no exception. The 1929 stock market crash and subsequent depression also damaged the town's economy. A few years before, in 1926, the Castleton State Bank had folded and merged with the Pretty Prairie State Bank. The townspeople began driving to Hutchinson to shop, forcing Castleton further downhill.[3]

For a brief time in 1951, life changed for Castleton residents when they were swept off their feet by Hollywood movie magic. Castleton became the site of director Henry King's two-million-dollar film, *Wait till the Sun Shines, Nellie*. The *Kansas City Star* gave the following description of the "event" on August 26, 1951:

You can put Castleton back on your map, in case it was omitted, as it has been from many maps in recent years. Just place a dot a little to the left of Kansas Highway #17, about twelve miles below Hutchinson. But perhaps you should label it, "Sevillinois."

After a half century of decline has reduced the population to fewer than 100, Hollywood money and make-believe have brought an exciting life and a new personality to this Central Kansas village. . . .

For the movie, Castleton has become the mythical town of Sevillinois. . . . The story is from the book, "I Heard Them Sing," by Fer-

The Castleton Railroad depot boarded up in 1958. This building was used in the film Wait Till the Sun Shines, Nellie.

dinand Reyher, reporting a town's life from 1895 to 1945, as seen through the eyes of the town barber, David Wayne.

It's a nostalgic piece, in which the barber experiences some human heartaches and joys and crises, as his town grows from the size of Castleton (1895) to Hutchinson (1945).

As the Castleton filming progressed, the wide, unpaved street in front of Hornbecker's pleasant stucco bungalow was lined on both sides with big transport trucks labeled "20th Century Fox." . . . To the west, across the street, Hollywood had taken over a modest white cottage. . . .

On the porch of the cottage, King sat in a long-legged canvas chair labeled "Director," a little apart from the bustle on the lawn. Yes, it was much more difficult and costly making pictures on location than it was in Hollywood, where every facility was immediately at hand, he agreed.

"But I think people go to the movies for motion pictures, not just canned dialogue," King said. "And God still designs the best sets."

One of the more permanent markers left by the movie people was a sign painted on a building that read "Sam Eichenberger Store."

The town's most prominent citizen, David Wallace, first worked at the Santa Fe shops in Dodge City and later became a master machinist and tool designer for the Buick Motor Company. He went to Chrysler Motors in 1929 and for sixteen years held the position of president of the Chrysler division. After Wallace broke his leg in 1939, he adapted a fluid drive to one-legged use long before such transmissions were common; and as a captain in the motor transportation branch of the army during World War II, he developed an outboard motor large enough to push floats and barges. Wallace also developed an air-raid siren that reportedly produced the loudest noise ever made by man. By 1961, he was considered one of the world's most outstanding inventors by his peers.

Little remains of Castleton today. The post office discontinued its service on June 28, 1957, and now the town consists of a few homes, two churches, a schoolhouse, and a Co-op complex with a gas station and elevator.

LERADO
Reno County

In the summer of 1886 it looked as if two railroads—the Rock Island and the Wichita & Rocky Mountain—would meet to form a junction somewhere in Bell Township in Reno County. Dr. J. A. Brady from Louisville, Ken-

A Fourth of July celebration in Lerado, 1887. Note the tall skinny saplings on Main Street.

A fanciful drawing of the Lerado Water Works "plant" that appeared in the Lerado Ledger *in 1888.*

tucky, thought that in all probability there would be a city built at that junction. In fact he believed so strongly that he began to build the town before either of the railroads had started construction. Thus was Lerado born. The settlers built the town on the same site occupied by the small hamlet of Netherland thirty-five miles southwest of Hutchinson.

By September 1886 construction had begun on a $24,000 brick hotel, the 100-room Hammel House; a brickyard was in operation, turning out 10,000 bricks a day; and the water works was using windmill power to supply the city with sufficient water. Logan Street, the principal thoroughfare, was home to the Lerado State Bank, a newspaper called the *Lerado Ledger*, a town hall, a church, an opera house, the Ely & Sons store, the W. H. Cheatum Meat Market, the Orlo Jenks drugstore, and four livery barns.

The city also had a park where the Lerado Band gave regular concerts. In

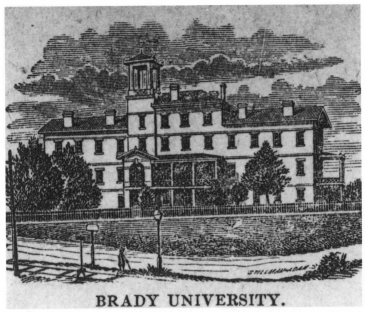

BRADY UNIVERSITY.

Lerado had grandiose schemes of being a big metropolis. This is an 1880s sketch of one such enterprise, Brady University.

fact the town had everything except a railroad. In 1887 Dr. Brady still believed that the railroads would intersect and that Lerado would be the division point. As luck would have it, the Rock Island built to Arlington and then swerved to the west through what is now Langdon and Turon, missing Lerado completely. The Wichita & Rocky Mountain Railroad, which was expected to build through Lerado, also failed to appear. The Denver, Memphis & Atlantic built instead and crossed the Rock Island tracks at Turon. On November 12, 1886, the *Hutchinson News* printed a map showing where the railroads were under construction. There was to be no railroad near Lerado, and in March 1887 the townspeople at Lerado called it quits and moved most of their businesses and homes across country to the new town of Turon. Seventeen buildings were moved at one time.

Today the site of Lerado is mostly farmland. The old school stands on the north side of the road and near the corner is the Odd Fellows Hall. Half a mile north is the Lerado cemetery. To the south is an abandoned grocery store with the doors wide open, and nearby is the ruins of another store now long gone.

Most of Lerado has disappeared; this is the last business building, a general merchandise store.

Lerado revived briefly in the early 1930s when an oil company erected a few derricks in the belief that the town was located near an area perfect for oil development. That was the extent of Lerado's possible rejuvenation. The visitor can find the remains of Main Street, now only depressions in the earth, and an active church. This is all that is left of Dr. Brady's dream; he left town for Kentucky years ago, a disillusioned and disappointed man.[1]

OLD KIOWA
Barber County

In 1872 most of the settlers in Barber County were fighting Indians. They constructed a stockade at Old Kiowa and another near Sun City. In August a party of about twenty-five Osage Indians appeared outside the town, claiming they were on a buffalo hunt. When they refused to return to their reservation, Captain Ricker, commander of the county militia, sent scouts to the area where the Indians were last seen, about fifteen miles northeast of Medicine Lodge. They encountered the Indians and killed four of them.[1]

That same year, E. H. Mosley, J. Lockwood, and R. Leonard moved to Old Kiowa. Mosley opened a store and had a small stock of goods, which he traded to the Indians. The buffalo hunters in the region also made his place their headquarters, and Mosley spent his spare time hunting buffalo with them and collecting hides for market. Lockwood and Leonard both built cabins and attempted to farm near the town, but the Indians were opposed to white men farming in that section of the county, and on July 30 they raided their ranches. In the fight that followed, the Indians killed Mosely, but the other two men escaped harm by hiding in one of the cabins. The Indians killed nearly all the stock at the ranches and then quickly left the area.

Despite the Indian troubles, settlers moved into Old Kiowa in 1872, and G. Hegwer opened the first general store in the spring of 1873.[2] The government established a post office in 1874; and A. W. Rumsey built a large mercantile store in 1876. Rumsey also owned a cattle ranch adjacent to the townsite. According to an 1878 gazetteer, the town had forty inhabitants whose principal occupation was the shipping of livestock, furs, hides, and cedar posts to eastern cities. Among other businesses listed in the gazetteer were the Kiowa House Hotel, another general store, and a justice of the peace. Nat Lane and C. H. Vautier built the livery stable in 1880; C. E. Stowell owned the blacksmith shop; Mike O'Shea opened a drugstore and a saloon; and Dr. Long was Old Kiowa's first physician. In 1883 the *Kiowa Herald* was published on a $150 press sent out from Kansas City. In spite of the scarcity of subscribers, most of whom couldn't pay, the newspaper outlasted the town.

Old Kiowa had a chance at a railroad. Officials from the Atchison, Topeka & Santa Fe came to discuss building arrangements with the town company. The men carried on negotiations for several days, but no satisfactory terms could be reached, and the railroad men left town. By then it was too late. "New" Kiowa was established on the railroad line four miles to the south.[3]

Abandonment of the old town began in September of 1884, and most of the inhabitants moved lock, stock, and barrel to the new site where business opportunities were better.[4] They even moved the cemetery. A few

An old store in Kiowa. The cabin door advertises Arbuckles coffee.

years later the site became a camping place for itinerant travelers. Although nothing remains of the Old Kiowa townsite, "new" Kiowa is a prosperous town today.

LAKE CITY
Barber County

The history of Lake City is the story of the Lake family and their one-hundred-year struggle to keep a community alive in spite of changing economic times that all but defeated the small country town.

The chronicle of the Lake family begins with Reuben Lake, the founder of Lake City. Reuben was born near Toronto, Canada, in 1839. After his parents died in 1859, he immigrated to Adams County, Illinois, where he stayed for five years. During the Civil War Reuben joined Company E of the Fiftieth Illinois Infantry. After his discharge in 1865, the lure of the West (and cheap land) brought him to Osage Mission, Neosho County, Kansas. But his adventuresome spirit didn't allow him to stay on that farm for long. In 1873, accompanied by Byron P. Ayres, mayor of Erie, he and eleven others traveled to the area of Kansas that later became Barber County. He observed that this region offered natural advantages for raising cattle and for a future trade center. Reuben filed a claim on a quarter-section of government land and located his homestead where Lake City now stands.

Just five months after Reuben settled in the Lake City area, the county was organized. Two months later he was appointed the first sheriff of Barber County. Before his term was over, he also served as county commissioner.[1]

The decade of the 1870s saw little in the way of development in Lake City. When Lake's stint as commissioner ended, he opened a general store and became the town's first postmaster. Getting the mail to Lake City was never easy, as mail service only came as close as Medicine Lodge. Lake appointed "official temporary mail carrier" anyone who happened to be going that way, and the appointee would then bring back Lake City's share of the mail. In order to handle business more efficiently, the townspeople established two stagecoach lines—one that ran from Medicine Lodge to Coldwater, and another that ran from Lake City to Ashland. Both lines carried the mail. Lake City drew its principal trade from the large cattle ranchers. The businesses in town handled supplies and significant sums of money for these big concerns.

The 1880s were boom years for Lake City, but the decade was not a prosperous one for Reuben Lake. He began in an enviable position; his store did well the first few years, and he succeeded in getting the town platted in 1881. He constructed an entire city block of brick buildings and lured several businessmen into town to occupy them. These men included W. M. Tackett, J. C. Cuppy, and the firm of Vernon & Swank, all of whom opened general merchandise stores. T. S. Updike opened a hardware store, and the Railer Brothers and Felter & Son built the livery stables. Every town needed a newspaper, so in 1883 Lake started the *Lake City Prairie Dog*. Later the name was changed to the *Lake City Bee*, but the change failed to spur subscriptions. In 1888 the paper moved to Medicine Lodge and became the *Barber County Index*.[2]

Lake considered education a necessity, and in 1886 he started a school in his home. Later a building was erected on the north side of town to serve the students. In the summer of 1887, lightning struck the school and completely destroyed it. A similar fate awaited the Methodist church—a church that was finished in 1886 but within a year had been destroyed by a tornado.

Personal misfortunes began to plague Lake during the late 1880s. His store caught fire and burned down in 1886. Six years later, his other store in the nearby town of Coats burned to the ground. A year after that, the hotel he built in Coats also was destroyed by fire. Not one to let disasters get the best of him, Lake fashioned a makeshift brick kiln and turned out brick made from native clay. From this material he constructed two more stores and a home in Lake City that cost him nearly $3,000.

But Lake's biggest problem was his bad land investments. Two serious drought years, 1889 and 1890, brought financial ruin to the local ranchers and eventually to Reuben. The homesteaders had charged huge bills at his store during those years, and they finally had to assign their claims to him in order to pay their debts before moving west. The Lombard Investment Company was the principal source of financing in the area at that time, and Lake was the principal borrower due to his many claim assumptions. Two more poor crop years, 1891 and 1892, brought ruin to both the Lombard company and Lake. Like dozens of others, he assigned his land holdings to Lombard, but the company still went bankrupt. Lake liquidated his stock of merchandise at Lake City, and after he paid his debts, all that remained was his home, the store building, and a few dollars. The Cherokee Strip opened about that time, and since he had nothing to lose, Lake decided to make the run. He homesteaded near Medford, Oklahoma, and remained there until 1907.[3]

Two other serious problems plagued Lake City: the railroad and the legislature. When the first railroad was laying track through Barber County, the townspeople presumed that it would go through Lake Township. Many residents invested their hard-earned cash in what they thought would be the building of grades and bridges, but when the railroad ultimately failed, they were unable to recover their money. Then in 1900 the Kansas legislature chose to vacate all but four blocks of the townsite. Lake City seemed doomed until 1906 when things in town began to look up again. A railroad line was finally coming! The Santa Fe was constructing a branch west from Medicine Lodge through Attica and Belvidere. The community was rejuvenated.

Settlers came back and built homes. Even Reuben Lake returned. After he sold his farm in Medford, he cleaned up his old store, restocked it with general merchandise, and put out the "Open For Business" sign. He stayed in Lake City until his death in 1917.

Reuben's store was soon followed by the Lake State Bank, two hardware stores, a lumberyard, a drugstore, a physician's office, a hotel, a livery stable/auto repair shop, a large brick schoolhouse, a short-order restaurant, a barbershop, a harness and shoe shop, a post office, and the Medicine Valley Alfalfa Mill and Elevator. A. J. Hargis, known as the "Alfalfa King of Barber County," owned an immense acreage just west of Lake City. The mill was constructed for his benefit, and for years the elevator enjoyed peak production from the crops produced in the immediate area.[4]

The Lake City Santa Fe Railroad depot, ca. 1935.

After Reuben's death in 1917, his oldest son Riley took over his holdings. Despite Riley's continued efforts to promote Lake City, the town did not develop for the son as it had for the father. Lake City did reach a peak population of about 300 in the 1920s, but the depression and drought in the "Dirty Thirties," plus the relocation of U.S. Highway 160 several miles to the south, caused more problems than the town could handle.[5]

Today Lake City has an elevator and a post office but little else. Dan Lake, Rusty Lake, and their families keep the name of the town alive, but the sleepy hamlet bears little resemblance to the town in its prime. The *Wichita Beacon* of August 9, 1959, best described the Lake City of today:

> The hot morning sun raised little heat waves, mirage-like, on the weed-lined chuck-holed main street.
>
> The flag flapped now and then, tired and dejectedly. . . . Across the street two men were working on a piece of farm machinery parked in the doorway of the blacksmith shop.
>
> That was the only sign of life . . . the only detraction from the air of complete disuse.

SUN CITY
Barber County

No one seems to know how Sun City got its name. The theories vary with the whims of the storytellers. One tale is that the first settlers arrived on

A street scene in Sun City, date unknown. The town was not developing very rapidly when this photograph was taken.

Sunday at sunrise; another, that they arrived at sunset. Yet others say the town was named after an Indian named "Sun," who just happened to pass through the site one day.

Sun City's first residents were George and Charlie Walker and an unnamed military officer, who together established a trading post in a dugout on the east bank of Turkey Creek in 1871. That winter a Colonel Griffin joined them, and they all engaged in the selling and trading of buffalo hides. At this time new settlements and land claims were rapidly being established southwest of Wichita, which led other pioneers to the Turkey Creek area. These settlers made money by selling cedar posts for fences and cattle pens and by shipping wagonloads of cottonwood sprouts to Wichita and Hutchinson to replace trees that had been destroyed by prairie fires.

In 1871 other dugouts appeared on Turkey Creek; over the next two years these were replaced by log homes. In 1872 the settlers officially platted Sun City, and in 1873 L. W. Bowlus erected the first business building, which was the scene of the first marriage in Barber County—that of John Garten and Melinda Rodgers on New Year's Eve, 1873. This community was also the site of the first births in the county—Charlie Adams and William Cochran, Jr., both born on September 3, 1873. It is uncertain who came first!

Bowlus was soon followed by other merchants, who built a stockade in 1874 that had a dual purpose—cattle and defense. Indian raids in the area had increased following the arrival of the settlers. In fact, Colonel Griffin, one of the town's earliest residents, became the first casualty. The Indians scalped and killed him while he was hunting buffalo. Sixty men organized a militia and transformed a buffalo hunter's camp into a makeshift stockade. They added a blockhouse in the center and surrounded it with rifle pits and picket fences. The men then built a stockade to the west, which when finished encompassed nearly five acres. Every night during an Indian scare the settlers in the area would bring their families to the stockade; in the mornings the men would accompany the militia and scout the vicinity to make certain it was safe to venture forth. If no Indians were sighted, the settlers would return to their claims. The scares were real enough—at least forty settlers lost their lives during Indian attacks just south of Sun City near the southern border of the state.

Sun City was quiet during the late 1870s, and economic progress sometimes seemed slow. In 1878 A. J. Johnson built a large mill near the headwaters of Turkey Creek. Johnson ground the wheat and corn into flour for the community; his customers paid him seventy-five cents for a fifty-pound sack. "Turkey Creek" flour soon became well known for its quality, and Johnson's sales market extended for miles throughout the region.

In 1872 Mark Twain's cousin, N. H. Clemens, arrived in Sun City and began selling buffalo hides for a living. In January 1875, while freighting supplies from Hutchinson, he and six other men were overtaken by a blizzard. Two of the men froze to death. Clemens's and Reuben Marshall's legs were so badly frozen that they had to be amputated. Another of the party, Harry Van Trees, lost all his toes to frostbite. In later years Clemens held several local positions, including county commissioner, sheriff, and doorkeeper of the state senate.

The 1880s were the boom years for Sun City. By 1889 the population reached nearly 1,500, and buildings lined both sides of Main Street for four blocks. These businesses included four hotels, a newspaper office, three livery stables, a bakery that turned out over a hundred loaves of bread each day, several saloons, three grocery stores, two dry goods stores, a hardware store, and a bank.

In 1888 a marble cutter named Roody came to Sun City. Residents believed that the gypsum rock in the area was really marble; indeed it resembled marble when polished. Roody made a good living cutting table tops, tombstones, and mantle pieces out of the gypsum. The red gypsum hills surrounding Sun City became the site of a business enterprise that employed a large portion of the local population. Commercial extraction of gypsum began in 1905 when a quarry and a fifty-four cam mill was constructed six miles northwest of town. In 1920 the quarry was moved southwest of Sun City and was eventually acquired by the National Gypsum Company. The mine employed 150 men, many of whom were Mexican la-

A Santa Fe train wreck near Sun City in 1915. Cattle were fortunately the only casualties.

borers. They lived in company houses west of town in a section nicknamed "Mexico." Other company workers lived in an area on the west side of Sun City known as String Town because of the "string" of identical shacks the laborers lived in. The company constructed two deep mines beginning in 1919—the second one, the "Pioneer," is the longest-lasting known gypsum mine still in operation. Collectively, the quarries gave Sun City the appearance of a Colorado mining boomtown rather than a Kansas boomtown. The mines allowed the community to survive the depression years of the 1930s without a financial recession.

The railroad arrived in Sun City shortly after the turn of the century. In 1906 the Denver, Kansas & Gulf Railroad laid track through town, ushering in a new commercial era by connecting Sun City to outside markets. The railroad became a major factor in shipping gypsum for nearly two decades.

Sun City also offered two major attractions that brought in people from all over the region during the early 1900s. One was natural; the other was promotional. On Bear Creek six miles south of town, stood the massive "Natural Bridge," a stone bridge fifty feet across and thirty-five feet wide between two rock formations twelve feet above the stream. For many years this formation was the focal point of quite a few gatherings and picnics. Unfortunately, in December 1961 the bridge suddenly and inexplicably collapsed.

Saunders Dry Goods Store in Sun City. A Model T Ford captivates the townspeople, ca. 1915.

The other attraction was known simply as "McLain's Roundup." From 1921 to 1938 Marion McLain sponsored the largest independently owned ro- deo in the world on his ranch near Sun City. For three days in July, thou- sands came to his show to witness some of the finest horse races and other outstanding rodeo performances ever held in Kansas. On a nearby hill he eventually built a large concrete grandstand with a seating capacity of 3,000. There was also an Indian encampment along the Medicine River, where Chief Maurice Medicine and his Cheyenne tribe from Canton, Oklahoma, conducted their ceremonies. The Brodbeck Carnival furnished rides and other amusements and held a dance each night. The extra attractions often included such characters as "Hiko the Wild Man," who would rip open a live chicken and eat the bloody, still-beating heart (shades of performer Ozzy Osborne?), and the "hypnotized" man who was "buried alive" for all three days of the roundup.

Other special rodeo events included relay and chariot races, wild cow milking, and trick riding and roping. Charlie Schultz and "Pinky" Geist, the clowns, provided plenty of laughs when they rode a "bucking Ford" automobile and performed other amazing stunts.

Marion McLain traditionally began the rodeo by making a grand en- trance with his two sons, Max and Mark. Following closely behind them in line were the clowns, the contestants, the trick riders, and the Cheyenne Indians. In 1939 the "Roundup" came to an end, but not without assuring many good memories. Today the Medicine River has washed away most of

The Gypsum Hills Celebration in Sun City always included Native American dancing. Here a crowd surrounds a performance on Main Street, 1950.

Tanks and armored personnel carriers dazzle a crowd of spectators on Main Street in Sun City, ca. 1950.

the midway, and the rest of the area is in a cultivated field. The grandstand still exists but is gradually crumbling into the hillside.

In 1935 Sun City had a population of 300, and supported three cafes, three gas stations, a post office, a hardware store, a lumberyard, a blacksmith shop, a barbershop, a meat market, two general stores, a confectionery, a drugstore, a garage, a telephone office, and a doctor. But by 1980 the population had dwindled to 126, and only six businesses and two churches were still active.

The scenery of the gypsum hills around Sun City is beautiful. Beginning in 1950 the citizens made an effort to mark the roads and trails with signs that describe the natural formations. While following the roads through the hills, you can visualize the rodeo and smell the saddle leather. Sometimes you may even hear the distant "toot-toot" of the calliope on the merry-go-round.[1]

COMANCHE CITY
Comanche County

James W. Dappert was a civil engineer in Comanche County when many of the towns were being surveyed. He was responsible for surveying Comanche City, and the accurate accounts of his undertakings in his "Old Pocket Day Book" offer one of the only known histories of this boomtown. Dappert made the following remarks:

> I did not get any cash pay for my services in surveying and plotting Comanche City but took my pay in deeds to 16 lots in the new town . . . until notified by the County Treasurer that the town had been abandoned and no taxes had been levied upon Comanche City which was 1904 or 1905.
>
> Actually, I never did visit Comanche City after we had gotten through with its survey, which was about March 13, 1886. I understood that during the years 1886-87 the town built up quite well and things looked favorable for quite a "Boom."

Comanche City, located fifteen miles south and six miles west of Cold Water, was first called Satanta and, according to Dappert, was also known as Nashville in its formative years.[1] The following excerpts from Dappert's day book recall Comanche City's first weeks:

> Presently, about April 1885, the new Comanche County became legally organized, and a whole set of county officials were to be elected. I then ran for

County Surveyor upon the Progressive ticket and Mr. Ed P. Lee was the candidate for County Surveyor upon the other ticket; and we two agreed to not
make any "Hot Contest" for the office, but did agree that whichever one of
us would be elected to the office, he would appoint the other one as his
Deputy Surveyor, as the prospect was good for a big run of business, as the
Government survey monuments had been largely destroyed by trampling
and herding of buffalo and cattle. . . . I was duly appointed as Deputy
County Surveyor.

Dappert was marooned in the Cold Water Hotel during the Great Blizzard of 1886 and then traveled to other adjoining counties to look for further work. Finally on February 18, 1886, he returned to Comanche City and
made the following entries in the day book:

Monday, February 22—A very nice day. Got up early and drove down to
Gaylord's and got ready to survey the new townsite of Comanche City.
Started the survey right after dinner. Wm. Bowman, Mr. Cook, and a stranger helped on the survey one-half day each. Drove back home to Schaeffer's
and stayed over-night.
Tuesday, February 23—Went on down to Avilla and surveyed on the new
addition there after noon. The people of Avilla were afraid that the new Comanche City would soon eclipse their town and urged me very strongly to
hurry and complete the survey and plat for them; also Mr. Woodworth was
in a great hurry to have me complete the survey of Comanche City. I did the
best I could to comply with their desires. . . .
Wednesday, February 24—Nice day. Went down to the new town of Comanche City. Stopped for dinner at Gaylord's . . . during the time I was engaged in the survey of the 320 acre townsite.
Sunday, February 28—Cool, disagreeable day. Worked all day on survey of
boundary lines. The people would not let me off, even if it was Sunday.
Tuesday, March 2—Worked the rest of the day upon the plat of Comanche
City, one-half day. It rained all afternoon and night. . . .
Friday, March 5—Worked on survey of Comanche City all day. Fred
Fulton, store-keeper for Mr. Dixon at Plano came up in the evening and he
brought me the box of cigars, but he could not change the 10 dollar bill that
I offered him, and just about the next day, his store was closed in bankruptcy
proceedings and then Fred said he could not take the pay; and that box of ci-
gars was never paid for.
Saturday, March 6, 1886—Warmer, worked on survey of townsite 9 hours.
Worked upon the town plat while in the evening. Fred Fulton came up in

the evening and told me about the closing of the Dixon store at Plano, and refused to take pay for the box of cigars.

Wednesday, March 10—Worked upon survey of the townsite all day, and wore my overcoat. In the evening, Jas. Ward came to Gaylords. He claimed that he had not yet been paid for his land and wanted to stop the survey. I paid no attention to him.

Saturday, March 13—On survey of Comanche City townsite and finished the survey by noon. I gave all the helpers statements and orders for payment of their wages, and then went to Avilla in the afternoon.

Unfortunately, details of the town's history and growth after the survey are sketchy. The settlers changed the name to Comanche and named the streets after Indian tribes. The government opened a post office in 1886, and one of the businessmen published a newspaper from 1886 to 1888.[2] During its boom period, Comanche City had brick buildings and was larger than either Protection or Cold Water, the two major towns in the county. The town's economy failed when a proposed railroad from Anthony to Comanche City never appeared. Buildings from the town were moved to Cold Water and Protection, and the site was vacated in 1905.[3]

HOPEWELL
Pratt County

The importance of a bank to a rural community can never be underestimated. Often the bank is the lifeblood of the town, and when it closes, the town never fully recovers.

A case in point might well be the small town of Hopewell, a relative latecomer to the area, not established until after the turn of the century. From 1901 to 1908, the post office name was Hopewell, but unfortunately the government closed the office until February 1916, when they reopened it under the name of Fravel. Fravel it remained until 1921 when it was again named Hopewell. The Farmer's State Bank of Hopewell, established about this time, had a shaky beginning. Part of the problem was the proximity of other banks in nearby towns. Byers, Trousdale, and Macksville all had large local banks. Competition was brisk. If the bank was not directly threatened, then other peripheral industries were affected. For example, the postmistress decided to retire in 1919, leaving the town without anyone capable of running the post office. An officer of the bank, foreseeing trouble in losing the service, contacted his senator and offered to move the post office into the rear of the bank building. Although designating a bank officer as postmaster was unheard of in banking circles, the postal department agreed to the idea, thus saving the post office, at least temporarily.

Hopewell had several businesses during the early 1920s, including a general store, a hotel, a blacksmith shop, a hardware store, and a lumberyard. A community hall was constructed as a meeting place for the various lodge organizations. Square dances, dinners, and political gatherings were also held in that building.

In those days, money for community activities was hard to collect. Lodge organizations would vie with one another, and in order to gain members, they often held contests. Two lodge groups in Hopewell decided to compete against each other in a rabbit hunt—the winner was to host an oyster supper for the loser. The winners corraled eight hundred rabbits and herded them to a buyer in the nearby town of Byers. The buyer had originally agreed to purchase only five hundred of the animals, but in the end he was coerced into taking the other three hundred. At the time, jackrabbits sold for seventy-five cents each on the market and cottontails for thirty-five cents. A good oyster supper was enjoyed by all.

The Farmer's State Bank continued in operation until 1923 when it was voluntarily liquidated due to a lack of depositors. The other businesses in Hopewell held on for awhile and then slowly closed one by one. By the 1930s, most of the town and its residents were gone.[1]

BYERS
Pratt County

Byers was founded in 1914 when the Anthony & Northern Railroad built through the area. When the day finally arrived for the opening of the new town, the track lacked over a mile of reaching the Byers depot site, but this small deterrent didn't keep Pratt County residents from attending the opening day ceremonies. They came as far as the track had been laid and then finished the trip on foot. Hundreds of people attended the big celebration that consisted of a political rally, a balloon ascension, a big dinner, entertainment by the Pratt city band, and last but hardly least, the selling of city lots. The city gave a free lot to Mrs. Hunley Warren, a prominent citizen who was instrumental in naming the town after O. P. Byers, the president of the Anthony & Northern Railroad. On that opening day alone, the town council sold over 100 city lots.

Many businesses opened during the fall of 1914. The Byers State Bank was incorporated; Elmer Reed put up an implement shed; Mr. McBride built a garage; Hugh Bernard erected a barber shop; and Mrs. J. B. Patter-

The Wichita & Northwestern Railroad depot, Byers, 1939. By then much of the town was gone. In the background is the Gano Elevator, one of several in central Kansas established by the giant Gano Company of Hutchinson.

son opened a millinery shop. Other businesses were Water's Drug Store, Sinclair's Grocery and Dry Goods, John Wood's Hotel, McHenry's Implement Company, King's Store, Henry Donner's Meat Market, Hoggett's Bakery, and two lumberyards.[1]

April 29, 1915, was another big day in Byers—four hundred more lots were sold. By this time over 400 people called Byers home. The town soon opened its post office, on May 6, 1915, and the mail came in each morning from Pratt on a railroad car called the "Jitney." John Conner founded a weekly newspaper, *The Byers Journal*, which he published until 1917 when he sold it to Alice Proctor.

Byers was not without crime. A murder occurred on December 16, 1915, when Lou Self shot and killed Robert Randle in a restaurant on South Main Street after an argument over an unpaid food bill.[2]

The town dwindled slowly until 1965, when the women took over the government. The previous mayor and five councilmen had held office for as long as anyone could remember, and in the meantime the chuckholes got deeper, the weeds grew taller, and nothing was being done to correct any of the problems. In April the people called for a special election, and the women candidates won by a landslide. Mrs. Roy Moore, the mayor, and her cabinet officially took over the business of the city government in May. Roy Moore, the mayor's husband, said, "I'm glad the women got in.

They meet and decide things and that's more than the men were doing. They're accomplishing something."

One of the first things the women did was approve a city budget of $1,000 a year. "Once we started cleaning up, everyone got busy," Mrs. Moore said. "The school even hauled its trash for the first time and people cleaned up their yards. . . . All we want to do is have a nice, clean little town and we'll have it." Mrs. Moore continued: "Another problem was our streets. They were so full of chuckholes one hardly could get a horse through them. Nothing ever was done about them. Since we took office, we've had three miles of them dragged and we still aren't through."

During the 1960s the women cleaned up the town and kept it going economically. "They've been calling us Petticoat Junction ever since the election so we're going to put lace curtains in the city hall windows just to please them," Mrs. Moore said.[3] But by 1984 the town had fewer than fifty citizens, almost no businesses, and just a few homes.

ZENITH
Stafford County

The story of Zenith is really the history of two towns—one a typical small agricultural town that catered to the needs of the local farmers; the other a rip-roaring boomtown that survived the depression of the 1930s due largely to the discovery of "black gold" in the area.

The first Zenith traces its beginnings back to 1886, when the Chicago & Northwestern Railroad constructed a section of track in the area known as the "Kinsley Branch." S. W. McComb, assisted by other local farmers, gave the railroad $700 to put in a 100-foot spur side track, which they named Zenith. At the junction of this spur, a corn crib fence was built around the track to hold the farmer's grain until the railroad cars arrived, thus putting an end to the need of hauling grain by team and wagon to Sterling.

The Kansas Grain Company built a grain elevator in Zenith in 1901; it was soon followed by a post office and a general store. One man, Fred Ramsay, was proprietor of all three operations. The mail was delivered cross-country by Raleigh Stewart, who quickly changed from a horsedrawn delivery service to a motorcycle when the technology became available. By 1896 the Santa Fe Railroad had established a depot and telegraph service and was making regular stops in Zenith.

In 1905 R. A. Boyd purchased several acres of land and platted a townsite, signaling the start of Zenith's first boom. Before long settlers and businessmen from all over the region established new stores there. Boyd built another general store, which was soon followed by the D. J. Fair Lumber Company, the Farmer's Elevator, two blacksmith shops, a creamery, a city windmill that provided the city water supply, a hotel, and the Zenith Bank. Two other grain elevators were built alongside the Farmer's Elevator: the Midwest and the Red Star, making three available to the local farmers.

In the early 1900s citizens made a priority of schools and churches. They held their Sunday school classes in the lumberyard until they established the United Presbyterian church in 1911. In 1914 they organized the Zenith school district and built a handsome brick grade school, which served the community until 1941 when a larger white stone building replaced it. The citizens also built a high school that was in operation for ten years until it moved to Stafford.[1]

As the years passed, the business district expanded and the Santa Fe Railroad built a new station and stockyards with a water well. In 1915 Bert McComb and Bill Johnson, owners of the Zenith store, joined in a partnership to sell automobiles. They acquired the only Buick and Studebaker dealership in the county and sold cars for years. Their sales rapidly increased as automobiles became more popular; in one month alone they sold twenty cars. Each year the duo sponsored a big parade that attracted hundreds of people. Their business eventually became too big for Zenith, and they moved the dealership to Stafford.

Each summer Zenith hosted its famous grand chautauqua. In August a big tent went up, and speakers and musicians from all over the country came to town. The chautauqua offered residents a welcome diversion in an otherwise hot, dry, and somewhat boring month.

Zenith began to falter in 1927. Much of the town's economic success had resulted from the efforts of S. W. McComb, an influential legislator and one-time county commissioner who had originally organized the school district and the bank. After his death in 1927, the bank closed and business in the stores and shops declined.[2]

Zenith maintained a stable population until one morning in September 1937. Drillers from the Standard Oil Company had been looking for oil in the area, and their search ended successfully at Harnett No. 1, one-half mile south of town. Almost immediately Zenith was transformed from a small farming community into an oil boomtown, and the community's citizens succumbed to oil fever. The first well came in at 800 barrels a day along with strong gas pressure. Land was leasing at a wild pace. Soon other oil companies came to Zenith, including Trans-Western, Skelly, Sinclair, Shell, Gulf, Vickers, Texaco, and Derby. By January 1, 1939, the companies had drilled a half-dozen wells in the Zenith field, and there were no dusters. The next year, wells were everywhere, and by December 1940 more than 100 derricks dotted the landscape. Drilling was so intense that on September 14, 1940, the government decreed that for safety's sake oil wells had to be surrounded by at least ten acres.[3]

What did this do to Zenith? The town's population and businesses boomed. On the south side of town, fifty buildings sprang up, including restaurants, gas stations, and shops. The January 3, 1939, *Kansas City Times* observed:

> "East side, west side, all around the town." That's the story of Zenith. . . . For today, it matters not which way you turn, there are the long rows of oil derricks that mark the most amazing development in any single Kansas oil field in 1938. The freight depot, long in listless lethargy, sprang into activity as timbers, rigs, machinery, tools, engines and ponderous wheels and things began to arrive. A half mile frontage along U. S. Highway 50, which courses past the southern edge of Zenith, was leased, and along that half mile front were stores, shops, equipment houses, where but a year ago was sandy pasture land.

In a few years, the daily production in the Zenith fields went beyond 200,000 barrels a day, and by the end of 1944, 335 wells were pumping in the area. The Zenith boom was so spectacular that, in spite of the depths to which the Kansas oil industry had sunk by the late 1930s, "in the face of shrinking activity elsewhere, [Zenith] continued lavishly."

For nearly twenty years the Zenith field and the town's residents prospered. Large quantities of natural gas, however, had been allowed to escape. After about fifteen years, water began to seep into the smaller wells, and most of the companies moved on to other more productive fields. In 1969 the remaining oil companies started a water flooding project whereby they pumped water into the old wells so as to force the inert oil to rise. By 1974, however, only seven wells were still in operation, yielding a mere ninety-seven barrels a day.[4]

By this time the businesses in town had dwindled to a store, a gas station, and a grain elevator. Today the town has declined even further to the days before oil changed everyone's lives. Now and again, the promise of a boom resurfaces, but the town will never be what it was before World War II.

TROUSDALE
Edwards County

"The Wheat Belt Town Site" was the original name of Trousdale. The town was named for Walter Trousdale, owner of the Trousdale Ranch. He hired J. W. Allison to survey a townsite, then he laid out an eighty-acre plat, forty acres on each side of Main Street. Trousdale also donated land for a school, a church, and a town park, and built a block of brick buildings that housed six separate businesses.

The town came to life when the Anthony & Northern Railroad laid track through the vicinity in 1916. The railroad was to run from Pratt to Kinsley with a branch from the Trousdale area extending to Larned and Hays. The company hoped to run the tracks to Anthony and Wichita, but without additional capital the railroad never got beyond Pratt.

P. T. Bates built the first store and post office; he and his family had to live in a tent until the structure was complete. Bates's store was followed by two blacksmith shops, the Trousdale State Bank, a railroad depot, a drugstore, a hardware store, a flour mill, three grain elevators, a meat market and produce house, a hotel, and a dry goods store. The townspeople placed a flagpole in the center of the street immediately south of the bank but later had it removed when cars kept hitting it.

The first religious services were held in temporary structures until a church could be built. One of those meeting places was in the office of a lumberyard. When the settlers organized a congregation, they requested donations from every participating member. A young boy attending the meeting held up his hand and said he would collect $75.00. True to his word, he raised the money and became the youngest charter member of the church. By 1917 a sanctuary had been completed that served all denominations until other churches could be built. This first church later became the Methodist church.

The ladies in the community wanted to build a park, so they bought a vacant lot next to the hotel and landscaped it. They had a cement tank constructed that served the town as a swimming pool. This park became a popular choice for town celebrations and picnics.

During the depression of the 1930s, Trousdale's citizens had to seek employment in the larger urban centers. In fact so many people moved to Wichita that there were more Trousdale residents there than in Trousdale. Most of the houses were moved to other towns such as Kinsley, Pratt, and St. John. In 1933 the bank, hotel, barbershop, produce house, and hardware store closed their doors, and the drugstore moved to Mullinville. The elevators closed, for there was no longer a railroad to haul their grain.[1]

World War II inflicted heavy losses on local boys who went overseas. Of twenty-three men from Trousdale drafted for service, seven lost their lives.

The Trousdale Post Office, lonely and windswept, 1966.

This percentage was markedly higher than in many other communities of the same size. When the men returned from war, no employment opportunities awaited them in town. Today the business district has declined to a few stores, several dwellings, and a small resident population.

7

NORTHWEST KANSAS

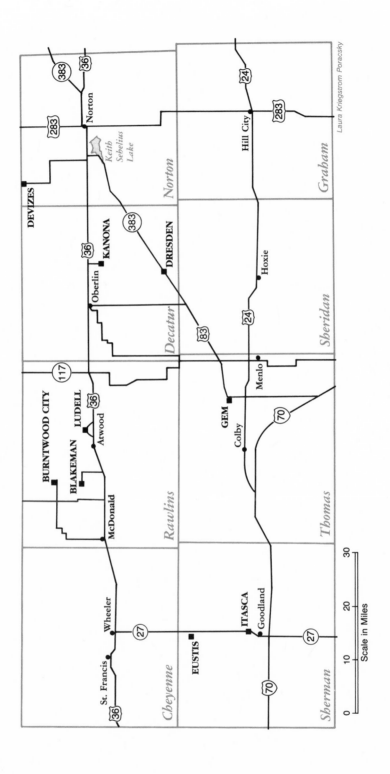

Laura Kriegstrom Poracsky

Scale in Miles

0   10   20   30

DEVIZES
Norton County

Devizes was the first settlement founded in northwest Norton County. Harry Zimmerman and Herbert Shaw established claims on the land about one mile west of Devizes in 1872, and a dozen other settlers followed the next year. Several merchandise stores and a post office comprised the early business district of the community. The town was named Devizes for Devizes, Ontario, the hometown of Ruben Bisbee, the first postmaster.

The town's most important industry was a flour mill, the first one in the county and the first ever on Sappa Creek when the settlers built it in 1877. They also built a sturdy dam about a half mile upstream that provided sufficient water power to operate the mill around the clock. For many years farmers from all over the county as well as Nebraska patronized it, which helped make Devizes a major trading center. L. M. Sherbune constructed a large general merchandise store on the hill overlooking the mill; he catered to the settlers who stopped in town to buy flour.

For thirty years Devizes boomed in spite of the lack of a railroad. In 1885 one railroad conducted a survey up Sappa Creek, and for several years thereafter the settlers expected and hoped that actual rail construction would begin. Grading for the road started to the north, however, in Orleans, Nebraska, and never went any farther west than Precept, another community that is now a ghost town.

During Devizes's boom, a murder shocked the community and kept it reeling for years. The "Albert Applegate murder" occurred on November 8, 1895. Just like in the westerns, a stranger came to town looking for Applegate. After questioning the neighbors as to his whereabouts, he found Applegate husking corn in his field and fired several shots at him. Applegate turned and walked directly toward the man. When he got within a few yards of the stranger, the man fired the fatal shot, hitting him in the head.

A neighbor, who had heard the shots, found Applegate a half hour later and took his body to his home, where the coroner conducted an inquest. The only clue to his murderer lay in a statement Applegate had made to a friend. He said he had caused the divorce of a couple in Colorado the year before and that the husband had sworn to hunt him down and kill him "if it took twenty years."

A posse searched for the murderer for weeks, but the felon appeared to have escaped. One day several months later, they received word that a man connected to the crime had been caught and imprisoned in eastern Nebraska. The man, William Heddy, was brought back to Norton and placed behind bars. Before the judge could schedule a trial, however, the sheriff found Heddy hanging in his jail cell, his bedsheets wrapped around his neck.[1]

Devizes reached its zenith in the 1890s with a general store, a post office, a creamery, a flour mill, and a blacksmith shop. But already signs of decline were evident. A notice in the Norton newspaper in the 1890s read: "The townsite of Devizes has been vacated by the commissioners on the petition of J. C. Martine of Chicago, the present owner of the land who thinks it can be put to better use." This turned out to be a hoax, and perhaps a bit premature, for just a few years later the town boasted a brass band!

The real end of the community came on September 30, 1916, when the Devizes general store caught fire. An alarm rang out, and all the neighbors gathered to try to put out the flames, but the store burned to the ground. With it went all hopes of a brighter future for Devizes. Another store opened after the fire and operated until the 1930s. After that the town disappeared.[2] Today the Devizes cemetery still marks the townsite, but most of the buildings are gone, leaving only depressions in the sod.

KANONA
Decatur County

Imagine what it would be like to own your own town. Actually, at different times, two or three people have owned Kanona in Decatur County. Gilbert Brown purchased Kanona in 1960 when the town consisted of nine buildings on a fifteen-acre tract. The only buildings in Kanona that Brown did not own were the schoolhouse, the grain elevator, and the telephone building. Among the remaining structures he purchased was a Methodist church sold to him under the odd stipulation that unless it was used again as a church it was to be torn down.

Brown paid about $10 a lot for his fifteen-acre tract plus an undisclosed amount that had already been spent on each of the nine buildings. When asked what he was going to do with his holdings, Brown remarked, "I'll do whatever I can. I've been trying to figure that one out!"[1] On July 10, 1960, a *Topeka Journal* reporter interviewed Brown, and when he was asked how it felt to own a town, Brown replied, "Not very good, but then it doesn't make me downcast either!" But Brown must have become dissatisfied with his town, for in April 1968, he sold it to Wayne Lohoefener of Oberlin. In an *Oberlin Herald* newspaper article dated April 18, 1968, Lohoefener said that he planned to turn the old blacksmith shop into a workshop and tear down some of the other buildings for the lumber. The church was still

A bird's-eye view of Kanona, 1909.

standing despite the previous stipulation that it was to be torn down.[2] By this time, Kanona was somewhat of a tourist attraction, and many travelers drove the two miles from Highway 36 southeast of Oberlin to see this "real-live" ghost town.

The history of Kanona can be traced to the early 1880s, when the town went by the name of Altory; the government established a post office there on September 13, 1881. In 1885 Kanona was platted by Anselmo B. Smith, who noted that "burr-oak stakes were driven well into the ground at the front corners of each lot and stones were planted low down in the ground at some places."

A few local residents cherished vivid memories of the town. Etta Brown, who was born in 1887 in a soddy three miles northwest of Kanona, shared the following childhood recollections of the community:

> Ma used to give my brother and me little buckets of eggs and we would run the three miles into Kanona to trade with Mr. Orbin [Charles Orbin was Kanona's first permanent merchant and general storekeeper].
>
> I remember that we always hoped there would be a little money left from the eggs, so we could buy some candy or cookies from the big barrels in Mr. Orbin's store. Ma always told us, if there was any extra to buy a can of tomatoes or something. But it really didn't make much difference because he usually scooped out the broken cookies from the bottom of the barrel and put them in a sack for us kids.
>
> The country sure looks bare out there nowadays. A friend and I drove out there the other day and there just isn't much left [in the 1950s].

Luther Capps and Frank Soderlund, both reared in the Kanona neighborhood, remembered the town as a busy village with a hardware store, a livery stable, a lumberyard, two general stores, a barbershop, and a hotel. In

Kanona buildings and residents, 1903.

1919 Art Laughlin built the bank, and the town constructed a new school in the middle of Main Street. At that time the population was about 150. Kanona was also a shipping point along the Chicago, Burlington & Quincy Railroad, which cut across its northern edge, and many of the more important businesses, including two elevators and the stockyard, set up near the tracks. The boom continued into the early 1920s, when two garages were built, as well as a movie theater, a hardware store, and two restaurants.

Bad times followed good. A fire in 1923 destroyed the pool hall, the barbershop, and the roof on the bank; the bank became insolvent in 1926. Another fire in the late 1920s burned the two general stores and a garage; and in 1949 a tornado damaged the school, the lumberyard, and many other buildings.

Today Kanona is a scene of desolation. Portions of an old concrete sidewalk wind through the weeds, and the old brick bank building with its windows boarded up is closed permanently. A long building that was once the blacksmith shop remains in fair condition. The only buildings still in use are the Co-op elevator, the residence of its manager, and the community building that was once the school. The church remains, but stray ani-

A train wreck in Kanona, possibly around the turn of the century.

mals are its only congregation. The fate of Kanona now rests with its solitary owner.[3]

DRESDEN
Decatur County

When the Rock Island Railroad laid track through Decatur County in 1888, it established the town of Dresden. Immediately the community boomed, mainly due to the railroad and the sudden influx of homesteaders. The settlers laid out five east-west streets and named them Kings Avenue, Kansas, Topeka, Decatur, and Jackson. First, Second, Main, and Railroad streets crossed the town north and south.

Merchants from other sections of northwest Kansas who saw favorable business opportunities in Dresden moved there in the first few months. Early establishments included a drugstore, a blacksmith shop, the Bowman Bank, the Leonard Implement Shed and Coffin Storage, the Yeakel Building, the McKinney merchandise store, Bainter's Hotel, a livery stable, a meat market, several grocery stores, and a newspaper, the *Kansas Sunflower*. Oddly enough, the meat market was located within only a few feet of the often fly-infested livery stable! The Odd Fellows lodge hall was the local gathering place for most events. The townspeople used the upper story strictly for lodge meetings, but they used the first floor for every community gathering from dances to church meetings.

The railroad and depot remained the center of activity for the town, for residents of Oberlin and other nearby towns who wanted to take the train to Kansas City or Denver had to come to Dresden. To accommodate the traffic between Dresden and Oberlin, an enterprising local businessman established a stagecoach run that made roundtrips daily. The old two-story Rock Island depot saw many years of use. Each time the lower floor wore out, a new one made of two-inch planks was placed over the old one. When the railroad finally demolished the building, the layered floor was over a foot thick.

Although Dresden residents frowned upon liquor, the local drugstore occasionally served a "quick fix." The town druggist had a young intern working for him who indulged in spirits; in fact he sometimes drank so much he passed out. One day several residents found him sprawled over the counter fast asleep. Their idea of a cure was to pick him up and throw him in the horse trough.

After the townspeople built a schoolhouse in 1916, they held a celebration and a baseball game. At that time Dresden had a winning ball team, which every other town wanted to best. As the game progressed, the fans consumed ever more liquor. At the end of the eighth inning, Dresden was ahead by two runs. The visiting team was at bat with two outs and a man on second base. The batter hit a grounder to the shortstop, who momentarily fumbled the ball. Seeing that the play was going to be close, the runner jumped feet first into the first baseman. Dodging the sharp cleats, the first baseman missed the ball and had to run several yards to retrieve it. Meanwhile the man on second scored. The other runner made it to second, then headed for third, but as he rounded third he ran headlong into the plaster cast worn by the previously injured third baseman, which knocked him out cold. He was only one base away from tying the score, but the umpire called him out. The crowd went crazy, narrowly avoiding an all-out riot.

The population of Dresden peaked at about 300 before the depression of the 1930s. But it was the loss of service from the Rock Island Railroad in 1960 that caused the town's eventual decline. Although today some buildings are deserted, a small resident population keeps utter desolation at bay.[1]

BURNTWOOD CITY
Rawlins County

The name of this community attests to the destructiveness of early prairie fires. Burntwood City got its name from a prairie fire that swept through the area in the 1860s. At that time, only buffalo hunters were around to tell the story; they described the fire as widespread and severe. One tree stump measuring fifteen by five feet smoldered for months. Only moderate re-growth had occurred by the time the first settlers came to the Rawlins County, but it was enough for a little firewood and to make ridge poles and posts.

The settlers were sometimes their own worst enemies when it came to fires. On March 17, 1887, Billy Doty decided to burn some trash, against the warnings of his neighbors. Billy replied complacently that St. Patrick would watch out for him. The fire that resulted from his carelessness raged south almost to Colby, then west into Colorado just short of Burlington. An-other devastating prairie fire started near McDonald in 1900 by a train on the Burlington branch. In 1902 a fire wiped out most of the trees in the area and destroyed the grapes, currants, and cherries that the settlers planned to use for jams and jellies that fall.

Fires, however, were not the only problem the first white inhabitants faced. The Cheyenne Indians were a constant threat to the buffalo hunters. In the 1870s the Indians attacked four hunters near the Burntwood City site. Although all four took refuge in a gully, the Cheyenne killed three of them. The one hunter that escaped went back later to bury his friends. He placed their bodies in the walls of the gully and piled plenty of dirt around them. Then he cut limbs from a tree and covered the burial site to discour-age hungry coyotes. The branches acted like a dam, impounding the runoff silt until the gully was completely covered. When the settlers broke the prairie for sod in the 1880s, erosion cut into the gully, which had already be-gun to wear away. After the drought years of the 1930s, rains washed the gully out into a deep canyon. By 1940 the hunter's bones were exposed in the canyon wall. Two local farmers discovered the remains, but they did not have the proper tools to rebury them. Several years passed before anyone returned to the site. By then the gully had widened even further, and the bones had completely disappeared.

Another Indian attack occurred on a prominent hill near the townsite. The Cheyenne surrounded a group of buffalo hunters who fortified them-selves in a buffalo wallow. After several hours of intense fighting, the hunters managed to disperse the Indians. In later years over a hundred car-tridge shells, mostly .54 caliber, and many arrow points were found on the ridge.

Burntwood City was established in an arid region dotted with springs; one such, known as Cold Spring, was ice cold the year round. There was another spring nearby called Dripping Spring, created by water seeping from an overhang of limestone. These springs were a favorite picnic spot, especially during the hot summer months. The less popular Rust Spring had amber-colored water spurting from a three-inch hole in the rock. This curious little body of water bubbled and gushed whenever it wished. Since it had the odor of sulphur, it was considered "bad water" by the suspicious Cheyenne, who used it only for snake and rabid animal bites. Rust Spring dried up in later years, leaving only a yellowish stain and a strange odor on the rock to mark its location.

Another interesting landmark near Burntwood City was the "Bone Banks," or gullies that once contained tons of buffalo bones. When the first settlers arrived, they found the huge deposits of bones and eventually sold them to local buyers. One man found an old skull, presumed to be Indian, among the animal bones. Archeologists from the Kansas State Historical Society excavated the area, and their findings indicate that the site was prehistoric.

During the early 1880s the Burntwood City site was traversed by cattle herds heading north to Ogallala, Nebraska, and to Wyoming ranches. Most of these cattle belonged to local ranchers who moved them from ranch to ranch, wintering them farther south in Kansas and grazing them north in Nebraska in the summer. The springs in the area and a large pond known as Dewey Lake afforded the cattle their last drink of water until they reached the Republican River.

In 1882 more settlers arrived in the Burntwood City area. By this time freighters had established a trail, known locally as the Stratton-Goodland Road, which they used extensively before the coming of the railroad in 1887. The trail grew in some places to be fifty to sixty feet wide, and the old wagon ruts eventually cut into the ground too deep for travel. Teams and wagons then had to straddle a rut or start a new one. With the coming of the Burlington & Missouri River Railroad, the freighters used the road less, soon deserting it completely.

Burntwood City started growing when the railroad began surveying a proposed route from its main line in Stratton, Nebraska, to Pueblo, Colorado. At that time, the town consisted of one sod house that served as a post office. But the community had one thing going for it: a location on flat, dry land that stretched for miles. Few creeks ran through the area that could cause the railroad additional cost or halt the progress of the work crews. The "town" didn't even have a well!

Once news of the railroad reached the area, the boom was on. A Doctor McIrvin nailed some boards over the counter at his house and called it a drugstore. The medicine under the counter included the ever-popular snake bite "cure." Charles Williams laid up sod for a large general store; the Hubbards started a restaurant where they "served grub"; and the Hovey family operated a livery stable. Then came the post office, lumberyard, and blacksmith shop. Burntwood City was beginning to look like a city.

Water for the town was a problem. The closest springs were nearly a mile to the east, and the settlers hauled water from them daily to be used for everything but bathing. The more particular folks would seine off the larvae and worms before drinking, but most everyone else thought these creatures just added to the flavor. The town modernized when all the merchants pooled their resources and dug a 240-foot well in the center of town. This well was a great drawing card for Burntwood City; settlers came from miles away with their water barrels and then stayed to gossip and to shop.

The town was just about to become important economically, when the railroad double-crossed everyone. The Burlington constructed a branch line from Orleans, Nebraska, to St. Francis, Kansas, leaving Burntwood City high and dry. The town could not survive this loss, which was compounded by competition from its new rival for the railroad, McDonald. One by one the businesses left for Bird City or McDonald. The last remnant of the town was the well, which soon filled with junk, and the city park, which consisted of a few scrawny trees that eventually wilted and died during drought years in the 1890s.

Today the site of Burntwood City is in a barren wheat field; shards of broken glass and a few square nails are the only tokens of life in the old town.[1]

BLAKEMAN
Rawlins County

At one time Blakeman competed with Atwood for the county seat. Had things gone Blakeman's way, the town would be the county seat today, and Atwood would be in the alfalfa field. At its peak, Blakeman was much larger than Atwood, with a population of nearly 500. The town had a flour mill, grain elevators, a bank, a newspaper, two hotels, several mercantile houses, and a large brick schoolhouse.

Blakeman's beginnings lay with the Lincoln Land Company, a Nebraska organization that intended to promote Blakeman at the expense of Atwood, a town approximately five miles away. Atwood had been successful in securing the county seat but had yet to acquire a railroad. The Lincoln Land Company asked the B & M Railroad, another Nebraska corporation, to lay track through Blakeman and bypass Atwood. The B & M agreed to construct a branch line from Orleans, Nebraska, to near Atwood, then west to Bird City and St. Francis in Cheyenne County. The road missed Atwood by a mile and went through Blakeman, and for many years Atwood was without a railroad depot. At Blakeman the B & M built a large depot, actually much larger than was necessary.

When the depression years of the early 1890s hit northwest Kansas, residents of Blakeman made their move. They sent a man to Atwood with heavy equipment and gave him instructions to begin moving buildings to Blakeman. This man actually did move several structures and set them up on Blakeman streets. After watching these buildings being removed for several days, Atwood citizens began to protest vigorously. They soon formed a mob and ordered the mover to cease his activities, which he did without causing trouble.[1]

Meanwhile Blakeman was also attempting by legal means to obtain the county seat. The town filed a petition before the county commissioners calling for an election to relocate the county seat from Atwood to Blakeman. The county commissioners, however, refused to call an election because the required three-fifths of the registered voters had not signed the petition. Blakeman residents and the B & M Railroad officials appealed the case to the Kansas Supreme Court, but the court ruled in favor of the county commissioners, effectively stymying the election campaign.

The fight over the county seat continued for some time, but the residents soon tired of the controversy. Many of the more influential Nebraska backers, as well as officials of the B & M Railroad, also gave up the cause.

By the early 1900s what Blakeman had attempted to do to Atwood was now being done to Blakeman. Several buildings were moved to Atwood, leaving behind only partial foundations. In May of 1910, the Lincoln Land Company sold most of the town to W. E. Thompson, who plowed up his portion of the townsite and planted alfalfa.[2]

Today a few structures remain, and a sign along U.S. Highway 36 indicates where Blakeman can be found. Atwood, by contrast, has survived as a prosperous farming community.

LUDELL
Rawlins County

The pioneers in the newly settled western communities were full of an enthusiasm almost as boundless as the prairies around them. George H. Hand, editor of the *Ludell Settler*, reflected this optimism in his writings. In the premier issue, October 18, 1884, Hand devoted five columns to news of Ludell's people, problems, and prospects. He included the following gems:

> The type for the first number of the *Settler* was set in a sod house, with the fleas and bed-bugs having a fall round-up on all the territory below our shirt collar . . .
>
> The dance in honor of the opening of the Ludell *Settler* building was well attended, and passed off in fine shape. As an index to the morality of the community, we will state that not a drop of anything intoxicating was indulged in; in fact, not a drop was to be had . . .
>
> Five new buildings put up within two weeks, five more contracted for . . .
>
> We buy, sell or trade anything that walks on four legs and eats buffalo grass . . .
>
> We want one hundred shocks of sorghum, on subscription. Wood of any length, green or dry, is just as good as cash on subscription—in fact, better. Rye, corn, hay, millet, potatoes, eggs, chickens, etc., will be credited on subscription to the *Settler*. We want to place the paper within reach of all, and shall endeavor to make it sufficiently interesting as a local paper to cause a healthy demand for it. Any one with a dollar and a half can act as a special agent . . .
>
> Richard Riley fell from a house the other day in company with a ridge-log. Dick wasn't hurt much and the ridge-log is recovering . . .
>
> On Sunday afternoon we counted twenty-seven men in front of one store in Ludell, eighteen of whom were land-seekers. They come in squads . . .
>
> The new schoolhouse should be furnished with the most improved bentwood furniture. Ludell wants no second-class articles, to cast away in a year. In fact we want nothing second-class in the town. If it is only a pig-pen or a chicken-coop, build it right, and then paint it.

The Ludell community was initiated in 1872 by August C. Blume, who homesteaded one half mile southwest of Ludell. Blume, one of the organizers of Rawlins County, was also instrumental in establishing the post office. He carried the mail twice a month for six months between Ludell and Cedar Bluffs, a distance of more than ten miles. During 1872 Blume constructed a toll bridge out of two cottonwood trees placed across a nearby stream. He charged each settler fifty cents per crossing—the price included equipment.[1]

The decade of the 1870s was too early for anyone to be settling in Rawlins County. Indian attacks persisted; in fact, an Indian raid in 1878 killed many of the first settlers in the area. Two years later, however, enough settlers had

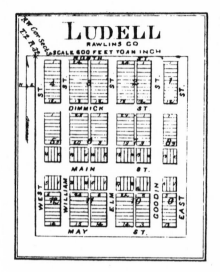

The nice square town plat of Ludell, 1887.

arrived that they were no longer afraid, and the community was beginning to take shape. That summer the town was formally laid out and christened Ludell—a combination of the names of the wives of the two founders—Luella and Della.

By 1884 and 1885 Ludell boomed in response to the prospect of the Chicago, Burlington & Quincy Railroad building through town. Andrew and Alameda Smith arrived in 1885 and built the two-story Smith Hotel. Andrew ran the livery stable a block south of the hotel, and Alameda was responsible for feeding as many as thirty-four boarders three times a day. As the railroad approached, the hotel bustled with activity. Not only were the railroad workers housed there, but so were the travelling salesmen and other railroad "hoppers" who worked the towns from one end of the line to the other. Alameda picked up a well-deserved reputation for serving good food. Salesmen would call ahead to reserve a seat for Sunday dinner if they were going to be in the area. Alameda's menu usually consisted of fried chicken, cream gravy, and potatoes, all for twenty-five cents. Everyday she baked dozens of loaves of bread and packed thirty lunches in gallon syrup pails for the railroad workers. She did the laundry outside on washboards in big tubs with water she heated in iron boilers.

Besides the hotel, Ludell had two grocery stores, two banks, a lumberyard, a blacksmith shop, two garages, a school, a Christian church, and of course, the newspaper.[2] The *Settler* kept track of all events, no matter how trivial, that affected the Ludellites. Here is a sampling of Ludell's prospects as expressed in the local news column in late 1884:

Strangers arriving at the rate of ten a day. They all take land, and seven-eighths of them will become actual residents. They are all financially prepared to take advantage of the rare opportunities offered for soon living in opulent ease in a rich, healthy, country; water as pure as crystal and air as refined as nature's most improved machinery can make. The climate is a cross between Florida and Maine. Society is a mixture of Western vim with New England purity . . .

The location of Ludell is lovely. . . . Come and see the country and people, is all we ask.

Although Ludell benefited from being a railroad shipping point, the town also had hopes of becoming the county seat, for which honor Ludell contended against Atwood. Atwood enjoyed a major advantage, for it was centrally located within the county. This, along with a large and loyal population, was enough to sway the county seat in that direction. Nonetheless, the county seat question arose several times over the next twenty years, especially in 1905 when the expensive courthouse at Atwood burned to the ground.[3] Almost before the ashes had cooled, residents of Ludell and Herndon began jockeying to pull the county seat away from Atwood. The *Topeka State Journal* of December 10, 1905, related the story in detail:

Although Atwood is the center of the county, and the logical place for the county seat, there is said to be a strong movement on foot to build the new courthouse at Herndon, in the northeast corner of the county, or failure in that, at Ludell about halfway between Atwood and Herndon.

In the Herndon-Ludell section of the county, there is a strong German population, and they are the ones that want the county seat changed. . . .

It is a hard job to move a county seat, however. There are a lot of legal requirements to be met, and it is difficult to get the requisite petition for calling a county seat election.

Actually, Herndon and Ludell residents were their own worst enemies; they were unable to rally together to back just one town. Both wanted the county seat, and in the end the courthouse remained at Atwood.

Their foiled dreams did not deter the residents at Ludell. The town remained an active railroad shipping point for many years. In fact, during the 1920s, Ludell was quite a swinging town thanks to Art Samson. Samson ran a dance hall so famous that it attracted nationally known jazz and big band artists who were touring across the high plains. Dancers from as far away as Kansas City made the long journey to Art Samson's at Ludell whenever they felt the urge. Art's hall was on the second floor of his garage business, and the mapleboard floor was specially designed for ballroom dancing.[4]

Another local boy who made good from the 1920s was Julius Myers. Myers got his start in New York City selling coal. He must have been good at it, for the business made him a millionaire. He later returned to his hometown of Ludell and opened a grocery store. Myers purchased food and miscellaneous items by the carload and sold the excess to grocery stores in nearby towns at a profit. Before long, several merchants in other northern counties were depending on Myers for their stock of goods.

The prosperity of merchants and businessmen like Myers and Samson was put to the test during the depression years of the 1930s when Ludell began to decline. Like residents of other small towns in those days, the Ludellites were suddenly out of work and forced to look elsewhere for jobs. Farmers in the area also suffered, and many went bankrupt and had to sell their land.[5]

Most of Ludell's businesses on Main Street have closed down since the 1930s, although a few buildings remain. The Smith Hotel has survived, though vastly remodeled, and the town is worth visiting for its interesting architecture. A resident population remains in Ludell, but it represents only a fraction of the town at its peak.

GEM
Thomas County

The "Gem of the Prairie" was a lively community that held high hopes of prosperity on the High Plains for many years, only to become a victim of the changing economics of the twentieth century.

Gem can trace its beginnings back to 1878. At that time, the first two families arrived in the area—the Andrew Reeds and the Martin Withams. Other settlers did not start coming to this part of the state until 1882. Many of these early pioneers lived in their wagons before they constructed their houses or soddies. One lucrative livelihood they indulged in was catching the wild horses that roamed the plains in plentiful numbers. Twenty or thirty could be caught at a time and sold for as much as thirty dollars each.

Early settlement also brought the pioneers many scares, most of which had to do with the Indians. One Sunday morning in 1882 word came to Gem that the Cheyenne had escaped from their reservation and would

Residents of Gem keeping the local creamery busy.

probably be in the area by evening. The settlers frantically hoarded what water they could, turned their chickens and pigs loose, and with their families, horses, and cattle, started immediately for Oberlin. When they reached the home of E.T. Smith on Sappa Creek, the settlers found several families had already set up camp, and they were persuaded to remain there. About seventy people were encamped with only a small amount of ammunition.[1]

At 3:00 p.m. that day, Frank Lord, a fifteen-year-old boy, started for Oberlin to get a supply of powder and ammunition. He returned before noon the next day with only a few dozen boxes of shells and one or two drams of powder, all the residents of Oberlin could spare. The men kept pickets on the surrounding bluffs watching for the Indians both day and night. About the time the settlers were well organized, the governor sent them a message stating that the Cheyenne had gone through eastern Colorado instead of western Kansas. The scare was over, and everyone returned home.[2]

The year 1885 was one of great excitement—the land rush was on! Thousands of settlers poured into the general area to homestead new lands. Their first winter, however, proved to be disastrous; 1886 brought two major blizzards and extremely cold weather. Many settlers lost their lives, and thousands of cattle perished in the heavy snows. Two years later, a town was established on a parcel of land owned by J. W. Ellsworth, who named this spread the "Gem Ranch." When the Rock Island Railroad built a right-of-way through the area, they shortened the name to "Gem." Thus were the town's ambitious beginnings.[3]

Families arrived in Gem and established businesses that catered to the railroad trade. In 1889 Charles Hardin came to town and opened the Gem Hotel. The hotel had a reputation for hospitality and good meals, the latter due to Mrs. Hardin's ability as a cook. It became a popular stopping place for salesmen and travelers, who always made an effort to spend the night in Gem. Meals could be had for twenty-five cents; overnight lodging, fifty cents. Jacob Riblett also came to Gem in 1889 and established a general store that operated for thirty-three years. His son opened a hardware and implement business that lasted several years. W. O. Eaton, a major town builder, was responsible for constructing and laying out much of Gem. He had a personal interest in the community and eventually owned many of the town's businesses.

For a short time, the farmers raised good crops, but by 1891 the hot winds and dust had ruined the land. Then the grasshoppers came and destroyed the fields further. In 1890 a severe drought on the High Plains caused many settlers to sell or mortgage their lands and to seek better opportunities elsewhere. For several years Gem's development was stunted, but around the turn of the century the town's economy began a rapid recovery. By 1906 Gem had two general stores, two hardware and implement stores, a drugstore, the Gem Hotel and livery barn, two elevators, two blacksmith shops, the Gem State Bank, a photograph gallery, and a regional telephone system.[4] In 1910 Gem even boasted a short-lived newspaper, the *Gem Leader*, a weekly published every Wednesday by Willard W. Scott.[5]

Fowler See, an inventor, owned one of the blacksmith shops. He was famous for two inventions—a riding harrow that was very popular with the local farmers and an apparatus designed to put passengers on and off trains without the train having to stop. The device was similar to a system used much later by most railroads to pick up mail. This particular invention created a great deal of excitement around Gem, as everyone thought that the Rock Island was going to buy the rights to it.

The railroad constructed a working model of the device at Gem alongside the tracks, and it took the passengers off the train as it went past the station at eight miles an hour. For some unknown reason, however, the Rock Island chose not to purchase the invention, and See's Gem Transfer Company went out of business.

The Gem Methodist church, focal point of the community.

Once again the climate and weather had a negative affect on Gem. From 1911 to 1913, the town endured a series of severe dust storms that impeded the growth of the community and caused many businesses to close. After these years passed, farm income became more substantial, and once again the town prospered. During the World War I years, farm prices were good, and for a while the town boomed.

The economic depression that overtook much of the country in the late 1920s had a severe impact upon Gem. And the early 1930s were even worse. Most of the farmers could not hold out under the combination of low farm prices, poor crops, and severe drought. Many were forced to sell their land, which in turn caused some businesses to close. In 1932 the Gem State Bank was forced to cease operations, and along with its demise several other related businesses failed. One by one the buildings on Main Street fell into disuse. After a fire destroyed the depot, the railroad discontinued passenger service. The advent of the automobile and better roads took the townspeople farther from home for their necessities.[6]

Today there is still a resident population in Gem and a few businesses, but the town never made any real economic comeback after the Great Depression. The "Gem" of the High Plains has a shining spirit but a cloudy future.

MENLO
Thomas County

Menlo was established in 1888 as a railroad town along a branch of the Union Pacific Railroad, which finally laid track in Thomas County after a slowdown in construction out of Salina. The townsite was first called Zillah and was located on the Sheridan–Thomas County line. One and one-fourth miles northwest a small settlement named Mystic was also established, which had a post office, a hotel, a blacksmith shop, a livery stable, and several dwellings. But Mystic did not have a railroad, so the citizens moved many of the buildings to Zillah when the Union Pacific arrived.

The government renamed the town Menlo in 1889 when it opened the post office, which was soon followed by a school in 1890, then a general store, an implement building, and a broom factory that operated for a short time. As more families came to live in the Menlo area, other businesses were needed. During the period from 1890 to 1910, a drug store, a hardware store, a doctor's office, a lumberyard, and the Farmer's Cooperative Creamery were added. The Shellabarger Grain Co. and the Robinson Grain Company constructed elevators in 1903. A settler by the name of A. Bailey built a machinery and blacksmith shop with a hall above it that served the community for gatherings whenever necessary. In 1904 Jacob Shroth built a

Main Street in Menlo, ca. 1910. Note the two bicyclists.

The cashier's cage in the Menlo State Bank, complete with plant and strategically placed spittoons, ca. 1910.

Menlo had a typical one-room country school, where all eight grades studied together, ca. 1910.

A patriotic playground scene in Menlo shortly after school consolidation.

large two-story hotel. In 1905 Fred Chrisensen, affectionately known as "Little Fred," opened a confectionery and short order business, which later became a variety store. The first newspaper in Menlo was the *Menlo Enterprise*, with Asa Scott as editor. Telephone service came to Menlo in 1905 when the Menlo Farmers Mutual Telephone Company was organized. Banking services also appeared that year with the incorporation of the Menlo State Bank. After weathering many financial panics, the bank finally sold in 1951. In 1909, rural mail service was established with Wilbur Maxwell and Lee Cummins as carriers. They first used horses and buggies, then later motorcycles.

The period of greatest business activity in Menlo was from 1910 to 1930. During the early 1920s the town boomed. It had a railroad depot, a two-story hotel, stockyards, three elevators, three general stores, a lumberyard, a hardware store, a meat market, a barbershop, five gas stations, a post office, a bank, a variety store, a blacksmith shop, a dress shop, a cafe, a creamery, the *Menlo Leader*, and a movie theater. The town was also noted for its windmills. Many of the town's approximately forty residences had their own windmill.

The first schoolhouse, built in 1890, was a frame building occupied until 1904 when a new larger frame structure was built at the north end of Main Street. At the time of school consolidation in the 1920s, other elementary districts joined with the Menlo district and they added a brick high school at that time. The enrollment reached about 200 elementary and 100 high school students. During these years students of the Menlo schools excelled in athletics and scholarship. There were two state championships in basketball and a finalist in the National Scholarship program. Enrollment dwindled, however, and the district dissolved in 1963, and the territory was added to adjoining districts.

Although Menlo was located in the center of a rich farming area, it declined from about twenty-five establishments in 1905 to three in 1975. During the 1930s the depressed economy caused the closing of many businesses. When the automobile became an important part of rural life, and good roads made it easier to reach the larger commercial centers, more businesses closed. The national trend of movement to urban areas led to the closing of the rest. To make matters worse, the older citizens retired and moved to the larger communities.

By 1975 the population was down to around forty, only one-seventh of its size during the town's boom years. Businesses by that time included only a post office, a church, a recreational center, and the Menlo-Rexford Cooperative Elevator. In the summer, transient workers added another twenty to the population count. Several abandoned buildings exist today on Main Street, making it one of Kansas's most photogenic ghost towns. Many structures, however, are on private property, and all trespassing signs should be respected by those who wish a closer look.[1]

EUSTIS
Sherman County

In the spring of 1885, P. S. Eustis, an agent of the Burlington & Missouri River Railroad, and O. R. Phillips organized the Lincoln Land Company and laid out a town they called Eustis.[1] In 1886 the town began to prosper. By July the government had established a post office, the Lincoln Land Company was a successful corporation, and J. H. Tait had started a newspaper called *The Sherman County Dark Horse.*

On September 20, 1886, Sherman County was organized, and the court named Eustis the temporary county seat. The town had only two opponents in the upcoming county seat election—Sherman Center and Voltaire, and for several months a clear-cut rivalry existed between Eustis and Sherman Center.[2] A prominent citizen who lived close to both Eustis and Sherman Center told the members of the Eustis Town Company that he was going to vote for Eustis in the next election. The officials realized the advantage his influence would have on other voters, so they immediately offered him $50 cash and $250 later if he could persuade his friends to vote for Eustis. He took the $50 and drove to Sherman Center, flourishing the money about town, telling everyone how he got it, and advising them to vote for Eustis. His actions caused quite a commotion among the citizens of Sherman Center. On November 8 Sherman County held its first election for the temporary county seat, and the voters chose Eustis by a wide margin. In several elections held previously Voltaire had won; however, the court had declared these elections fraudulent. Eustis now had its own county officers, and they were busy constructing a courthouse.[3]

By July 1887 Eustis had a peak population of 500. The town had a public school, three banks, and two weekly newspapers, the *Dark Horse* and the *Sherman County Democrat*. Other businesses included a brick manufacturing plant, an insurance office, two groceries, two lawyers, three general stores, six real estate offices, two lumber companies, a livery stable, two dressmakers, two blacksmiths, two painters, a shoemaker, three drugstores, two hotels, a furniture store, two hardware stores, two physicians, two restaurants, a meat market, a billiard room, and a harness maker.[4]

At the next election held in the spring of 1887, Eustis again was chosen the temporary county seat. After the votes were counted, about fifty men drove to Eustis from Sherman Center. The county officers at Eustis barricaded the unfinished courthouse and prepared for a fight. They presumed that these citizens from Sherman Center were coming to take the county records, but actually they only wanted everyone in town to know that the books were fraudulent.[5] The men from Sherman Center left without a fight; they had come to prove a point.

On August 23, 1887, a county committee met at Eustis, and their business concerned the election of a permanent county seat. Had the Eustis town company argued well before the committee why the town should be the county seat, it might still be on the map. But they let the opportunity slip away. Propositions were submitted by Voltaire, Sherman Center, and by B. Taylor, a private individual who owned land near the center of the county. The committee wanted the town they recommended to run for the county seat and to build a courthouse and a jail free of cost to the county. The only town that met these requirements was Eustis.

Eustis had a courthouse already underway, and the citizens had said, unofficially, that when they completed the building, it would be turned over to the county. But the Eustis town company failed in its presentation in August, and at the next meeting a new town company from the Goodland townsite won the admiration and respect of the county committee. The county held an election that fall, and the results were seventy-five votes for Goodland, twelve for Eustis, three for Voltaire, and three for B. Taylor and his privately owned land.[6]

Although Goodland won the election, Eustis had the county records, and the court still recognized the town as the temporary county seat. Eustis claimed fraud on the part of Goodland and threatened to contest the election. Possession was nine points of the law, especially in a county seat fight where about the only principle involved was money. The town company placed guards at every road, and they halted and questioned everyone coming into town.

By this time the citizens had almost completed the courthouse at Eustis and had hidden the county records in the second story of another building across the street. City officials stationed a company of armed men in this building and gave orders to shoot anyone who attempted to take the books. They were to ask no questions, just shoot the first man who mounted the stairs.[7]

The officials at Goodland decided to strike back. They hired a group of armed cowboys to ride to Eustis and capture one of the county commissioners. These men forced the frightened official to enter the building, mount the stairs ahead of them, unlock the safe, and remove the books. The cowboys loaded the records and some furniture into waiting wagons and rode away without firing a shot.[8]

A few weeks later the citizens of Eustis moved the entire town to Goodland. In one short month Eustis had gone from boom to bust. Today only a few foundations and deserted cellars remain of what could have been the county seat of Sherman County.[9]

ITASCA
Sherman County

Itasca (sometimes called Leonardville) was first named Leonard after pioneer Thomas P. Leonard. The town was laid out and platted in December 1885 by R. R. Frisbee, W. B. Swigart, C. C. Reynolds, Thomas Leonard, and John D. Hays of Oberlin, who had formed an organization known as the Sherman County Land Association. Other prominent businessmen decided to settle there, and the community began to boom. In the spring of 1886 the citizens built a school, a drugstore, a real estate office, the Commercial Hotel, and a livery stable. The hotel contained sixteen rooms and was one of the largest in the western part of the state. The town company offered lots to anyone who would build structures on them. Before long the town had seventy-five houses, all nicely painted.

A reminiscence that appeared in the *Goodland Herald* on December 27, 1934, gives some insight into the founding of the town while relating the story of a group of people stranded in Leonard during the Great Blizzard of March 25–27, 1886:

> After about two hours battling the (blizzard), our horses brought us at last to the little prairie settlement. . . . We went into the restaurant and there we found about 140 men huddled together in the little 16 x 24 feet boxed frame building. They had burned all the coal and Mr. Leonard magnanimously instructed the men to saw up the lumber in the lumber yard to burn in the stove. Several thousand feet of perfectly good new lumber was burned in this way.
>
> Finally, late Sunday afternoon after what seemed to be an indeterminable length of time, the storm abated. . . . But what a snowy old world it was!

During the summer of 1886, the townspeople of Leonard tried three times to secure a post office but were refused each time because other towns had similar names. At a special meeting on August 16, the board of trustees decided to change the name of the town from Leonard to Itasca. The U.S. Postal Department agreed on the name and placed Itasca on the map.

A newspaper, the *Sherman County Republican*, was published in Itasca in 1886. About this same time, the county held an election to determine the county seat. Itasca made a bid for the seat, but was unsuccessful, perhaps because transportation to and from Itasca was a problem. The products sold in the town had to be hauled across country from Fort Wallace, a distance of thirty-two miles.

At its peak, Itasca had 500 residents. When the railroad entered the county late in 1886, it became evident that Itasca was not on the list of railroad centers since the tracks missed the town by several miles. That fall most of the businesses were moved to Sherman Center and Eustis, with the exception of the Commercial Hotel and the Swigart Building, which remained until they moved to Goodland in 1887. Today nothing remains of Itasca.[1]

8

WEST CENTRAL
KANSAS

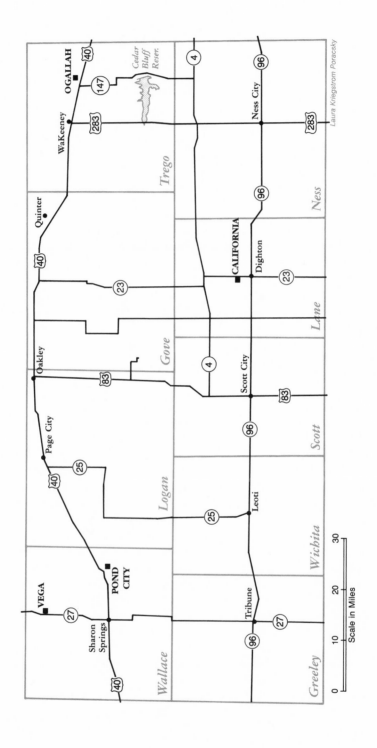

OGALLAH
Trego County

One of the finest reminiscences I have had the pleasure of reading is the description of Ogallah by Christopher C. Yetter, one of the town's first residents. He describes what life must have been like for the earliest white inhabitants of the region of Kansas west of Hays. Here are the highlights of his story, extracted from *The Club Member*, 1908:

> Twenty-nine years ago (1879) on a cold, dismal day in the early part of February, the writer with his effects, which consisted primarily of faith, hope, and courage, was landed at a blind siding then known as Ogallah. . . . It was late in the evening, a stiff breeze was driving the sleet and snow spitefully into our face no matter what way we turned.
>
> A longing look in every direction for some place of refuge for the night was met only by the most bland and supreme desolation we had ever beheld. The threatening clouds above, the bare earth below, and two streaks of rust called the Kansas Pacific Railroad, was all we could look up to build our future hopes upon. Separated by 600 miles from our family and with such a prospect in sight we reflected, had a man not as well be caught in an ocean without compass, rudder, or sail? In fact, had he not as well be drowned?
>
> The coyotes were too numerous in those times to allow us to indulge in outdoor slumber at night. Forty brass bands at high-tide parade could not equal in noise a few hundred of those coyotes. . . .
>
> . . . In hunting up the settlers, and to better acquaint ourselves with conditions, we came upon a family in a little boarded-up-and-down cabin whose first year's experience is worthy of some notice. A few weeks after erecting their first domicile there swooped down on them one day a small cyclone which lifted the house up into the air, taking the wife and one child with it to the height of fifteen or twenty feet, then going to pieces, the man being out somewhere near. As the fragments of the house scattered around, the man soon discovered the wife holding to the child in the torrents of rain then coming down. After gathering them up and providing the best shelter that he could for them he ventured to inquire of the wife if she wanted to go back where they came from. Her answer was not if she had to take the same route she had been over awhile before—meaning the straight up route. . . .[1]

Christopher Yetter stayed in Ogallah for many years, but not without suffering personal hardships. His wife and two children followed him to Ogallah in the spring of 1879, a year noted for its severe storms and hail. His garden and crops were beaten to the ground, desolation was everywhere, and to add to his troubles, his wife became very sick. These trials soon passed and in the years that followed, Yetter became a successful business-man, a deacon in the local church, and a member of the G.A.R. [Grand Army of the Republic] post.

How did Ogallah get its name? One theory is that it came from Fort Ogallah, an earthwork fort constructed a few miles east of WaKeeney by surveyors working in the county in 1867. Another story tells of a Kansas Pa-cific train that stopped at a siding to let a woman off, and as she viewed the vast expanse of unbroken prairie, she exclaimed with excitement, "O Golly, how far I can see!" The railroad officials modified the expression and called the siding "Ogallah." Other sources say the town was named for the Ogalala Sioux Indians, which is probably the most likely explanation, for Ogallah means "Big Hill" in the Sioux language.[2]

In 1878 families began to settle in the area and establish permanent homes. The first buildings included a stone structure known as Orten's Store and a depot for the Kansas Pacific Railroad. Early town meetings were held in the freight room of the depot and ranged from business and social gatherings to Christmas performances. A blacksmith shop was also built that year; it served as a classroom for the first school. The Yetters operated a hotel known as the Yetter House. Rooms cost twenty–five cents a night, or a weekly rate of $4.00 including board. Lizzie L. Wurst opened a grocery and dry goods store that she advertised as the "Wurst Store in town, but the best place to trade."[3]

The January 17, 1880, issue of the WaKeeney *Western Kansas World* in-cluded an illustrated write-up of Ogallah and vicinity, showing the town's rapidly growing business district. At that time there were fifteen buildings on the townsite and many more planned. During the next thirty years Ogallah grew steadily and by 1920 the population was listed at 125. Several more general merchandise stores were constructed, also a lumberyard, two grain elevators, a large hardware store, the Ogallah State Bank, a creamery, a doctor's office, and a drugstore. In 1909 Bill's Half-Way Place, a hotel owned and operated by William Clup, opened for business. What made this hotel interesting were the advertisements that placed it 337 miles from Denver and 337 miles from Kansas City. Thus it truly was a "half-way place."

A variety of "entertainments" was available to Ogallah residents. A liter-ary society met in the schoolhouse, and the members discussed the latest books, news articles, and the women's suffrage issue. Neighborhood "sings," spelling bees, Christmas parties, and musical performances were all popular, and chautauquas were held in Ogallah nearly every summer from 1917 to 1933. A large room over the hardware store provided space for roller skating and dancing. A company of entertainers from nearby Ellis even performed the opera "Queen Esther" in this room. In 1916 a stock company was formed to solicit funds for a meeting hall. Such a building was eventually constructed across from the railroad depot, and a variety of events was held there, including memorial day programs and movies. When times got tough, the building was sold and converted to other uses.

From 1925 to 1932 the Ogallah Community Club sponsored all kinds of civic enterprises such as a town band, parent-child banquets, old settlers reunions, 4-H club projects, and baseball teams. The club was also responsible for electrifying Ogallah, laying curbs, and paving streets. The Ogallah Community Club marked the finest years of Ogallah, and its demise signaled the end of the town. In 1929 the population reached a flourishing 150, but then the depression came and with it drought and dust storms. Businesses experienced a deep recession from which they never recovered, and eventually they had to close their doors. The economic recovery promised during the war years never appeared.[4]

One high mark in Ogallah's history was the discovery of oil one mile south on the Fred Schoenthaler farm in May 1951. The good news spread, and within three years, over one hundred oil producing wells dotted the landscape around Ogallah. Three oil companies—the Texas Company, Mid-States Oil Company, and the Stanolind Oil Company—leased claims in the area. More families moved in, and it appeared that the town might make a comeback. In addition, the U.S. Corps of Engineers began in 1949 to construct Cedar Bluff Reservoir. This dam also brought a few families to Ogallah and prompted the opening of service-related businesses for recreation-minded folk who liked to boat, fish, and camp. Among other changes in town were the tavern and the race track. Since neither business was acceptable to the established families in the community, both soon closed for lack of customers.[5]

In a few years, after the oil boom slacked off, the town declined again, and this decline was permanent. Today Ogallah has a resident population and a few businesses catering to travellers who wander off Interstate 70, but most of the earlier businesses have disappeared, and the town has not benefited noticeably from its proximity to a major highway. The ghost-town hunter can benefit, however, as this is one town that can be reached without meandering off the beaten path or driving a four-wheel drive vehicle. Follow the signs, and enjoy a quick trip back in time!

CALIFORNIA
Lane County

In Kansas history "California," a common place name in the nineteenth century, designated at least five separate communities; none of them exist today.

The town of California in Lane County, located two miles north of Dighton, was the best known of the five. It had three other official names: Bell City, Gould City, and Lucretia. Residents also sometimes called it "Belltown." Ed Bell, the founder, was a man who chased, captured, and sometimes killed wild horses. Unfortunately, he often killed more tame horses than wild ones. Bell became the first postmaster in California when the government established a post office there in 1879.[1]

W. H. Lee was editor of the town's newspaper, the *Lane County Gazette*, a small two-column, four-page paper. Like most other editors in those early days, he went to extreme lengths to start a boom in the town. Lee must have been good at his work for he soon expanded the *Gazette* to a large six-column folio. In his first issues he didn't commit himself politically, but Lee showed his Republican leanings in the later issues.

The original paper had only two advertisements, one by J. H. Pelham "dealer in Groceries, Provisions, and all other necessaries kept in a first class store," and an ad describing the merits of the *Gazette*. The paper revealed the town's frontier characteristics in its story on the new schoolhouse, as in most new communities the all-purpose local meeting place—"a box house . . . 14 by 20 in size. When completed it will be used for Sabbath School, church services, and all public meetings. This is a commendable enterprise and it is to be hoped that the people all over Lane County will follow the example as soon as possible."

Lee wrote a front-page column about the murder of John Bowers in Wichita County. He said that the man accused of the act had been apprehended and taken into custody by the California townspeople, who delivered him into the hands of the law in Trego County. The accused, however, had been allowed to depart in peace because "the governor, attorney general, and other prominent officials" had decided "there was no law, either government, State, or County, in this part of Kansas to punish murderers." The editor stated that although he regretted the offense, he regretted much more the fact that such criminals were permitted "to run at large without hindrance." Although not in favor of mob rule, he asked "would it not be well for the citizens to adopt some plan of bringing criminals to sure and speedy justice?"

Lee published the last issue of the *Gazette* on March 23, 1882. Soon thereafter other businesses closed, and the death of California was complete.[2]

• ——————————————— **VEGA** ———————————————— •
Wallace County

Many Kansas communities originated as ethnic colonies. An emigrant land
company would purchase large sections of land and then lure various ethnic
groups to settle there. Vega was just such a place. The Vega townsite was
one of several proposed communities created by the Southwestern Swedish
Townsite Company. This company operated in both Kansas and Nebraska
and brought thousands of Swedes to the high plains of both states in the
late 1880s.

Vega was more actively promoted by the townsite company than most of
their other colonies. They published an interesting pamphlet entitled "The
Queen of Western Kansas," in which they listed all the lots available for
purchase in Vega. On the back page they described the community and its
advantages:

> The beautiful townsite of Vega is situated in Wallace County about 200 miles
> east of Denver, Colorado, and 400 miles west of Kansas City, Missouri, on
> fine rolling prairie land. The Montana, Kansas and Texas line of the railroad
> is now in the course of construction and will pass through the town and tele-
> graph wires having already been put up to within 25 miles of the place.
>
> Many can be had at a reasonable rate from the Building and Loan Associa-
> tion of Sharon Springs, Kansas.
>
> The townsite of Vega: Is situated in the midst of what will no doubt be
> the largest Swedish settlement in America. About five lots have already been
> bought up by Swedish people who will settle there and improve the land.
> The land lies very beautifully; the soil is very productive. . . . no better
> farming land is to be had anywhere in the state. There is plenty of good wa-
> ter to be had at a moderate depth and good market for farm products.

In spite of the active promotion, the townsite company never successfully lured many Swedes to this part of Kansas. Granted, they established
the town as promised, and it did have several businesses and a rail connection, but little else. In the early 1900s, the few Swedish emigrants who had
settled there went elsewhere. Despite good soil and good water, it was, after
all, the high plains of western Kansas, and its climate was not one that
many emigrants could endure. A few settlers found their way back to the

Lindsborg area in central Kansas, where a much larger Swedish population had congregated. Others moved farther west into Colorado. By 1908 even the post office had been discontinued.[1]

Today little marks this attempt by the Swedes to colonize the Western High Plains. Nor did the Swedish townsite company have any better luck in Nebraska or elsewhere in Kansas. Certain ethnic groups came to Kansas in great numbers, but they acculturated with other similar groups and probably moved to several different places in a lifetime. Vega was just one brief stop on a journey.

POND CITY
Wallace County

Pond City and the Pond Creek Stage Station were both located about two miles west of Wallace; the stage station was situated a short distance south of the present highway that crosses Pond Creek.

After the massacre of the Cheyenne at Sand Creek in Colorado, troubles with the Indians increased across the western plains, making it extremely dangerous to venture to the Colorado gold fields. The army therefore established some military posts for the protection of travelers and stage drivers on the Smoky Hill and Santa Fe trails. Camp Pond Creek was one of the posts under the orders of General Grenville Dodge, commander of all forts in this section of Kansas.

In February 1866 General William Sherman ordered two companies of infantry and cavalry sent to the Pond Creek Station for the protection of the stage lines. One official, William Bell, said that during his three weeks stay at Pond Creek, he was attacked twice by Indians.[1] Bell wrote the book, "New Tracks in North America," in which he described the station in 1867:

> Standing side by side, and built of wood and stone, are the stables and the ranch in which the drivers and hostlers live. . . . A little subterranean passage, about five feet by three, leads from the stables to the house. Another one leads from the stables to a pit dug in the ground, about ten yards distant. . . . Another narrow subterranean passage leads from the house to a second pit, commanding the other side of the station; while a third passage runs from the corral to a larger pit, commanding the rear. In both houses, many repeating Spencer and Henry breechloading rifles—the former carrying seven, the latter 18 charges—lie loaded and ready to hand; while over each little fort a black flag waves, which the red man knows well means "no quarter" for them. When attacked the men creep into these pits, and, thus, pro-

tected, keep up a tremendous fire through the portholes. Two or three men, with a couple of breechloaders each, are a match for almost any number of assailants. . . . The Indians are beginning to understand the covered rifle pits, and the more they know of them the more careful they are to keep at a respectful distance from them.

In 1866 life for the soldiers at the Pond Creek Station was decidedly dreary. By the time they had completed their quarters, winter had set in. Only the arrival of stagecoaches broke the daily monotony, and they ran on irregular schedules. The snows that winter meant trouble for both Pond Creek and the next station at Monument. The soldiers had only brought enough rations to last until midwinter, and unless additional supply wagons could get through, the men would face starvation. To make matters worse, the pork and bacon had spoiled, and the hardtack had mildewed. As more snow covered the ground, the horses also began suffering for lack of forage.

About a week before Christmas, the men sighted a buffalo herd and killed eight of the animals, but by Christmas the buffalo meat was all gone. The food shortage became so severe that in early January the men walked fifty miles to Monument for supplies. The conditions at Monument, however, were just as critical, so they joined forces and marched to Fort Fletcher. Thus was Pond Creek abandoned until early spring when the command reestablished the post.

Indian harassment continued. One of the worst encounters occurred on June 26, 1867, near the post. *Harper's Weekly*, July 27, 1867 featured an account of the battle:

The war on the Smoky Hill Route through Kansas continues with great fury. On the 26th of June last a band of 300 Cheyennes, under a chief called Roman Nose attacked a station two miles from Fort Wallace and ran off the Overland Stage Company's stock. They then advanced toward the fort, when Company G of the 7th Cavalry . . . went out to meet them. The Indians fell back to the brow of a hill two miles from the fort, then turned and awaited the attack. The cavalry charged at a gallop, and were met by a counter charge. The Indians, with lances poised and arrows on the string, rode at them with great speed, and a hand-to-hand fight followed, in which the savages displayed unlooked-for daring. With their overwhelming numbers they succeeded in driving the cavalry back to the fort, with a loss of seven men killed, several wounded, and half the horses captured or killed. Roman Nose was very conspicuous in the fight, dashing into the midst of the fray on his powerful gray horse. He carried a spear, with which he unhorsed a soldier, and was about to spear him as he lay on the ground, when corporal Harris struck the savage with his sword, which he had in his left hand. Roman Nose turned upon him but as he did so Harris placed the muzzle of the Spencer rifle which he carried in his right hand at the breast of the savage and fired. With the blood spouting from his wound, the Indian fell forward on his horse. . . . After the battle there were found to be 8 men killed and 7 men injured.[2]

An old mountain man named Bill Comstock, sometimes called the "Natty Bumppo of the Plains," entertained the men at Pond Creek with his wild stories of Indians and western outlaws. Comstock stayed at Pond Creek several months before heading out across the plains, but unfortunately, his adventures ended for good just a few miles away from the post when he was killed by a band of Cheyenne.

The Pond Creek Station assumed the name of Pond City in 1868. One of the military scouts from Fort Wallace, E. Whitney, mentioned in his diary that he "played cards, wrote letters and other things in the morning and went to Pond City in the afternoon," where all the saloons and gambling houses were located. Whitney also noted in his diary that there were "a bunch of Indian raids on Pond City in 1868, too numerous to go into detail."[3]

In 1868 Pond City became the first county seat of Wallace County. The census of the county taken on April 17 showed a population of 609, including the military post. A charter for the Pond City Land and Town Company was applied for on January 22, 1869, and the incorporators were John Whiteford, Richard McClure, W. H. Bush, Harrison Nicolls, and Charles Fee.

In August 1869 John Whiteford wrote from Pond City to Governor Samuel Crawford that the Indians had attacked the Comstock and Drisco farms, killing a farmhand at the latter. He told how Mrs. Drisco, dressed in her husband's clothes, then grabbed a gun and crawled under her bed. As the Indians entered the house, she fired, driving them out into the yard. There Mr. Drisco and another farmhand shot at them from a more fortified position. After the Indians retreated to a hill at the rear of the house, the three escaped to Pond City.

The Indians attacked a hay camp at Pond City on August 20, driving off the oxen and mules. On August 27 Whiteford again wrote the governor about the dire situation at Pond City, stating that they were hemmed in and had no wood or hay. The women and children had retreated to the stone buildings in town for protection. The men were all willing to fight but had no horses or arms. The Indians were well supplied with guns and ammunition from the government.[4] Indian depredations continued around Pond City through 1869.

Excitement at Pond City centered on the saloons and brothels, at least until the town of Wallace took over the liquor traffic. One of the more memorable incidents concerned Sharp Grover, a famous Indian scout, who was shot by a man named Moody in a saloon brawl. Although Grover was not armed when he was killed, Moody was allowed to go free, for he claimed he had shot in self-defense. Moody said he "thought" Grover had a gun when he started toward him uttering a flow of "abusive epithets."[5]

On August 26, 1869, the *Time and Conservative*, Leavenworth, covered another interesting incident:

At Pond City this morning about two o'clock, John Langford was taken out by the Vigilance Committee to be hung for his crimes. On ascertaining his certain fate, he told them he did not want them to hang him, and that he would hang himself; so he pulled off his boots, put the rope around his neck, climbed the tree and jumped off. Before doing this he acknowledged to killing six men, and said if he had his fate postponed a few days he would have killed as many more. On being requested to make his peace with his Maker, he replied that if he had a Maker, it was a damned poor one, as he had experienced considerable trouble in the last few years. He also said he would meet them all in hell, but none of them should gain admission except with hemp ropes ornamenting their necks.

The count of the people at Pond City taken on July 6, 1870, showed a total of forty persons. These citizens abandoned the town when the railroad built through Wallace. A local newspaper dated October 11, 1934, described the remnants of Pond City:

Mr. V. A. Kear informs us that one mile east of what is now Pond Creek bridge, there used to be a station called Pond Creek station. . . . This old site is now and has been farmed over for the past three years by Wilbur Collins of Wallace. In digging around Sunday, Mr. Kear found many relics. He found about a dozen .58 caliber revolver shells, one .58 caliber bullet, and an old canteen. On the site of the old station he found many signs and evidence that there had once been buildings there.[6]

Today the site can be found on the south side of U.S. Highway 40 on privately owned farm land. Cellar holes and remains of dirt fortifications are still visible. The stage tender's building remains intact on the Madigan ranch, ten miles north and four west of old Wallace. Bullet holes can still be seen in the siding, evidence of the Indian attacks.

9

SOUTHWEST KANSAS

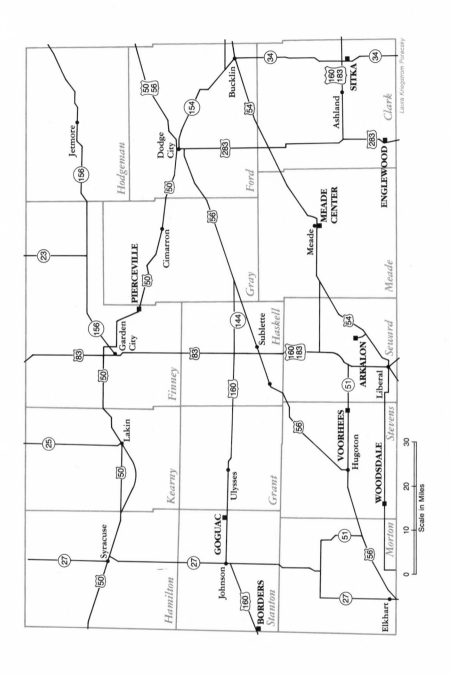

Jetmore

156

Hodgeman

50
56

154

Bucklin

34

34

160
183

SITKA

Ashland

54

Dodge City

283

Clark

50

23

PIERCEVILLE

Cinarron

50

56

Ford

MEADE CENTER

ENGLEWOOD

283

Meade

Gray

Garden City

156

Meade

144

Sublette

Haskell

54

Seward

83

83

160
183

ARKALON

50

Finney

160

51

Liberal

Lakin

25

VOORHEES

56

Hugoton

50

Kearny

Ulysses

Grant

WOODSDALE

Stevens

Syracuse

GOGUAC

51

Morton

27

27

56

27

50

Johnson

160

Elkhart

Hamilton

BORDERS

Stanton

Scale in Miles

0   10   20   30

PIERCEVILLE
Finney County

In 1872 Pierceville was farther west than any frontier town in southwestern Kansas. In the vast area around Dodge City and south of the Union Pacific Railroad, and for many miles into Colorado and the Indian Territory, there were no other established habitations of white men. This isolation gave rise to several incidents that marked the town as a place of historical interest.

Early in the spring of 1872, three years before Dodge City became a cattle town, the Barton brothers drove 3,000 head of cattle up from Texas over the Western Trail. These men were the first to bring in a trail herd to feed on the government ranges in western Kansas and the first to establish a ranch headquarters along the Arkansas River near the site of Pierceville. This ranch was chosen by the Santa Fe officials as a railroad townsite and named in honor of Charles and Carlos Pierce, members of the railroad company. As soon as the crew completed a survey, 500 workmen ate their meals and bunked in boxcars while they laid the rails. The railroad hired hunters to supply the workers with meat from the herds of buffalo and antelope that roamed the plains.

About the time the railroad completed laying tracks through Pierceville, Thomas O'Laughlin opened a store that became a popular spot for hunters, cowboys, section crews, and any adventurers who happened to be in the region. He traded his goods for buffalo meat, and then traded the meat for provisions, clothing, and ammunition. A post office opened in Pierceville on June 10, 1873, and George Clossen was postmaster. The town then outranked Dodge City for the title of "Cowboy Capital," because the first cattle herds brought into western Kansas came down the Arkansas River from the west directly into Pierceville.

For a year the town flourished. Then came July 3, 1874, a day that dawned clear and bright, the sun blazing down on the adobe buildings. A few citizens and some cowboys lounged in the shade, wondering if anyone would drift in to help them celebrate the "Fourth" the next day. As if in answer to their idle conversation, some buffalo hunters suddenly came into view spurring their horses at top speed. They brought news of the Indian fight at Adobe Walls, Texas, a few days before and warned them that a band of these angry Indians was heading north, making for the settlements along the Santa Fe Railroad.

Mrs. Ellen O'Laughlin, wife of Thomas, described these troubled times in a letter to her niece, Mrs. B. C. Hurst:

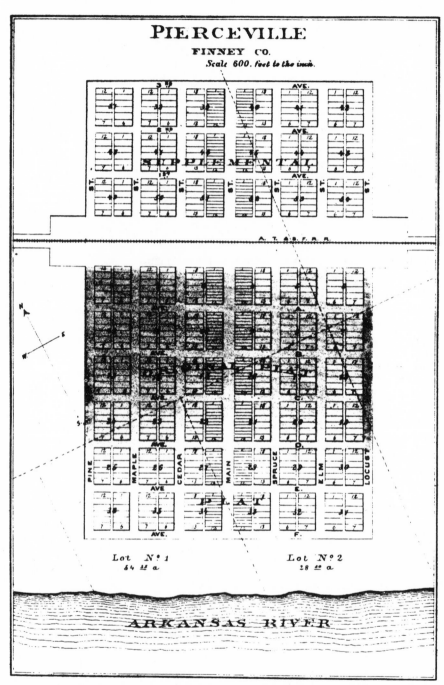

According to this 1887 plat of Pierceville, the original townsite was located south of the Santa Fe Railroad tracks. Soon the town developed rapidly north of the tracks as well. Today little remains of the original townsite.

Immediately after hearing this news my husband hitched the horse to a wagon. We loaded it with some bedding and a few clothes. We put our son and daughter in the wagon and drove to a cow camp run by the Bancrofts, near Pierceville, and stayed there that night. At this camp there were fifteen men, but I was the only woman. The men did not seem to be worried about a possible attack by the Indians, and left the horses staked out around the camp all night. The next morning they went out to bring them in, but they were on the watch for Indians. Suddenly a fast moving body of color loomed in the distance in the sandhills south of the river, and as the thing began to take shape it looked like horses galloping in the air. . . . Presently they had to admit that it was no optical illusion—it was Indians! A number of mounted warriors decked out in all their savage war paint!

The men did not wait to gather in the horses but raced back to the camp. This cow camp was built of pickets chinked with mud. The men knocked the chinking out just enough to get their guns through so that they could fire at the Indians. As soon as the Indians got within range and before they got to the horses they fired at them. The Indians turned and ran toward our store south of the railroad track.

We watched the Indians from Bancroft's cow camp. They rode around the store and dugouts several times before they went into the store. When they found that no one was there they went in, took what they wanted and set fire to it. . . .

About this time there was a sharp blast of a whistle, and a Santa Fe train came puffing into sight. A number of Indians mounted on fleetest ponies ran down the track to meet it, but the train never stopped. The savages continued to chase it, but the noise they made seemed like pandemonium broke loose, above the shrieks of the steam whistle. They fired at the train, and into the windows with arrows and revolvers. It is not known whether any of the crew or passengers were hurt, for none of them ever returned to tell the story.

Bancroft, who was in charge of the camp, rode down to the railroad, hastily threw a rope over the telegraph wire, and pulled it to the ground. He sent the following dispatch by touching the ends of the wires together: "For God's sake, come to Pierceville. Surrounded by Indians." He had intended the message to reach the soldiers at Fort Dodge, but an agent at Granada, Colorado, heard the transmission and quickly sent a railroad engine to their rescue. But long before any help arrived, Pierceville lay smoldering in ruins, and the Indians were on their way back to their own territory.

During the next four years no one made any effort to rebuild the town. The site served only as a campground for Indians or for the drivers of the trail herds. Then in 1878 John Stowe built a cabin, a man named Vermillion started a store, and the post office reopened. By this time several small towns existed farther west, but Pierceville had the only coal chute on the railroad, and the settlers came for miles around to get their coal and do their trading.

In 1879 William Harvey operated a general store in the Vermillion building; R. W. Sholes had a general store; William Newlin opened a real estate office; and John Brown was the village blacksmith. The Barton brothers started a ferry, so people south of the Arkansas River could now trade at Pierceville. The Bartons made trips across the river whenever teams and wagons or horsemen appeared on the opposite bank and hailed the ferry. One day in the fall of 1886, the ferry started across with five tons of coal. A strong wind was blowing and carried the boat along rapidly. They dropped the sail as usual within thirty feet of the bank, but the ferry failed to stop and shot completely over the bank, wrecking it beyond repair.

N. J. Collins came west from New York with a modest amount of money to start a wheat ranch. During the summer of 1879, he built "The Summit," a twelve-room, three-story house above a full basement of native rock. A spacious portico extended from each story, and standing on the hill overlooking Pierceville, the house towered like a castle above the plains. For several years Collins planted his wheat, but no rains came, and the land dried up. He said he had "a vision that it was going to take a long time to tame the wild sod and the still wilder weather conditions," so he abandoned the Summit and moved to Dodge City. For the next few years the big house stood empty, and stories circulated that it was haunted. Its flapping shutters and swinging doors seemed moved by unseen hands. Even those in need of shelter shunned the place. Then after the business boom of 1886, so many people lacked housing that four families moved in, but they left just as soon as the boom was over. Once more the Summit stood deserted. As time passed, the house gradually fell to ruin, and some local citizens hauled away the lumber and other building material to use in smaller houses.

By 1886 the population had reached 400. At this time the county built a bridge across the Arkansas River and opened a road to the south. The weekly *Pierceville Courier* reported that there were lumber yards, real estate offices, a restaurant, a hotel, a harness business, hardware stores, a doctor and druggist, carpenters, a blacksmith, a surveyor, and the Laclede Hotel in town.

In the early 1900s a steel and concrete bridge replaced the old wooden structure over the river, and the city erected several school buildings. In 1920 Pierceville built a new district grade school and a fireproof high school at a cost of $17,000. Until recently these same structures still served the declining community. In 1930 the population of Pierceville was 166.

Today Pierceville is a semighost, first the victim of an Indian raid, then of time itself.[1]

ENGLEWOOD
Clark County

Picking up bones to keep from starving.
Picking up cow-chips to keep from freezing.
Picking up courage to keep from leaving.
Way out west in No-Man's Land.[1]

"No-Man's Land" was just south of Englewood, a prosperous little town in the southwest corner of Clark County. Founded in 1884, it was located fifty miles south of the notorious Dodge City. The Tuttle Trail passed five miles west of the town, and another trail came straight down from Dodge City to Englewood. In 1885 the settlers formed a town company and elected N. E. Osborn, president; B. B. Bush, secretary; Grant Hatfield, treasurer; Howard Friend, E. A. Rieman, and S. S. Mills, directors.[2]

In those early days many cowboys and settlers traveling down the Tuttle Trail rode over to Englewood to "wet their whistles" with firewater. They would get drunk, terrorize the citizens, steal horses and cattle, and then slip across the border into "No Man's Land." It took a long time for the lawmen to come from Dodge City, and when they did arrive, they were much too late. Finally a group of vigilantes formed a committee in the Cherokee Strip to help protect the settlers. If they caught a suspect, they hanged him to the nearest tree and then buried him immediately.

The town was booming when the Santa Fe Railroad was laid out in 1887. At this time the business houses were on Douglas Avenue beginning at the Cattle King Hotel and extending in a three block square to the St. Elmo Hotel. The businesses consisted of a bank, three general stores, three hotels, three livery stables, a jewelry store, a dance hall, two restaurants, a drugstore, two blacksmith shops, a post office, and a skating rink, as well as three doctors, a lawyer, a preacher, a city marshal, and a deputy sheriff. In the mid-1880s, the population reached nearly 2,000.

A masquerade ball in Englewood complete with fiddlers. Sorry, no spitting allowed.

In 1932 pioneer Albert Easley wrote about the cowboys in the early days of Englewood:

> They would ride to a ranch, get a job, work awhile, maybe a long time, maybe they'd leave all of a sudden. As a rule they were good hearted, but were on the dodge of the law. They had their principles, maybe a little less than a lot of folks. They gambled, but not with kids. They drank whiskey, but would not give a kid a drink.

In 1885 the outlaws became very defiant. When John Folley, the deputy sheriff and also the leader of an outlaw gang, made an arrest, he would make the city marshal turn the prisoners loose by threatening him with his gun. Few outlaws were ever convicted.

Outlaws did not wreak the only havoc in town. Inattention and drunkenness created their own tragedies. The town newspaper, *The Englewood Chief*, of July 9, 1885, reported: "After the Fourth of July celebration at Beeson's Grove, seven men were cleaning their guns, one man by the name of Kinzer, bending over to see how far the hammer would go back was fatally injured and died. The body was packed in ice, taken to Dodge, and shipped to Indiana." And in August 1885 the following item appeared in the paper:

S. P. Scalland was a cowboy from the territory, and W. T. and Charles Peck were merchants from Vesta. The Peck brothers drove their team and wagon in front of the dance hall about 12 or 1 o'clock. When Scalland, who had been drinking, objected to their going home, all began to quarrel, several shots were fired, and Scalland was shot through the bowels and died soon after. The Peck brothers were fined $500.

Fred Edwards, a Mexican from Texas, came to town the winter of 1885. When he was four years old someone kidnapped him and threw him in with the roughest kind of people. He could change from a kind man to a real fighter in a moment's notice. Willis Long, city marshal of Englewood, wanted to quit and asked Edwards to take his place. The morning after he was in office, he went out on the street and, as he told it:

I was surprised. There were sixteen out-houses along the street. It sure made me feel bad. Well, I waited till two o'clock. The gang, eleven in all, was standing in front of the post office. John Folley looked awfully big. They all laughed at me. I told them to move the houses back to where they got them. I gave them one hour. If they did not I would have the Governor send me 100 State Soldiers. A lawyer told them it would go hard with them if the state took a hand. Every house was moved back in its proper place.

One of the gang, John Brisco by name, came to me and said I'd better resign or I'd be killed and Folley would use my head for a football.

The next morning, Folley walked across the street and told Edwards if he arrested one of his gang, he'd kill him, and simultaneously he drew his gun. Edwards, knowing he meant business, drew his gun first and shot Folley. Of course, Folley's gang, hearing the gunshots, was sure the "greaser" was dead, and a crowd gathered. It surprised the gang to see their leader lying lifeless in the street. The townspeople were relieved to see that their marshal was still alive.

In March 1886 Edwards shot and killed a cowboy named Sconce in the Cattle King Hotel. Sconce had been drinking and gambling, and Edwards claimed he shot in self-defense. A few months later, Charlie Cole, a young cowboy, rode into town and proceeded to get drunk. Others who were drinking dared him to ride his horse up the wide back stairway of the Cattle

A school scene in Englewood, ca. 1900.

King Hotel. With plenty of cursing and yelling he rode the pony upstairs and into the hall with the intention of riding down the front stairs, but Edwards heard the commotion in the hall and fired his gun. The report was deafening inside the building, and the pony took off down the back stairs with one jump and bolted out of town.

The following year Bill Dalton of the notorious Dalton Brothers dressed up like a professional gambler with a high hat, white shirt, black tie, and checked pants, and he stayed a week at the St. Elmo Hotel. He must have behaved himself, for no record exists of any trouble in town that week.[3]

The town continued to grow into the 1900s, but trouble was not far in the future. During the depression businesses began to fail, and the Dust Bowl years upset the balance of nature, plunging the area into a deep economical decline. Englewood barely hung on. There were no new stores, and the town's youth drifted elsewhere. By the 1950s, the remaining businesses folded and the school closed its doors.

In 1981 Mayor Robin Roberts was still doing what he could to hold the town together. He had the only service station and tavern in Englewood. There were still two elevators and the post office, but these were about all the businesses left in town. Englewood, once an "end-of-the-track" town, is now nearing the end of its line.[4]

The first residence in Sitka, built in 1884.

SITKA
Clark County

Today Sitka is one of the most impressive Kansas ghost towns, with abandoned buildings and ghostly passages. But Sitka was not always thus. In 1909 the town was platted into forty square blocks. This translated into 1,019 city lots to be sold as home and business sites by three of the town's movers and shakers: George Harvey, Paul Clark, and Charlie Wallingford. Prices were a cool $25 a lot.

The citizens of Sitka had much to brag about. The town had a large commercial trading area that included Oklahoma Territory and the Bluff Creek neighborhood. It had one of the largest stockyards on the Englewood branch of the Santa Fe Railroad and was located in the heart of a great wheat and alfalfa belt.

The first sale of town lots in March was well advertised in Ashland's *Clark County Clipper*. Full page ads had headlines bragging of "The Beginning of A Great City." Many lots were sold and buildings went up overnight. The first two were grain elevators, one capable of holding 15,000 bushels. Sitka's market area for cattle and grain shipping soon expanded fifty miles to the south and twenty-five to the north. At its peak, the town had nearly 300 people, two lumberyards, two grocery stores, three livery stables, six feed yards, and two hardware stores.

Unfortunately, time was not generous to Sitka. Its market area diminished with the advent of other railroad towns. Businessmen moved elsewhere when the depression and drought years brought hard times. In 1959 fire raged through the downtown section, destroying the Sherman general merchandise store, the post office, some outbuildings, and the L.A. Haydock residence. This was the final blow after years of barely surviving.[1] Today Sitka still stands in a rich agricultural and oil region, but the ghost town profits not. It's worthwhile to take the time to visit Sitka and tour a neglected but beautiful part of Kansas.

MEADE CENTER
Meade County

> One of the things that attracts the attention of a traveler is the rapidity with which some of these new towns are pushed forward. Meade Center in Meade County is a striking example of this. It is located on the west side of Crooked Creek, near the center of the county. The first building was raised on the 20th of May (1885). On the 20th of July there were 88 houses erected, and the last Meade Center paper reports 139 buildings with a population of near 500.

Thus wrote Jeremiah Platt, a circuit rider in Meade County.[1] Meade Center had quite a boomtown start, typical of the early days in western Kansas. Today, the county seat of Meade contains Meade Center, a victim of annexation.

In the 1870s the settlers in the region around Meade Center experienced their share of unrest, beginning with what was known as the "Lone Tree Massacre," one of the most famous Indian attacks in the history of Kansas. In the summer of 1874 an expedition of twenty-two surveyors made camp a short distance east of the old "Lone Tree," a well-known landmark on the east side of Crooked Creek six miles southwest of Meade Center. Captain Oliver Short's party planned to survey the exterior lines of the township, and they were scheduled to be away from their base camp for the entire week.

On August 24, 1874, Captain Short chose his crew, which consisted of his fourteen-year old son Daniel, James Shaw and his son J. Allen, Harry Jones, and John H. Keuchler. Harry Short, Captain Short's other son and the chainman for his father, was supposed to stay in camp. Two days later on August 26 when the other surveyors spotted Captain Short's wagon standing alone on the east side of Crooked Creek, they armed themselves and rode ahead to the empty wagon. There they found the bodies of Captain Short and his five men lying on the ground in a row, just where the Indians had left them. The oxen were dead in their yokes with their hindquarters cut off, and the camp dog lay dead beside its master. Captain Short, his son Daniel, and Harry Jones had been scalped, and the heads of the others had been crushed. The pants' pockets of all were turned inside out. There were twenty-eight bullet holes in the wagon and eight bullets found in the water barrel.

The men put the bodies in Short's wagon and hauled them back to camp, where they buried them at sundown about a hundred yards southeast of the "Lone Tree." They dug one grave three feet deep for all the victims and wrapped them in tent cloth. The men took time to carve initials on rough stones and place them at the head of each body. Years later, the bodies were disinterred and buried with their families in separate locations.[2] The famous old cottonwood known as "Lone Tree" was blown down in a windstorm in June 1938, and most of the wood was hauled to Meade, where it was stored in a local warehouse.[3]

Sometime in the 1870s Meade Center became known as Meade City, but in 1885 the name changed again when the town company filed the "Meade Center" charter. That October, by court order, the city of Meade Center was incorporated, but by 1889 the name had been changed to Meade, the name by which the county seat is known today.[4]

ARKALON
Seward County

Abe K. Stouffer, editor of the *Arkalon News*, wrote in 1888 that the town was "graciously situated on the Cimarron." From the day he left Fargo Springs, Stouffer's allegiance lay with Arkalon. He waged a bitter editorial battle trying to help the little town become the Seward County seat, which unfortunately went to the larger community of Liberal. Liberal is still there today; Arkalon is all but gone.

Arkalon was founded seven miles below Fargo Springs on the Rock Island Railroad line. The government established a post office there on May 9, 1888, and the Arkalon Town Company with M. A. Low as president signed the plat of the town on May 10. Since lots were cheap, some 3,000 people either invested in or moved to Arkalon. Many of these settlers were former residents of the nearby towns of Fargo Springs and Springfield. Unfortunately, Arkalon had ecological problems that soon crippled its chances for survival. The country surrounding the town was too hilly to make it a

A street scene in Arkalon showing a burro pack train loaded with supplies in front of the bank building, ca. 1900.

suitable marketing point, and the area was pocketed with deep sand and sagebrush too deep for the teams that had to pull heavy loads in and out of the river valley.[1]

Despite these natural problems, Arkalon remained an important shipping point for about twenty years. This business probably would have continued had it not been for the 1914 flood in the Cimarron River valley. The water destroyed an important bridge at Arkalon that was later replaced downstream by a monstrosity everyone called the "Samson of the Cimarron." After the flood, the Chicago, Rock Island & Pacific Railroad moved most of its operations to Liberal. Thereafter the depopulation of Arkalon was rapid. Many of the people who had originally come from Fargo Springs moved again, this time to Liberal. By 1920 only a few families still lived on the townsite. The post office, one of the last services left, closed in 1929.[2]

Today all that remains of Arkalon are a few deserted buildings. From a point inside one of the dilapidated buildings, one can see the wildwood that now graces the area where some early day horticulturist sought to plant fruit trees on the banks of the Cimarron. A few cottonwood trees, dwarfed and twisted from their struggle for survival through the "dirty 30s," also remain in the old orchard. On the crest of the hill to the south lies the small, well-kept prairie cemetery where many old settlers rest. This hill also offers a view of the areas where Springfield and Fargo Springs once

Interior view of the Custer General Store in Arkalon. Like many general stores of its day, anything was available, often hanging from the ceiling!

On May 7, 1914, a flash flood rolled down the Cimarron River, catching a locomotive by surprise on the Arkalon Bridge. Both bridge and train fell into the river, many of the cars sinking in several feet of quicksand.

stood and overlooks the present activity of the Panhandle Eastern oil station north of the great Cimarron bridge.

Life and death in western Kansas continues. Fargo Springs, Springfield, and Arkalon all succumbed to Liberal, the final victor in the conflict for the Seward County seat.[3]

WOODSDALE
Stevens County

Samuel Wood, a prominent Topeka attorney, founded Woodsdale in 1885. At that time the nearby town of Hugoton had been chosen as the temporary county seat. Wood was annoyed at this selection and began legal proceedings in Topeka to try to prevent the organization of the county. Back in Hugoton, Wood was considered an outsider who was seeking to interfere with what the townspeople believed to be their firmly established rights. Suddenly, in August 1886, Wood mysteriously disappeared.

In order to eliminate Wood until a temporary county seat could be selected, Hugoton's supporters had had him arrested and taken to Oklahoma. These officials accounted for his absence by saying that they had persuaded him to abandon his legal battle with the county, and he had gone into Indian Territory on a hunting trip. His friends did not believe this explanation, and they immediately organized a search party and headed south. On their way they found a note that Wood had secretly dropped by the trail. Thus assured they were on the right track, they hurried on and caught up with Wood's captors, who surrendered him without incident. Upon his return to Woodsdale, Wood filed civil and criminal proceedings against his abductors, but for "lack of evidence" the judge dismissed the charges without a trial. In 1887 state legislators passed a bill legalizing the organization of Stevens County, and in the ensuing fight for the county seat between Hugoton and Woodsdale, Hugoton was (temporarily) successful.[1]

Another dispute between the two towns arose from an election to vote bonds for a railroad that the citizens of Woodsdale favored and the Hugoton people opposed. In June 1888 the Rock Island proposed to build two lines, one to run in the northern and the other in the southern part of the county, leaving Hugoton halfway between the two roads. In fact Woodsdale officials were attempting to "kill" Hugoton. The interested parties held a meeting at the nearby town of Voorhees to discuss this issue. That evening a fight occurred when Sam Robinson, marshal of Hugoton, struck Woodsdale's undersheriff, Jim Gerrond, with his revolver. Nothing more serious took place at that time, but within a few days Sheriff Gerrond issued a warrant charging Robinson with assault and battery. The sheriff placed the warrant in the hands of Ed Short, marshal of Woodsdale, who proceeded to Hugoton and attempted to arrest Robinson. The two marshals engaged in a gunfight, but the Hugoton men, who outnumbered Marshal Short two to one, ran him out of town.

In late June 1888 the county held a railroad bond election. Before the votes could be canvassed, a controversy erupted over the returns from one precinct. The people felt that if a conflict was to be averted when they counted the votes, they would need protection from an outside source. The county sheriff wired Governor John Martin asking that a militia be sent to keep the peace. General Murray Myers and two companies of men went at once to the area and found each town to be a fortified camp, the inhabitants itching for a fight. Believing that bloodshed was a distinct probability, he promptly disarmed both forces. After the election commission completed the canvass of the election returns, the excitement subsided, and the warrant for the arrest and prosecution of Marshal Robinson was dropped—at least for the time being.

A month passed without incident, then on July 22, when Woodsdale's Marshal Short was at Voorhees, he learned that Hugoton's Marshal Robinson was with a hunting party in the Cherokee Strip. Short returned to Woodsdale and with the assistance of several friends started out in pursuit of Robinson. Again he planned to serve Robinson with the warrant for his arrest. At Goff's Creek in Oklahoma, the group came upon a local farmer who told them where to find the Robinson party. Short then sent word ahead to Robinson to surrender, warning him that he could not escape. Orin and Clarke Cook, two of Robinson's men, advised him to get away as quickly as possible. After Robinson fled on his horse, Short sent a message to Woodsdale's Sheriff John Cross, who immediately started south with five deputies to help Short capture Robinson.[2]

In the meantime the Cook brothers reached Hugoton and organized a posse that headed back south, where they encountered Short and chased him out of the area. Sheriff Cross and his deputies failed to find either Short or Robinson and started back to Woodsdale. "Kid" Tonney, one of Cross's deputies, described the ensuing massacre:

> About 9 o'clock at night we reached a camp of haymakers at the head of Wild Horse Lake, eight miles south of the Kansas line, . . . Eaton and Wilcox got up into a wagon nearby to rest. The rest of us were laying on the hay. . . . We were surprised by the appearance of Robinson and his men. They commanded us to surrender and hold up our hands. . . . Robinson said: "Sheriff Cross, you are my first man," and fired at him with a Winchester killing him instantly. He then turned and said: "Hubbard, I want you," and shot him also.
>
> At the same time J. B. Chamberlain, one of the commissioners of Stevens County, took my revolver from me, stepped back a few feet, leveled his Winchester and fired. As he did so, I, having my hands up, made a sudden movement and received a flesh wound in the shoulder, the force of the ball knocking me down. I played dead.
>
> Robinson's party then discovered Eaton and Wilcox who, hearing the firing, had got out of the wagon. Eaton ran several hundred yards before a shot hit him. Cross, Eaton, Hubbard, and Wilcox were all shot again to be sure they were dead. Robinson and his crowd pulled me around by the foot to see if I was dead. Chamberlain assured them that I was, as he had given me a center shot. . . .

After they had been gone a short time, I got up and got my horse and started for Voorhees, about 15 miles to the northeast. . . . On reaching there I found the news of the bloody tragedy had preceded me, and men had gone after the bodies of the slaughtered men. An officer started to take me to Liberal so that I could get out of the country, as it was feared that the Hugoton crowd would hunt me up and kill me, but I was too weak to stand the trip, and was secreted in the cornfield of a physician until friends from Woodsdale arrived and took me away.

Robinson and his gang, after escorting the haymakers, returned to the scene of the butchers and discovered that I was gone. They set out to hunt me but went in exactly the opposite direction to the one I took.

After the shooting of Cross and his men, several of the citizens of Hugoton threatened to burn down the town of Voorhees and drive its inhabitants out of the country because they had assisted me after I was wounded. Excitement was at fever heat, and state officials, together with eight companies of Kansas National Guard were ordered to Stevens County, and martial law was proclaimed. It lasted a month.[3]

A few arrests were made in this case, but apparently no court had jurisdiction since the crime took place in "No Man's Land." Finally, however, a trial was held in Stevens County, which ended in a conviction of the accused felons. Later the court ordered a reversal of the decision, stating that the attorneys in charge of the prosecution were "too zealous."

At the time of the homicides, S. B. Bradford, the state attorney general, investigated the murders personally. He wrote a report of his conclusions to the governor in which he expressed the unqualified opinion that the killings were deliberate murder, but the governor considered Bradford's conclusions to be hearsay and discredited them. At a Supreme Court hearing, this gubernatorial proceeding was declared in error, and the court ordered a new trial. The U.S. Attorney General became convinced that the district attorney had given too much "leeway" to Wood and had him removed from the case. However, energetic efforts by Wood's attorneys to have the prosecution discontinued were successful, and there the matter ended.[4]

After winning the next election, Hugoton became the county seat, and Woodsdale began its decline. Sam Wood made the mistake of visiting Hugoton that year, and someone shot him in the back. After his death, the city he had founded slowly faded away.[5]

Today the Woodsdale site is in an open field where some cellar excavations are still visible. Nearby is the old cemetery containing a few marked graves. Ten miles to the northeast is Hugoton, a county seat with a history of misdeeds.

VOORHEES
Stevens County

Voorhees, the one-time "queen" of Stevens County, was established in 1887 about twenty miles west of present Liberal. Apparently, the first structure in town was a hotel—the St. Nicholas. Constructing the St. Nicholas was no small venture, for it was a two-and-a-half-story building measuring seventy feet by seventy feet! It held the town company headquarters and was the business center in town for years. Shortly after the hotel was built, C. E. Wright started the *Voorhees Vindicator*, which carried colorful advertising both for the town of Voorhees and the St. Nicholas.

A large advertisement appeared in the paper in October 1887 asserting that the town company "is a strong and influential corporation, being composed of the world-renowned town builders of Southwestern Kansas, the members of which have not only gained local distinction but a number are of national celebrity!" The paper also noted that Voorhees was named for Daniel Voorhees of Indiana, a member of the town company.

From 1887 to 1891 Voorhees boomed. Some 225 lots sold during the town's history, the first three going to W. H. Mayberry of Kenton, Kentucky, for $166.24. A post office, a school, a hotel, a livery barn, and several brick buildings composed the business district. The town company platted over 129 acres for the townsite and laid out several streets, including the main streets of Ingalls and Matson Avenues. A hand-dug well provided water for the town as well as for the St. Nicholas Hotel. In 1888 water was piped from the well directly to the rooms of the hotel, a major engineering feat in southwest Kansas at that time.

If the St. Nicholas Hotel was still around and could talk, its stories would astound us all. The hotel offered "French cuisine," courtesy of the French chef, Peter Castene. Apparently some members of the town company went all the way to Cincinnati to lure him to Voorhees. He developed a reputation for fine cooking and for the good supply of fine liquors, champagne, beer, and whiskey he kept on ice below the hotel. Food supplies were often limited, and Castene at times had to settle for "rotten eggs and spoiled jackrabbits." One of his suppliers, Warren Farmer, sold jackrabbits to Castene for forty cents each and a drink of whiskey. Castene would hang them until they got soft like butter, and then he would cook them. Farmer supplied him with only a few jackrabbits at a time in order not to overstock

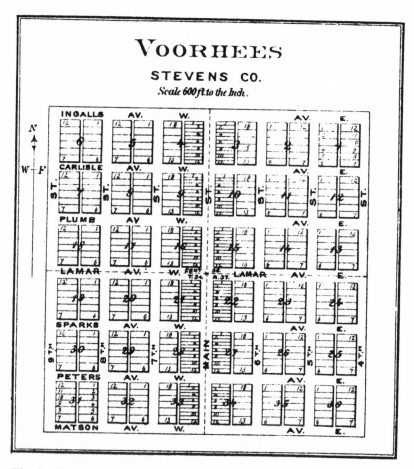

The plat of Voorhees honored two Kansas politicians with street names—Senator John J. Ingalls and Governor Preston B. Plumb. Today nothing remains of this one-time county seat contender—it lost to Hugoton.

the market and keep the price high. Jess Dunn, who operated the Voorhees grocery store, also sold supplies to Castene. One day Dunn sold him some rotten eggs in what both parties considered a good deal. Later that week a travelling salesman visited Dunn, and after they had transacted their business, Dunn invited the man to the St. Nicholas for dinner. The two enjoyed a fine meal of tasty eggs and fried rabbit. Just as they were finishing their feast, Dunn suddenly remembered the rotten eggs he had sold to Castene, and he promptly became deathly ill![1]

The St. Nicholas hosted many gatherings. A joint debate was held there concerning the election for bonds for railroads that were to extend from Liberal west through Voorhees and another northwest through Woodsdale. These railroads would benefit Voorhees but miss Hugoton, the other competitor in the county. During the debate, Sam Robinson, U.S. deputy marshal at Hugoton, became enraged and threatened violence. Although J. C. Gerrond, a Woodsdale supporter, warned him to calm down, the two had a fist fight before they left the hotel that night.

Voorhees attained a peak population of about 135 before the town began to decline. One of the town company's last efforts to avoid extinction was to petition the federal government to place a land office there for the district west of Liberal. The office would have brought more people to the community and insured the town's existence for several more years. The government failed to act on the petition, and Voorhees began an economic downtrend in the mid-1890s. [2]

Today three trees remain to mark the townsite. The place has been almost completely obliterated and only a few depressions indicate where buildings once stood. Except for some broken pieces of metal or glass that surface occasionally, Voorhees is little more than a memory.

GOGUAC
Stanton County

Founded on the high plains of western Kansas, Goguac was an agricultural center forty-five miles southwest of Garden City. The settlers formed the town company in 1889; W. J. Cross was president and V. C. Quick, secretary. One of the county's earliest newspapers, the *Stanton Telegram*, was published at Goguac by C. W. Cross, but as soon as the town was firmly established, they changed the name of the paper to the *Goguac Telegram*. Most of the local news items consisted of reports of land failings, law suits, and sheriff's sales. In early 1889 the *Telegram* noted that a Mrs. Ross had dug a well on her claim; the herd law of Stanton County had been repealed; and T. P. Grissom, postmaster, advertised that he was holding letters for Thomas McCready, Henry Nicola, L. A. Beom, Alice Prouty, and Nancy Burton. According to the newspaper, the townspeople at Goguac were expecting three railroads to be built through the area in the near future.

Throughout 1889 the newspaper editorials printed by the *Johnson City Journal* and the *Goguac Telegram* became almost slanderous at times. The *Journal* reported the following:

Editor Cross of the Telegram was quite wrathy at the Journal last week. He frothed at the mouth and blubbered around like a mad dog. He evidently hasn't sense enough to pound sand in a rat hole or he wouldn't fill his columns with such uninteresting, illiterate, abominable, licentious and libelous matter that he does. In his article on the county printing he not only intentionally lies but shows himself below the dignity of a gentleman. The best thing for him to do is soak his head in a strong solution of concentrated lye, bathe his body in high water, take one box of blue mass pills and retire to some quiet place where in his dreams he can communicate with rats. Our columns are too valuable to waste further space upon such a brainless attempt as he makes defending the people of Stanton County.

The following week the *Telegram* responded to the *Journal*'s accusations:

There are many times when a man gets so low in his ideas of journalism as to be beneath contempt but we feel in justice . . . to call attention to the foul manner in which the Journal man has attacked us. Our facts stand undisputed. He has not answered any statement in a mannerly way. He rants and raves in such a manner as to create suspicion of his sanity and his article makes one wonder how he happens to be in Johnson City running a paper rather than in some insane asylum or school for the feeble minded. . . . We could hardly expect any better from this hypocritical demogogue-like mongrel cur in a manger.

As for the town of Goguac, it had financial problems when the long-expected railroads failed to arrive, and during the depression of the 1890s, many people moved their homes to other more prosperous towns. Today nothing remains of the townsite.[1]

BORDERS
Stanton County

Another "Gem of the Prairie" was the wild and woolly cattle town of Borders, a short-lived addition to the Kansas ghost town list.

The National Cattle Trail was the last major trail to make an imprint in the Kansas sod; it was declared a "trail" by an act of Congress after bitter legislative debates in Texas, Kansas, and Colorado. The terminus of the trail was the town of Trail City, two miles west of Coolidge in Hamilton County. As thousands of head of cattle began arriving in Trail City, other western Kansas merchants became eager to take advantage of this goldmine and organized a committee to "share the wealth."

A group of citizens from Cimarron, Garden City, Dodge City, and Coolidge platted a town twenty-eight miles south of Trail City in Stanton County and christened it "Borders." On April 1, 1887, they filed a petition for the incorporation of Borders; the capital stock of $30,000 was to be divided into 3,000 shares at ten dollars each. Once they platted the townsite, they were quick to proclaim to the world, and especially to the trail drivers, that Borders existed just for their benefit.

Borders was named for Colonel Joseph H. Borders of Coolidge, one of the directors of the town company and owner of the Coolidge State Bank. The town company advertised that Borders was located on a stage line, the cattle trail, a proposed irrigation canal, and a railroad. They publicized the town as the future commercial center of the southwest. The promoters set aside several lots for those who would go into business and build substantial improvements there.

On August 12 the *Border Rover* began weekly publication. The first issue contained an extensive description of the town's bright future:

> Borders . . . is the liveliest and most successful town in Southwest Kansas. Situated on the state line, and is absolutely without a rival or peer!
>
> The town company which is composed of the best element of the world—renowned town builders of Southwest Kansas, have spared no means to make booming Borders one of the best towns in Kansas, and have built a hotel at a cost of $3,500, which challenges everything in that line south of the Arkansas River for comfort, beauty, and architecture.

The promoters established Borders a bit too late to take advantage of the cattle trade on the National Trail. The year 1887 was a dismal one for cattle. The market for Texas stock was sluggish. Although more than 90,000 head sold at Trail City that season, at least 70,000 returned to their home state. Meanwhile the government opened a block of land in southeastern Colorado to public settlement, and homesteaders moved in and quickly closed that portion of the trail. In addition, the ranchers in the area were reeling from losses caused by a blizzard the previous winter. They were without credit or money to restock their herds, causing thousands of cattle to be driven back to Texas for lack of a market.[1]

Within a year Borders was gone, not unlike its better known counterpart, Trail City. The town was not without an impressive list of backers; it was not without experienced planners; it was not without ambition. What

Borders lacked was a firm economic foundation—the cattle trade—which was already dwindling by the time the town was established. Most of the town's promoters went on to be successful businessmen in western Kansas; they just didn't get rich in Borders.

NOTES

INTRODUCTION

1. This quotation was taken from William Elsey Connelley's introduction to "Some of the Lost Towns of Kansas," *Kansas Historical Collections* 12 (1911–12): 426.

CHAPTER ONE: NORTHEAST KANSAS

Palermo, Doniphan County

1. *Troy Kansas Chief, Illustrated Doniphan County Supplement* (Troy, Kans.: *Kansas Chief*, 1916), p. 225. This is an authoritative source on Doniphan County communities, especially steamboat towns.

2. Ibid., p. 226; *Troy Kansas Chief*, January 9, 1941.

3. *Troy Kansas Chief, Illustrated Doniphan County Supplement*, p. 225.

4. *Troy Kansas Chief*, January 9, 1941.

5. Ibid.

Bendena, Doniphan County

1. *Troy Kansas Chief, Illustrated Doniphan County Supplement*, April 6, 1916, p. 178.

Kickapoo City, Leavenworth County

1. Kansas State Historical Society (KSHS), comp., "Doniphan County Clippings," vol. 3, n.d., p. 87.

2. Ibid., pp. 87–88.

3. Louise Barry, *The Beginning of the West* (Topeka: Kansas State Historical Society, 1973), pp. 253–54.

4. Ibid, p. 306.

5. Ibid., pp. 309–10.

6. KSHS, "Doniphan Clippings 3," p. 87.

7. Barry, *Beginning*, pp. 471–72.

8. It was not the oldest, but probably one of the oldest. The Rookery at Fort Leavenworth predates this structure by at least a decade.

9. Barry, *Beginning*, p. 1204.

10. A. Andreas, *History of Kansas* (Chicago: Andreas Publishers, 1883), 1: 459.

11. *Western Treasures and Eastern Treasures Magazine*, 4 (August 1976): 52.

12. Jesse Hall and LeRoy Hand, *History of Leavenworth County* (Leavenworth, Kans.: Standard Publishing, 1921), p. 320.

13. Andreas, *History of Kansas*, 1: 459.

14. *Western Treasures and Eastern Treasures Magazine*, 4 (August 1976): 52–53.

15. Cyrus K. Holladay, "Wyandotte County and Kansas City, Kansas," *Kansas Historical Collections* 3 (1891): 397.

16. Andreas, *History of Kansas,* 1: 459.

Bain City, Leavenworth County
 1. *Kansas City Times,* March 30, 1964.
 2. *Lawrence Journal-World,* March 24, 1964.
 3. *Kansas City Times,* March 30, 1964.

Quindaro, Wyandotte County
 1. Andreas, *History of Kansas,* 2: 1229–30.
 2. Alan W. Farley, "Annals of Quindaro: A Kansas Ghost Town," *Kansas Historical Quarterly* 22 (1956): 10–15.
 3. Andreas, *History of Kansas,* 2: 1229–30.
 4. Farley, "Annals of Quindaro," pp. 12–17.
 5. Ibid.; "Quindaro Study," unpublished study by Kansas State Historical Society's Historic Preservation Department concerning the acquisition of the Quindaro site as a state historic site, 1991.

Six Mile House, Wyandotte County
 1. Farley, "Annals of Quindaro," pp. 17–18.

Padonia, Brown County
 1. A. N. Ruley, *History of Brown County* (Hiawatha, Kans.: World Publishing Co., 1930), p. 19.
 2. *Topeka Daily Capital,* July 16, 1917.

Ash Point, Nemaha County
 1. *Pony Express Courier* (Seneca), August 1935.
 2. Ghost Town Files, Reference Division, KSHS, Center for Historical Research.

Neuchatel, Nemaha County
 1. *Onaga Herald,* June 4, 1891.
 2. *Nemaha County Journal-Leader,* August 1, 1974.
 3. Ibid.

Blaine, Pottawatomie County
 1. *Topeka Capital-Journal,* September 25, 1966.
 2. Ibid., and interview with Blaine High School reunion participants, June 15, 1992; Pottawatomie County Historical Committee (PCHC), "Blaine," in *Early History of Pottawatomie County* 1854–1954 (Wamego, Kans.: Pottawatomie County Historical Committee, 1954), p. 21.

Louisville, Pottawatomie County
 1. Note mentioned in *Kansas Historical Collections* 17 (1928): 77.
 2. Pottawatomie County Centennial Committee, "Louisville," in *Early History of Pot-*

tawatomie County 1854–1954 (Wamego, Kans.: Pottawatomie County Centennial Committee, 1954), p. 16.

3. PCHC, *Early History of Pottawatomie,* pp. 16–17.

4. *Topeka Capital-Journal,* February 14, 1960.

5. Kansas Automobile Association, *The Club Member* 7 (1908): 22–23.

6. Ibid.

7. PCHC, *Early History of Pottawatomie,* pp. 16–17.

8. *Topeka Capital-Journal,* February 14, 1960; Andreas, *History of Kansas,* 2: 976. I also
wish to thank members of the Wamego Historical Society for interviews conducted during a monthly meeting, July 12, 1977.

Afton, Marshall County

1. *Marysville Advocate,* November 30, 1967.

2. *Marysville Advocate,* December 7, 1967.

3. Ibid.

Bigelow, Marshall County

1. The date has been generally given as 1851, although some sources, such as the Grant
Ewing one, indicate the date as June 9, 1842.

2. *Marysville Advocate,* November 17, 1977.

3. *Topeka Capital-Journal,* January 17, 1960.

4. *Marysville Advocate,* December 30, 1965.

Bala, Riley County

1. Winifred N. Slagg, *Riley County Kansas* (Manhattan, Kans.: Winifred Slagg, 1968),
pp. 159–72.

2. *Clay Center Dispatch,* October 10, 1951.

3. Slagg, *Riley County,* pp. 159–72; *Manhattan Mercury,* June 12, 1978.

CHAPTER TWO: EAST CENTRAL KANSAS

Monticello, Johnson County

1. Andreas, *History of Kansas,* 1: 639.

2. Ibid.

3. *Johnson County Sun,* June 11, 1975. A final remark—unfortunately, many of the original records pertaining to Hickock's term as sheriff have disappeared; today these local
government records would lend valuable insight into his early law enforcement career.

Paris, Linn County

1. Note in *Kansas Historical Collections* 12 (1912): 430–32.

2. Andreas, *History of Kansas,* 2: 1116.

3. Ibid.

4. *Kansas Historical Collections* 12 (1912): 430–32.

5. *Pleasanton News,* March 2, 1905; *Fort Scott Tribune,* August 16, 1957.

Moneka, Linn County

1. Spiritualism was popular at this time. It advocated that all reality is in essence spiritual or ideal.

2. William E. Connelley, "Some Lost Towns in Kansas," in *Kansas Historical Collections* 12 (1912): 429.

3. Note in *Kansas Historical Quarterly* 23 (1955): 202.

4. Andreas, *History of Kansas*, 2: 1116.

5. Note in *Kansas Historical Quarterly* 27 (1959): 190.

6. Connelley, "Some Lost Towns," p. 429.

7. Note in *Kansas Historical Collections* 15 (1922): 201.

Lone Star, Douglas County

1. Martha Parker and Betty Laird, *Soil of Our Souls,* (Lawrence, Kans.: Coronado Press, 1976), pp. 146–52.

2. Ibid., pp. 152–58.

3. Paul Nieder, "Rise and Fall of Lone Star, Kansas," July 16, 1975, unpublished manuscript located in Spencer Research Library, University of Kansas, Lawrence.

Potwin Place/Auburndale, Shawnee County

1. Potwin Place Improvement Association[?], "The Summer Years, Potwin Place" (pamphlet), 1985, pp. 1–2.

2. Interview with Douglass Wallace, Topeka, July 15, 1977.

3. Shawnee County Historical Society (SCHS), *Potwin Place* (Topeka: Ives Printing Co., 1968), 45: 94–97.

4. Interview with Douglass Wallace, Topeka, August 22, 1992.

5. SCHS, *Potwin Place,* pp. 97–98.

6. Ibid., pp. 99–100.

7. Interview with Douglass Wallace, Topeka, July 15, 1977.

8. SCHS, *Potwin Place,* pp. 100–103.

Willard, Shawnee County

1. *Topeka State Journal,* March 3, 1937.

2. Interview with Vitasco D. Jones, February 17, 1976.

3. *Topeka State Journal,* March 3, 1937.

Richland, Shawnee County

1. KSHS, comp., "Shawnee County Clippings," vol. 1, p. 314, from *Topeka Mail & Breeze* article, May 1896.

2. *Topeka State Journal,* November 27, 1954.

3. *Kansas City Star,* July 21, 1968.

4. *Kansas City Star,* August 16, 1967.

5. *Topeka State Journal,* November 27, 1954; I also wish to thank Bradley Trimble, Richland resident, for the interview on July 4, 1987.

110 Mile Creek, Osage County

1. *Topeka Journal,* April 28, 1928.
2. C. R. Green, *Early Days in Kansas* (Burlingame, Kans.: C.R. Green, 1913), 13: 65.
3. *Kansas City Star,* January 22, 1928.
4. Green, *Early Days,* p. 65.
5. *Topeka Journal,* July 1, 1927.
6. Roger Carswell, *The Early Years of Osage County* (Newton, Kans.: Mennonite Press, 1982), p. 16; *Overbrook Citizen,* May 11, 1961; *Kansas City Star,* January 22, 1928.

Arvonia, Osage County

1. *Lebo Enterprise,* August 21, 1958.
2. Note in *Kansas Historical Quarterly* 43 (1977): 454–57.
3. Harlan Hamman, ''History of Arvonia'' (pamphlet, no publisher, 1963), pp. 1–4.

Fostoria, Osage County

1. *Osage County Chronicle,* March 1, 1987.
2. *Burlingame Enterprise-Chronicle,* July 22, 1976.

Old Strawn, Coffey County

1. Strawn Centennial Committee, ''Strawn,'' 1972, pp. 1–4.

Miller, Lyon County

1. *Emporia Times,* August 12, 1965.
2. *Emporia Gazette,* February 7, 1935.
3. Ted McDaniel, ed., *Our Land, A History of Lyon County, Kansas* (Emporia, Kans.: Emporia State Press, 1976), pp. 66–73.

Dunlap, Morris County

1. Jessie Parrish, ''Dunlap,'' in *Centennial, Council Grove, Kansas, 1825–1925* (Council Grove, Kans.: Council Grove Centennial Committee, 1925), p. 61.
2. Ibid.
3. Ibid.
4. *Emporia Gazette,* May 3, 1962.
5. Parrish, *Centennial Council Grove,* p. 61.; I also wish to thank 1991 Topeka West High School oral history students, who conducted an extensive oral history of residents in the Dunlap area that proved useful; also, for further research on the black schools in Dunlap, the scholastic census records have survived in the register of deeds office, providing very extensive information.

Skiddy, Morris County

1. *White City Register,* October 28, 1937.

CHAPTER THREE: SOUTHEAST KANSAS

Freedom Colony, Bourbon County

1. The best source for information on this community is H. Roger Grant, "Portrait of a Worker's Utopia: The Labor Exchange and the Freedom Colony, Kansas," in *Kansas Historical Quarterly* 43 (1977): 242–60; also special thanks to Gene DeGruson of the Pittsburg State University Special Collections Library for his insights.

Rollin, Neosho County
   1. *Topeka State Journal,* July 9, 1951.
   2. *Topeka State Journal,* February 14, 1973.
   3. Ibid.
   4. Fulton Lewis, Jr., "Washington Report," *Topeka Daily Capital,* July 9, 1951.

Cato, Crawford County
   1. The best source on Cato available is Michael G. Christensen, "Cato: First Settlement In Crawford County," in *Papers in History* (Pittsburg, Kans.: History Club, Pittsburg State College, May 1970).

Farlington, Crawford County
   1. KSHS, comp., "Crawford County Clippings," vol. 3, p. 68.

Croweburg, Crawford County
   1. Edward T. McNally, *Pittsburg Almanac, 1876–1976* (Pittsburg, Kans.: no publisher, 1976), pp. 237–38.

Monmouth, Crawford County
   1. KSHS, comp., *Crawford County Clippings*, vol. 3, n.d., pp. 104–5.
   2. Ibid.
   3. Ibid., p. 357.
   4. B. Close Shackleton, *Handbook on the Frontier Days of Southeast Kansas, Kansas Centennial, 1861–1961* (Pittsburg, Kans.: B. Close Shackleton, 1961), p. 41.
   5. KSHS, comp., "Crawford County Clippings," vol. 5, pp. 154–55.
   6. F. W. Blackmar, *Cyclopedia of Kansas History* (Chicago: Standard Publishing Co., 1912), 2: 299.

Treece, Cherokee County
   1. Arrell Gibson, *Wilderness Bonanza: The Tri-State District of Missouri, Kansas and Oklahoma* (Norman: University of Oklahoma Press, 1972), p. 28.
   2. American Guide Series, *Kansas* (New York: Viking Press, 1939), p. 508.
   3. Ibid.
   4. Ibid., pp. 97–98.
   5. Ibid.
   6. Gibson, *Wilderness Bonanza,* p. 195.
   7. American Guide Series, *Kansas,* p. 508.
   8. Gibson, *Wilderness Bonanza,* p. 95.
   9. Ibid., p. 195. I wish to thank Arrell Gibson for all his help in 1986 with the writing of

NOTES 289

this book and in answering interview questions concerning the Tri-State District while in Sacramento, California.

Le Hunt, Montgomery County

1. The best source on LeHunt is Robert K. Ratzlaff, "LeHunt, Kansas: The Making of a Cement Ghost Town," in *Kansas Historical Quarterly* 43 (1977): 203–16.

Votaw, Montgomery County

1. Charles Clayton Drake, *Who's Who—A History of Kansas and Montgomery County* (Coffeyville, Kans.: Charles Drake, 1943), p. 38.

2. *Coffeyville Journal*, August 24, 1969.

Hewins, Chautauqua County

1. *Independence Daily Reporter*, May 28, 1967. I would also like to thank Mrs. Irma Kidwell of Lawrence for her insightful remarks concerning Hewins during interviews in the summer of 1980.

Boston, Chautauqua County

1. *Wichita Eagle*, January 15, 1956; note concerning Boston in *Kansas Historical Collections* 16 (1925): 217–18.

Delaware Springs, Wilson County

1. *Fredonia Daily Herald*, October 20, 1961.

Kalida, Woodson County

1. *Chanute Tribune*, June 5, 1871.

2. *Toronto Republican*, September 20, 1962.

3. Woodson County Historical Society (WCHS), "In the Beginning," vol. 1, no. 2 (1968): 14–20.

4. *Toronto Republican*, September 20, 1962.

5. WCHS, "In the Beginning," pp. 18–20.

Defiance, Woodson County

1. WCHS, "In the Beginning," pp. 14–20.

Reece, Greenwood County

1. *Leon News*, October 27, 1944.

Smileyberg, Butler County

1. *Augusta Daily Gazette*, August 13, 1974.

Rosalia, Butler County

1. Harold J. Borger, *A Pictorial History of Rosalia,* 1869–1935 (El Dorado: Harold J. Borger, 1972), pp. 117–18.

2. Ibid., pp. 41–42.

3. Ibid., p. 43.

4. Ibid, pp. 111–12.

CHAPTER FOUR: NORTH CENTRAL KANSAS

Strawberry, Washington County

1. Maurice Gieber, "Strawberry, Kansas, 1868–1951," (Washington, D.C.: Maurice Gieber, 1990), pp. 5–8. I wish to thank everyone involved in the dedication of the Strawberry monument on the townsite August 12, 1990. Several good interviews were conducted there, as well as with the Throop family of Washington and Wamego during February 1991.

Salem, Jewell County

1. Harry Ross, *What Price White Rock?* (Mankato, Kans.: Harry Ross, 1937), pp. 43–45.

2. C. Clyde Myers, "Salem, A Town That Boomed, Then Faded," in *Kansas Historical Collections* 17 (1928): 384–86.

3. Ibid.

4. Ross, *What Price White Rock*, pp. 43–45.

5. Ibid.

6. Andreas, *History of Kansas,* 2: 973.

7. Ray Myers, "Historical Sketches of Smith and Jewell County and Old Salem," unpublished manuscript in Manuscripts Section, Collections Division, KSHS, Center For Historical Research.

8. Myers, "Salem, A Town That Boomed," pp. 384–86.

Hunter, Mitchell County

1. KSHS, comp., "Mitchell County Clippings," vol. 2, pp. 228–29.

2. *Topeka State Journal,* May 23, 1917.

Asherville, Mitchell County

1. Horseless Carriage Club, "Souvenir Booklet, National Midwest Tour of the Horseless Carriage Club, May 21–23, 1954," (pamphlet, 1954).

2. KSHS, comp., "Mitchell County Clippings," vol. 2, pp. 156–58.

Tipton, Mitchell County

1. *Beloit Call,* May 24, 1951.

2. KSHS, comp., "Mitchell County Clippings," vol. 2, pp. 224–28.

3. *Beloit Call,* May 24, 1951.

Simpson, Mitchell County

1. *Simpson News,* November 2, 1939.

Lake Sibley, Cloud County
    1. Blackmar, *Cyclopedia of Kansas*, 2: 93.
    2. Dee Brown, *The Galvanized Yankees,* (Urbana: University of Illinois Press, 1963), p. 163.
    3. Note mentioned in *Kansas Historical Quarterly* 1 (1932): 326.
    4. De B. Randolph Keim, *Sheridan's Troopers on the Borders* (Philadelphia: David McKay, 1885), p. 33.
    5. Ghost Town Files, KSHS, Center for Historical Research.
    6. Note mentioned in *Kansas Historical Quarterly* 38 (1972): 375.
    7. Ghost Town Files, KSHS, Center for Historical Research.
    8. Note mentioned in *Kansas Historical Collections* 12 (1912): p. 9.
    9. Note mentioned in *Kansas Historical Quarterly* 3 (1934): 280.

Industry, Dickinson/Clay County Line
    1. KSHS, comp., "Dickinson County Clippings," vol. 2, pp. 65–66.
    2. *Clay Center Times,* February 11, 1904.
    3. KSHS, "Dickinson County Clippings," vol. 2, p. 65. I'd like to thank Constance Menninger for bringing to light the Menninger connection to this ghost town.

CHAPTER FIVE: CENTRAL KANSAS

Holland, Dickinson County
    1. *Wichita Eagle-Beacon,* August 31, 1981.
    2. KSHS, "Dickinson County Clippings," vol. 2, pp. 60–61.
    3. *Wichita Eagle-Beacon,* August 31, 1981.

Elmo, Dickinson County
    1. *Hope Dispatch,* April 17, 1958.
    2. KSHS, "Dickinson County Clippings," vol. 5, p. 75.
    3. *Hope Dispatch,* April 17, 1958.

Abram, Lincoln County
    1. *Lincoln Sentinel,* November 9, 1939.
    2. Ibid.
    3. Andreas, *History of Kansas,* 2: 1421.
    4. Ghost Town Files, KSHS, Center for Historical Research.
    5. *Lincoln Sentinel,* November 9, 1939.

Carneiro, Ellsworth County
    1. *Wichita Eagle,* December 8, 1975.

Allison's Ranch, Barton County
    1. Ray Schultz, "Allison's Ranch," in the Kansas Anthropological Association *Newsletter*, 15 (1969): pp. 1–3.

2. Family Heritage Society, *Family Heritage Album in Barton County, Kansas* (McPherson, Kans.: Family Heritage Society, 1973), p. 12.

3. R. M. Wright, "Personal Reminiscences of Frontier Life," in *Kansas Historical Collections* 7 (1902): 48.

4. Schultz, "Allison's Ranch," pp. 3–6.

Zarah, Barton County

1. Ghost Town Files, KSHS, Center for Historical Research.

2. *Hutchinson News Herald,* November 12, 1950; Andreas, *History of Kansas,* 1: 769.

Galatia, Barton County

1. Family Heritage Society, *Family Heritage Album in Barton County,* p. 386.

Boyd, Barton County

1. *Great Bend Tribune,* May 28, 1972.

2. Ibid., October 10, 1954.

3. Ibid., May 28, 1972.

Hitschmann, Barton County

1. *Hutchinson News,* September 27, 1986.

Raymond, Rice County

1. *Lyons Daily News,* April 12, 1961.

Frederick, Rice County

1. *Salina Journal,* September 14, 1980.

2. *Kansas City Times,* December 2, 1954.

Paradise, Russell County

1. Family Heritage Society, *Family Heritage Album, Russell County, Kansas* (McPherson, Kans.: Family Heritage Society, 1973), pp. 32–33; *Hays Daily News,* April 6, 1980; *Russell Record,* December 18, 1897.

Yocemento, Ellis County

1. *Hays Daily News,* May 24, 1959.

2. Ibid.

3. *Ellis Review,* February 17, 1972.

4. *Hays Daily News,* May 24, 1959.

5. Ibid.

6. *Ellis Review,* February 17, 1972.

7. *Hays Daily News,* May 24, 1959.

Alexander, Rush County

1. *Rush County News,* Special Diamond Jubilee Edition, December 1949.

CHAPTER SIX: SOUTH CENTRAL KANSAS

Geuda Springs, Sumner County

1. *Arkansas City Traveler,* May 13, 1959.
2. *Kansas City Times,* March 28, 1955.
3. *Arkansas City Traveler,* May 13, 1959.
4. *Wichita Eagle-Beacon,* June 15, 1981.
5. "Geuda Mineral Springs" (pamphlet, no date).
6. *Oxford Register,* July 11, 1968.
7. *Arkansas City Traveler,* October 26, 1954.
8. *Wichita Morning Eagle,* December 14, 1947.

Bluff City, Harper County

1. *Leavenworth Times,* March 5, 1928.
2. Bluff City Centennial Committee, *A History of Bluff City,* 1886–1986 (Bluff City, Kans.: Bluff City Centennial Committee, 1986), pp. 2–5.
3. *Wichita Eagle-Beacon,* June 29, 1981.
4. Bluff City Centennial Committee, *History of Bluff City,* pp. 4–10.

Cameron/Camchester, Harper County

1. Gwendaline and Paul Sanders, *The Harper County Story* (Harper, Kans.: n.p., 1968), p. 100.
2. Ibid.
3. *Wichita Eagle-Beacon,* November 28, 1971.

Old Clear Water, Sedgwick County

1. *Clearwater Echo,* February 19, 1903.
2. *Clearwater News,* October 9, 1952.

Marshall, Sedgwick County

1. Floyd R. Saunders, "The Small Town and Its Future," in *Kansas Historical Quarterly* 35 (1969): 2–3.
2. *Cheney Sentinel,* August 24, 1950.
3. O. H. Bentley, *History of Wichita and Sedgwick County* (Wichita, Kans.: O.H. Bentley, 1910), p. 36.

Waterloo, Kingman County

1. Irene Bergkamp, "Waterloo in Galesburg Township, in Kingman County, Kansas" (Kingman, Kans.: Irene Bergkamp, 1971), pp. 5–10.
2. Kingman County Historical Society, *Kingman County Kansas and Its People* (Dallas, Tex.: Taylor Publishing Co., 1984), p. 71; *Leavenworth Times,* December 5, 1934.

Castleton, Reno County

1. Andreas, *History of Kansas,* 2: 1,379.
2. *Hutchinson Daily News,* May 24, 1970 and July 23, 1961.

3. Ibid., July 23, 1961.

Lerado, Reno County

1. *Hutchinson News,* September 30, 1934. I would also like to thank David Baylor of Hutchinson Public Radio for interviews and follow-up questions concerning both Lerado and Castleton during the months of November and December 1989. Also, see James Sherow, "Small Town Origins in Southwest Reno County," in *Kansas History* 3 (1980): 103–10, and Alfred B. Bradshaw, *When the Prairies Were Young* (Turon, Kans.: Arthur J. Allen, 1957), pp. 23–28.

Old Kiowa, Barber County

1. Andreas, *History of Kansas,* 1: 211.
2. KSHS, comp., "Barber County Clippings," vol. 3, p. 170.
3. Ibid., p. 179.
4. Ghost Town Files, KSHS, Center for Historical Research.

Lake City, Barber County

1. Barber County Historical Society (BCHS), *The Chosen Land, A History of Barber County, Kansas* (Dallas, Tex.: Taylor Publishing Co., 1980), pp. 59–60.
2. *Wichita Beacon,* August 9, 1959.
3. BCHS, *Chosen Land,* pp. 59–60.
4. *Wichita Beacon,* August 9, 1959.
5. BCHS, *Chosen Land,* pp. 59–60.

Sun City, Barber County

1. BCHS, *Chosen Land,* pp. 65–69.

Comanche City, Comanche County

1. Ghost Town Files, KSHS, Center for Historical Research.
2. *Protection Post,* March 21, April 11, April 18, and April 25, 1947.
3. Coldwater Diamond Jubilee Committee, *Kansas* 75th Anniversary Booklet (Coldwater, Kans.: Coldwater Diamond Jubilee, 1959), p. 12.

Hopewell, Pratt County

1. Family Heritage Society, *Family Heritage Album of Pratt County, Kansas* (McPherson, Kans.: Family Heritage Society, 1976), pp. 16–17.

Byers, Pratt County

1. Family Heritage Society, *Family Heritage Album of Pratt County,* p. 16.
2. *Pratt Tribune,* October 14, 1964.
3. *Kansas City Times,* September 21, 1965.

Zenith, Stafford County

1. *Stafford Courier,* September 12, 1974.

2. *Kansas City Times,* January 3, 1939.
3. *Stafford Courier,* September 12, 1974.
4. *Kansas City Times,* January 3, 1939.

Trousdale, Edwards County
1. Edwards County Centennial Committee, *Edwards County Centennial,* 1873–1973 (Kinsley, Kans.: Edwards County Centennial Committee, 1973), pp. 31–35.

CHAPTER SEVEN: NORTHWEST KANSAS

Devizes, Norton County
1. Charles Abernathy, *Pioneering the Prairies* (Newell, Iowa: Bireline Publishing Co., 1975), pp. 31–34.
2. Charles Abernathy, *Devizes* (Newell, Iowa: Bireline Publishing Co., 1982), pp. 36–39, 76–77.

Kanona, Decatur County
1. *Topeka Journal,* July 10, 1960.
2. *Oberlin Herald,* April 18, 1968.
3. Ibid.

Dresden, Decatur County
1. Flavius M. Foster, *So This Is Dresden, Kansas?* (Dresden, Kans.: Flavius M. Foster, 1980), pp. 10–19.

Burntwood City, Rawlins County
1. E. S. Sutton, *Sutton's Southwest Nebraska and Republican River Valley Tributaries* (Benkelman, Nebr.: E. S. Sutton, 1983), pp. 253–57.

Blakeman, Rawlins County
1. *Topeka Journal,* May 22, 1910.
2. Ibid., May 26, 1910.

Ludell, Rawlins County
1. KSHS, comp., "Rawlins County Clippings," vol. 2, pp. 98–99.
2. *Atwood Citizen-Patriot,* March 8, 1979.
3. KSHS, "Rawlins County Clippings," vol. 2, p. 99.
4. *Atwood Citizen-Patriot,* March 8, 1979.
5. Ibid.

Gem, Thomas County
1. Bill James and Marge Brown, *A History of Gem, Kansas* (Colby, Kans.: Prairie Printers, 1970), pp. 1–10.
2. *Sherman County Herald,* May 5, 1987.

3. Ibid.

4. Thomas County Historical Society, *Land of the Windmills, Thomas County, Kansas* (Dallas, Tex.: Taylor Publishing Co., 1976), pp. 114–15.

5. James and Brown, *History of Gem,* pp. 8–10.

6. *Sherman County Herald,* May 5, 1987.

Menlo, Thomas County

1. Thomas County Historical Society, *Land of Windmills,* pp. 51–53.

Eustis, Sherman County

1. Note in *Kansas Historical Collections* 8 (1904): 50.

2. Kirke Mechem, *Annals of Kansas* (Topeka: Kansas State Historical Society, 1954), 1: 14.

3. Note in *Kansas Historical Collections* 8 (1904): 50.

4. Ghost Town Files, KSHS, Center for Historical Research.

5. Note in *Kansas Historical Collections* 8 (1904): 56.

6. Ibid., p. 57.

7. Ibid., p. 58.

8. Ibid., p. 59.

9. Ibid., p. 60.

Itasca, Sherman County

1. Frank Perkins, "History of Sherman County, Kansas," thesis for University of Colorado, Boulder, Colorado, 1935, pp. 56–58; *Goodland Herald,* December 27, 1934.

CHAPTER EIGHT: WEST CENTRAL KANSAS

Ogallah, Trego County

1. *Club Member* (KAA) 6 (1908): 4.

2. *WaKeeney Western Kansas World,* March 4, 1954.

3. *Topeka Capital-Journal,* December 27, 1954.

4. *WaKeeney Western Kansas World,* March 4, 1954.

5. *Topeka Capital-Journal,* December 27, 1954.

California, Lane County

1. Ghost Town Files, KSHS, Center for Historical Research.

2. *Lane County Gazette* (California), January 29, 1880.

Vega, Wallace County

1. Blackmar, *Cyclopedia of Kansas,* 2: 841.

Pond City, Wallace County

1. *Oakley Western Times,* October 13, 1932.

2. Ibid.

3. Ibid.

4. Note in *Kansas Historical Collections* 17 (1928): 248.

5. Homer W. Wheeler, *Buffalo Days* (Indianapolis: Bobbs-Merrill, 1925), pp. 247–48.

6. Note in *Kansas Historical Collections* 17 (1928): 248.

CHAPTER NINE: SOUTHWEST KANSAS

Pierceville, Finney County

1. Leola Blanchard, *Conquest of Southwest Kansas* (Wichita, Kans.: Eagle Press, 1931), pp. 193–203.

Englewood, Clark County

1. This is an excerpt from a song entitled, "The Song of NoMan's Land," author unknown.

2. *Clark County Clipper,* November 14, 1940.

3. Ina Cole Ford, "Clark County Historical Society Notes," collection of September 12, 1940, Manuscripts Section, Collections Division, KSHS.

4. *Wichita Eagle-Beacon,* October 5, 1981.

Sitka, Clark County

1. *Clark County Clipper,* December 26, 1959.

Meade Center, Meade County

1. Note in *Kansas Historical Collections* 29 (1943): 384.

2. Note in ibid. 18 (1932): 266–67.

3. Note in ibid. 24 (1938): 336.

4. Note in ibid. 29 (1943): 384.

Arkalon, Seward County

1. *Hutchinson News-Herald,* January 15, 1956.

2. KSHS, comp., "Seward County Clippings," vol. 2, pp. 6–7.

3. *Hutchinson News-Herald,* January 15, 1956.

Woodsdale, Stevens County

1. Note in *Kansas Historical Collections* 19 (1933): 55–56.

2. *Spearville News,* August 8, 1935.

3. Ibid.

4. Note in *Kansas Historical Collections* 19 (1933): 55–56.

5. *Topeka Daily Capital,* December 1, 1929; *Liberal News,* December 14, 1934.

Voorhees, Stevens County

1. *Hugoton Hermes,* February 3, 1983.

2. Ibid.; KSHS, comp., "Stevens County Clippings," vol. 1, pp. 157–60.

Goguac, Stanton County
   1. *High Plains Journal,* October 1, 1960.

Borders, Stanton County
   1. *High Plains Journal,* August 16, 1951.

SELECTED
BIBLIOGRAPHY

Andreas, A. *History of Kansas*. 2 vols. Chicago: Andreas, 1883. Reprint available through Atchison County Historical Society.

Athearn, Robert G. *In Search of Canaan: Black Migration to Kansas, 1879–80*. Lawrence: Regents Press of Kansas, 1978.

Barry, Louise. *The Beginning of the West*. Topeka: Kansas State Historical Society, 1973.

Blackmar, Frank W. *Cyclopedia of Kansas History*. 3 vols. Chicago: Standard Publishing Company, 1912.

Emporia State University. "Some Ghost Towns of Kansas." *The Heritage of Kansas Series*. Emporia: Kansas State Teachers College, 1961.

Everts, L. H. *The Official State Atlas of Kansas*. Philadelphia: L. H. Everts & Co., 1887. Reprint available through Shawnee County (Topeka) Genealogical Society.

Federal Writers' Project, comp. *The WPA Guide to 1930s Kansas*. With a new Introduction by James R. Shortridge. Lawrence: University Press of Kansas, 1984. (Originally published as *Kansas: A Guide to the Sunflower State* [New York, 1939].)

Fitzgerald, Daniel C. *Ghost Towns of Kansas*. 3 vols. Holton, Kans.: Bell Graphics, 1976–1982.

————. *Ghost Towns of Kansas: A Traveler's Guide*. Lawrence: University Press of Kansas, 1988.

————. "Town Booming: An Economic History of Steamboat Towns along the Kansas-Missouri Border, 1840–1860." M.A. thesis, University of Kansas, Lawrence, 1983.

Ghost Town Files. Manuscript Division, Kansas State Historical Society, Topeka.

Hintz, Forrest. *Some Vanishing Towns of Kansas*. Wichita: *Wichita Eagle-Beacon*, 1982.

Kansas State Gazetteer. Detroit: R. L. Polk & Company, various dates.

Kansas State Historical Society, comp. "County Clippings" volumes. Available for all Kansas counties.

Kansas State Historical Society [William Elsey Connelley]. "Some of the Lost Towns of Kansas." *Kansas Historical Collections* 12 (1911–1912).

Wilder, Daniel. *Annals of Kansas, 1541–1885*. Topeka: T. D. Thacher & Co., 1886.

INDEX